LIBRARIES THAT BUILD BUSINESS

ALA Editions purchases fund advocacy, awareness,
and accreditation programs for library professionals worldwide.

LIBRARIES THAT
BUILD
BUSINESS

Advancing Small Business and
Entrepreneurship in Public Libraries

EDITED BY MEGAN JANICKI

Public Policy and Advocacy Office

CHICAGO | 2022

MEGAN JANICKI is the project manager of the Libraries Build Business initiative with the Public Policy and Advocacy Office at the American Library Association. Prior to her work with ALA, Megan worked in a variety of adult education, workforce development, and social service roles in Washington, DC. She holds a master of education degree in learning, diversity, and urban studies.

© 2022 by the American Library Association

Extensive effort has gone into ensuring the reliability of the information in this book; however, the publisher makes no warranty, express or implied, with respect to the material contained herein.

ISBN: 978-0-8389-3840-9 (paper)

Library of Congress Control Number: 2022934323

Cover design by Kimberly Hudgins.
Text design by Karen Sheets de Gracia in the Freight Text and Gotham typefaces.

♾ This paper meets the requirements of ANSI/NISO Z39.48–1992 (Permanence of Paper).

Printed in the United States of America
26 25 24 23 22   5 4 3 2 1

CONTENTS

Acknowledgments *ix*

Introduction: How Libraries Build Business
Megan Janicki and Marijke Visser *xi*

PART I: STRATEGIES AND CONSIDERATIONS TO GET STARTED

1 Considerations for Small and Rural Libraries
Brandon West, Susan M. Preece, Rachael Svoboda, Michael Sekaquaptewa, and Taneesa R. Hall *3*

2 Identifying Stakeholders, Building Partnerships, Finding Funding, and Sustaining It All
Julie M. Brophy, Lori Hench, Karly Feinberg, Diane Luccy, Sheldon Burke, Danielle Milton, Stacey Goddard, Atlas Logan, Adam Pitts, and Christopher Bourret *13*

3 Equity, Diversity, and Inclusion in Library Entrepreneurship Programs
Adriana McCleer, Madeleine Ildefonso, LaKesha Kimbrough, and Michael Sekaquaptewa *29*

4 Specialized Library Supports for Entrepreneurs
Ryan Metheny, Andrea Levandowski, Sara Brown, Tony Orengo, Nathaniel Burnard, Marra Honeywell, Julie M. Brophy, Rachael Svoboda, and Brandon West *41*

PART II: CASE STUDIES FROM THE FIELD

Small Business and Entrepreneurship Programs in Public Libraries

PROGRAM 1 **Supporting the Local Economy: Developing Business and Job Seeker Services from Scratch**
Lesley Cyrier and Emily Glimco, Addison (IL) Public Library *55*

PROGRAM 2 **BIPOC Business Community and Connections: Small Business—Big Impact**
Adriana McCleer and Yee Lee Vue, Appleton (WI) Public Library 61

PROGRAM 3 **Taking Budding Entrepreneurs from Business Idea to Business Plan: The Entrepreneur Academy**
Julie M. Brophy, Baltimore County (MD) Public Library 69

PROGRAM 4 **Empowering New Businesses with a Business Plan Competition: PowerUP!**
Maud Andrew and Arcola Robinson, Brooklyn (NY) Public Library 78

PROGRAM 5 **Built to Last: Built in Broward**
Sheldon Burke, Broward County (FL) Library 86

PROGRAM 6 **Rochester—Innovation Was Born Here: Business Insight Center**
Jennifer Byrnes, Central Library of Rochester and Monroe County (NY) 93

PROGRAM 7 **The Entrepreneurial Mindset: Encore Entrepreneurs and Key Advanced Entrepreneurs**
William Kelly, Cuyahoga County (OH) Public Library 100

PROGRAM 8 **Becoming a Resource Hub: The Dallas B.R.A.I.N**
Heather Lowe, Dallas (TX) Public Library 106

PROGRAM 9 **Pathway to Entrepreneurial Success: The Stamford Small Business Resource Center**
Elizabeth Joseph, Ferguson Library (Stamford, CT) 113

PROGRAM 10 **One-to-One Support for Micro-Entrepreneurs: Business Help at Your Library**
Taneesa R. Hall, Ferguson (MO) Municipal Public Library 119

CONTENTS **vii**

PROGRAM 11 **A New Start: Entrepreneurship for the Formerly Incarcerated**
Adam Pitts, Atlas Logan, Ronald M. Gauthier, Ann Serrie, and Andrea Devereux, Gwinnett County (GA) Public Library 125

PROGRAM 12 **Cultivate Small Business with BeanStack: Cultivate Indy**
Brandon West, Independence (KS) Public Library 132

PROGRAM 13 **Build Your Business Brand through Community Engagement: Invest in Yourself**
Audrey Barbakoff, King County (WA) Library System 140

PROGRAM 14 **Building Support for Rural Entrepreneurs: Wyoming Library to Business—A Statewide Initiative**
Rachael Svoboda, Laramie County (WY) Library System 147

PROGRAM 15 **Connect with Immigrant Entrepreneurs: Sea Un Vendedor Ambulante Exitoso/ Successful Street Vending**
Madeleine Ildefonso, Los Angeles (CA) Public Library 155

PROGRAM 16 **Taking a Shot with SCORE: Entrepreneur Workshop Series**
Stacey Wicksall, Macedon (NY) Public Library 161

PROGRAM 17 **Opening the Doors to Economic Success: The Miller Business Center**
Sophia Serlis-McPhillips and Elizabeth Malafi, Middle Country (NY) Public Library 167

PROGRAM 18 **The MAGIC Touch: Management and Government Information Center**
Katherine LaVallee and Eva Gunia, Prince William Public Libraries (Woodbridge, VA) 174

PROGRAM 19 **Develop an ESOL for Business Owners Class: Small Business Hub**
Christopher Bourret, Providence (RI) Public Library 180

PROGRAM 20 **Entrepreneurs Launch and Grow: The Entrepreneurial Launch Pad**
Diane Luccy and Mary Kate Quillivan, Richland Library (Columbia, SC) *187*

PROGRAM 21 **Biz.ability Workshops: Tools to Empower You**
Geeta Halley, Round Rock (TX) Public Library *195*

PROGRAM 22 **Business Networking through Community-Building: SBPL Building Business**
Ahmad Merza and Molly Wetta, Santa Barbara (CA) Public Library *201*

PROGRAM 23 **Be a Neighborhood Champion: Small Business Boot Camp**
Danielle Milton, Stacey Goddard, Crystal Miller, and Sarah O'Hare, Spokane County (WA) Library District *208*

PROGRAM 24 **Meet Them Where They Are: Small Business Outreach**
Jennifer Hyun-Lynn Gibson, St. Louis County (MO) Library *215*

PROGRAM 25 **Untethered and on the Move**
Meg Delaney, Miramelinda Arribas-Douglas, Linda L. Fayerweather, and Zachary W. Huber, Toledo Lucas County (OH) Public Library *222*

PROGRAM 26 **Support Rural Business: Employment and Business Entrepreneur Center**
Susan M. Preece, Topsham (ME) Public Library *230*

Resources *237*

Index *241*

ACKNOWLEDGMENTS

The editor wishes to thank the following for their contributions to this book: all featured authors and contributors and the libraries and organizations they represent; the Public Policy and Advocacy Office at ALA, especially Dr. Alan Inouye for guidance, Katherine Varela for manuscript assembly and organizational support, and Kathi Kromer for general leadership; Amelia Bryne for editorial expertise; Marijke Visser for critical review and development; editors Patrick Hogan and Jamie Santoro with ALA Editions; and the Libraries Build Business cohort libraries for their leadership. We thank the Libraries Build Business initiative, with support from Google.org, and the American Library Association, for the opportunity to highlight and advance small business and entrepreneurship initiatives at public libraries.

Libraries Build Business logo

INTRODUCTION

HOW LIBRARIES BUILD BUSINESS

Megan Janicki and Marijke Visser

The entrepreneurship services described in this compendium reflect some of the best and brightest programming of public libraries across the nation. These business development programs address the unique challenges and opportunities of each community and show that these inspiring programs need not be the exclusive domain of large or well-funded libraries. The Libraries Build Business project is a powerful example of how today's libraries and seasoned library professionals advance innovation and economic growth, especially in libraries serving entrepreneurs from underrepresented groups.

—PATRICIA "PATTY" WONG, ALA PRESIDENT 2021–2022

On any budget and scale, your library can help underrepresented entrepreneurs launch a viable business idea that addresses a community need. The American Library Association's Libraries Build Business initiative demonstrates endless possibilities for impactful programs your library can implement, including one-on-one business consultations, classes and workshops, equipment lending, and more.

We invite you to explore the experiences of library staff and the twenty-six unique programs profiled in this book for inspiration in developing your own small business program tailored to your local context.

Integrating into the Entrepreneurial Ecosystem

Libraries have a distinctive role to play in the small business ecosystem and can effectively partner to complement, rather than compete with, existing business services in the community. Because of the library's established reputation as an inclusive and safe place for anyone, it is a natural candidate for welcoming aspiring and existing entrepreneurs into the local infrastructure of entrepreneurial services and opportunities.

Libraries offer low-barrier access to basic technology, equipment, and information, making it easy for an entrepreneur to explore or test out a business idea before committing or investing in it. This is a key advantage for low-income or underrepresented entrepreneurs, who may lack the capital to start or sustain their business ventures. With strategic partnerships, libraries can also make referrals and help entrepreneurs get connected. This sense of belonging and inclusion is vital to sustaining a small business venture; library-initiated networking and introductions can be a critical link to success. Providing access to the resources and services necessary to get a business off the ground firmly establishes the important role of the library in fostering equity, diversity, and inclusion for entrepreneurs.

Beyond the benefits to individual entrepreneurs, library services for entrepreneurs and small business owners have a direct benefit for your community. Small businesses are a core ingredient in a thriving community with a strong economy. They are nimble and responsive to local interests and needs, which helps cultivate a sense of place. Supporting small business owners and entrepreneurs pays dividends, infusing new energy into the community and bolstering economic development in your area, making it a vibrant place to live and work.

Developing and expanding programs and services for entrepreneurs is an important opportunity for your library, too. Economic development is a priority for both the country and our locales; as libraries continue to innovate for twenty-first-century impact and support business services, they can demonstrate their current and future relevance in a changing world. When library staff develop their expertise and skill sets in this area, they expand the library's reach to new and different users. This reach can prove invaluable in fostering an engaged community of library users and supporters. In the process of advocating for entrepreneurs in their communities, libraries continuously seek resources and build capacity, staying on the cutting edge of innovative tools and best practices for locally relevant entrepreneurship. Libraries also make the case for themselves as reliable partners by leveraging their resources to get involved in larger economic development and vitality conversations. This willingness to engage with local economic challenges and opportunities and develop new library services is critical to advocating for libraries with local, state, and national stakeholders, partners, and patrons, and highlights why libraries are worthy of investment.

Like all library programs, library-led small business efforts are responsive to local stakeholders and program participants. The programs operate in a cycle of continuous improvement based on feedback and needs assessment data. Working with local stakeholders, you can develop a highly customized program that is tailored to the specific interests of your community. This approach to small business development programming enables libraries to refine their model and reach more patrons; it also furnishes library staff with the data to make informed decisions about how to prioritize staff time and financial resources.

Our experiences with ALA's Libraries Build Business (LBB) initiative demonstrate that any library can and should get involved with entrepreneurship. As you read this book, you'll discover that any library, no matter their size or budget, can provide critical resources and support to small businesses and entrepreneurs. And, you won't be doing it alone—we have a community of peers working together to share their promising strategies and advice, ask each other questions, and share resources. The programs you read about in

What If You Don't Have a Business Background?

by Julie Brophy, Baltimore County Public Library

Business support can seem overwhelming if you don't have a business background. But if you think about business-related questions as another type of reference question and spend a little time learning the language, before you know it you and your staff will be sufficiently confident and competent to help local small business owners. That's been our experience at the Baltimore County Public Library. Our staff are not specialists, not even age-level specialists; we're all generalists. When we became more intentional about small business support, we made sure our staff was set up for success so our customers would be, too. We looked for free or low-cost trainings to attend, and we worked with partners to bring a free version of their public workshop to some staff. Those staff then trained others. The result: staff who can support small businesses in our area and feel more assured doing so.

this book are really happening, and those library workers can help you get started. We're all in this together.

ALA's Libraries Build Business Initiative

With over 17,000 public libraries and library systems across the country, most Americans have a library nearby. Local libraries like yours offer programs that enable equitable access to services and resources, including both physical spaces and needed technology. Every day, libraries offer programming that is relevant to the day-to-day lives of those in the community, including small business owners and entrepreneurs. Libraries engage deeply in workforce development initiatives and cultivate a vibrant network of stakeholders. They are strong partners for the small business and entrepreneurship communities.

With this in mind, the American Library Association, in partnership with Google.org, invested $2 million to develop the LBB initiative to discern promising library-led models for entrepreneurship and small business programs and services, with an emphasis on low-income and underrepresented entrepreneurs.

Meet the Libraries Build Business Cohort

From nearly ninety applicants, a cohort of thirteen public libraries from across the country was selected to implement their own small business and entrepreneur programs tailored to the needs of their local context:

- Appleton (WI) Public Library
- Baltimore County (MD) Public Library
- Broward County (FL) Library
- Ferguson (MO) Municipal Public Library
- Gwinnett County (GA) Public Library
- Independence (KS) Public Library
- Laramie County (WY) Library System
- Los Angeles (CA) Public Library
- Providence (RI) Public Library
- Richland (SC) Library
- Spokane County (WA) Library District
- Topsham (ME) Public Library
- Yakama Nation Library (Toppenish, WA)

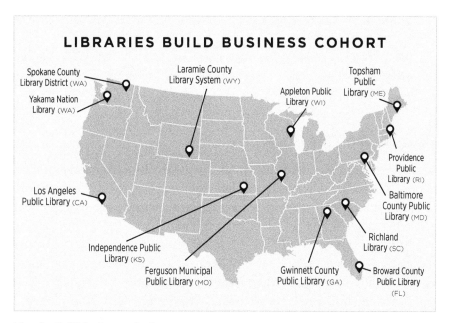

Libraries Build Business cohort map

The selected libraries represent all types and a wide geographical variety (small, medium, large and urban, suburban, rural). Their engagement, vision, and leadership as part of the Libraries Build Business initiative provide a lasting contribution to the field by way of their development of resources, tools, and promising strategies and models to share with other libraries that want to support entrepreneurship.

Throughout the duration of the initiative, the cohort libraries have built up local capacity and expanded their services for small businesses and entrepreneurs, with a focus on businesses owned by people from low-income and underrepresented groups. Their programs funded by the Libraries Build Business initiative are geared toward aspiring and existing entrepreneurs and business owners who reflect the makeup of local communities, including entrepreneurs of color, women, immigrants, tribal communities, veterans, and formerly incarcerated individuals. This commitment to equity, diversity, and inclusion is integral to the LBB approach to business and entrepreneur services and is a core piece of our vision for thriving local communities.

Through this initiative, we have set out to demonstrate the library's role in the local small business ecosystem—as a key partner, access point, and resource center for aspiring and existing entrepreneurs to conduct research, gather resources, learn skills, create, network, and ultimately launch their vision successfully.

Want to know more? You may want to read our Playbook or join our growing peer learning community—connect with us at www.ala.org/advocacy/workforce/grant.

How to Use This Book

Your library can and should offer programs and resources for local entrepreneurs. This book is intended to inspire and equip library workers who are interested in starting, growing, or adapting small business and entrepreneur programs, services, and resources in their library.

Part I of this book offers a few chapters on the considerations and components of building a successful library-led entrepreneurship program in your local context. In chapter 1, the authors highlight the unique challenges facing small and rural libraries that typically don't have the same access to resources, funding, and staff as large library systems in metropolitan and suburban areas. We also acknowledge the unique role that libraries can play in small and rural communities, which may not have access to many business and entrepreneurship support services. In this chapter we feature examples from small and rural libraries, including a case study from the Yakama Nation Library, a tribal library in Washington state. Chapter 2 showcases the core components and essential strategies for successful program development—partnerships, stakeholders, funding, and program sustainability—through the lens and expertise of our Libraries Build Business cohort libraries. Chapter 3 highlights our ALA and Libraries Build Business commitment to equity, diversity, and inclusion (EDI). It features the work our cohort libraries have done across these themes to integrate equity, strengthen business services, and ultimately bolster our primary goal of creating more inclusive business communities and, in turn, cultivate a vision for justice in communities across the country. Finally, chapter 4 showcases expertise and promising strategies from other library types or perspectives. These include contributions from the LA Law Library, the New Jersey State Library, and academic libraries, as well as a window into innovative practices in youth entrepreneurship programming from the Orange County Public Library and the Allen County Public Library.

In part II of the book, we profile business programs and services from twenty-six public libraries around the country. The selected libraries were identified from the Libraries Build Business cohort and from an open call for submissions. Each profile attempts to offer an easy "recipe" for readers to consider adapting or replicating in their local context. We provide the key ingredients—budget considerations, resources, partnerships—and the goals behind each approach to help readers assess their needs, current resources, readiness, and best fit. You will find profiles from libraries across the country that are working in a variety of contexts and offering a wide range of programs—including business resource centers, workshops and classes, mentorship, networking, and access to high-quality equipment and technology. These programs address an array of business needs, including writing a business plan, marketing and outreach, and more. We hope these examples will inspire readers to apply some of these ideas to their own offerings and to join our growing community of colleagues in the field.

PART I
Strategies and Considerations to Get Started

Considerations for Small and Rural Libraries

Brandon West, Susan M. Preece, Rachael Svoboda, Michael Sekaquaptewa, and Taneesa R. Hall

Small and rural libraries are important institutions in their communities that connect residents with a wider world of resources. On average, individuals who call rural America home are never more than 4.9 miles away from one of the more than 4,000 rural libraries in this country, and over 30 million individuals are served by rural libraries.[1] In other words, rural libraries have widespread reach and are key service providers for many groups, including entrepreneurs. In fact, your library has probably been offering some sort of small business help without even knowing it. Your library's existing space and services are often just what an entrepreneur needs. While a dedicated small business initiative might be new to your small or rural library, your interest in this topic shows that you have an entrepreneurial mindset. This way of thinking will allow you to overcome challenges, be decisive, and accept responsibility for the outcomes.

Opportunities and Limitations Facing Small and Rural Libraries

Rural and small libraries have unique opportunities and challenges related to their size, location, and geography compared to urban libraries. Unlike their urban counterparts, which typically have multiple departments, rural libraries rely on small staffs, flexibility, and—above all—their commitment to the communities they serve. Rural libraries are much more than just a "book warehouse." They are evolving and adaptive community centers that provide programming for all ages, offer upskilling opportunities, and facilitate access to technology and Wi-Fi, social services, and community gathering space. Their library staffers are charged with connecting an increasingly diverse audience to resources in an ever-more digital world where those who lack full access are left behind.

While libraries are important to many communities, rural communities typically have more limited resources and infrastructure and view their local library as an essential one-stop-shop for access to programs and services. Libraries connect their rural community to a world of possibilities, including economic development opportunities. The Independence Public Library in Kansas, for example, is located over an hour from the nearest Small Business Development Center (SBDC). This distance makes it almost impossible for underrepresented populations in the rural community to access the SBDC's resources. Consequently, the Independence Public Library works with the SBDC to connect patrons who aren't able to travel to the center with the resources they need.

Small and rural libraries have the opportunity to develop relationships, build rapport, and understand their communities on an intimate level. This means that these libraries often know what is needed and can step up to the plate to aid their communities in difficult economic times. In Topsham, Maine, when the local Naval Air Station closed, many people were not only displaced from their employment but from their homes as well. There were resources available from the federal government to help, but accessing them was a challenge. Many people preferred to go to a place that they knew for assistance, such as the public library. As people arrived with questions, the Topsham Public Library used its knowledge of the community and external resources to help residents navigate the challenges they faced. In another example, the Yakama Nation Library responded to community needs by designing a culturally responsive program for local makers and entrepreneurs who have different perspectives on business ownership and economic development. The experiences of these two libraries, as well as other participants in the Libraries Build Business program, inform the insights in this chapter for all small and rural libraries that seek to offer their communities economic and entrepreneurial support.

Special Considerations for Small and Rural Libraries

When starting an economic development initiative at a rural library, one is often faced with a variety of challenges and considerations, including funding, perceived lack of expertise, and limited space, to name a few. Yet, with some groundwork and creative thinking these challenges can all be turned into opportunities to propel your new endeavor.

Building Capacity by Working Together

When it comes to funding, most small and rural libraries don't have access to a grant writer to pursue funding, or have other staff to commit to the grant requirements. However, rural libraries can still access otherwise out-of-reach resources and programming by networking and partnering with outside organizations. Libraries can also partner with other libraries to share resources.

The Laramie County Library System, for example, partnered with the Wyoming State Library to expand a LibGuide with Wyoming-specific business resources and to create a web page for the Wyoming Library to Business (WL2B) initiative. WL2B also partnered with the Wyoming Women's Business Center, which creates marketing materials and promotes business stations for entrepreneurs at various rural libraries throughout the state. Through this partnership, WL2B could offer virtual personal consultations, programming, and outreach for women-owned businesses in rural communities. Additionally, the Wyoming Small Business Development Center Network provided photography light boxes to each participating public library to help rural small-business owners create professional pictures of craft items. Each library in the WL2B initiative also receives one-on-one training on strategies for connecting its patrons with organizations, programs, and resources to further their business interests. In sum, these collaborations expanded the capacity of the Laramie County Library System, making it possible to provide rural residents with better business assistance and more resources than the library system could have done on its own.

Digital Inclusion and Access

Collaborating with other libraries and organizations can expand your rural library's offerings, connect you with more individuals, and provide a quality of service that matches or exceeds your urban counterparts. However, rural libraries must go even further than just providing programs and events for entrepreneurs. Many library patrons in rural areas do not have access to the internet at home. This challenge brings an added layer of complexity for rural libraries. Virtual programs and resources will not reach and benefit those who don't have quality access to the internet. The Topsham Public Library in Maine has helped to bridge the technology divide by providing low-income residents who want to establish or grow a small business with access to technology and the internet at the library. No longer can a business compete without an internet connection, so library Wi-Fi, hotspots, computers, and laptops are critical supports for some. Not only do libraries provide access to the internet, but they are often the only local organization offering free basic computer help for all, especially in rural areas. This is important for would-be entrepreneurs and business owners who are comfortable with the library and who might feel intimidated by approaching an economic development organization for computer help.

Library Space Considerations

All libraries, and especially small ones, need to consider the challenges and opportunities afforded by their physical spaces. How many staff are needed to operate the building? How many staff members are interested in working with the local business community? Can a storytime and a business program occur at the same time? And if not, can the library adjust its programming? Does your library have enough desk coverage to enable staff members to leave the building for some period of the day to attend a business event at another location? These are some of the questions that must be considered in the process of planning your small business program.

As your business and entrepreneurship offerings grow, having a designated space for these programs and resources becomes increasingly important. And yet, many small libraries have very limited space to begin with. For this reason, your library spaces need to be nimble, adaptable, and multipurpose. For example, small library meeting spaces can serve as conference rooms for business meetings by request, especially when they're outfitted with appropriate technology and equipment. Your library also has several options for making resources mobile. The Wyoming Library to Business stations, for example, can be built on a cart so they can be moved and stored as needed. Somewhat differently, in Missouri, the Ferguson Municipal

Public Library's Entrepreneur and Job Skills Center gets local entrepreneurs, small businesses, and job seekers the information and resources they need to succeed by creating packets which are available at the reference desk or on a wall display.

Start Small

Especially in smaller libraries, keeping things simple and taking small steps may be your best bet. For example, you could provide a small collection of books and a computer with resume-building software, or entrepreneur resources like a template for a business plan. Or a thirty-minute "show and tell" for entrepreneurs and business owners, with time set aside for questions, can serve as the beginning of a two-way communication and help the library identify local business needs. People might have needs that the library can already easily meet—for example, a quiet space and a laptop.

Most importantly, be realistic with yourself when it comes to your time and staff resources. Staff may not have dedicated time to devote to a small business program, but you can still be helpful to local entrepreneurs by doing things like highlighting relevant resources in a display or promoting your partners' services. Knowing what is happening in your community and beyond is just as important as providing individual services. A great way to start is by creating a simple handout that has three components:

- First, what is on the shelf? What physical resources do you have in your library? (A list of business-specific Dewey numbers is a great resource.)
- Second, what is available online via the library? What business resources are available through library databases such as GALE or ProQuest?
- Third, who is a community expert? Which local organizations are available and most appropriate for the business patron? The library can refer its patrons to these services.

Also, remember that building capacity begins with asking for help. Call your local chamber of commerce, SCORE (Service Core of Retired Executives) office, or other organization and ask for advice. People who work in job and entrepreneurship support are often very happy to share their programs and resources. In Maine, public libraries have connected with a network of state-funded CareerCenters to reach those who have various job, small business, and entrepreneurship needs. Counselors for the CareerCenters have found that they are able to reach a different group of people through the public library than they were previously serving; and the needs of library-referred individuals are somewhat different than those who come from regular channels to the centers. This connection is valuable to the CareerCenters, the public libraries, and the community as a whole. No one wants to have to reinvent the wheel when we can be more successful working together. So, when embarking on partnerships, think of it as a win-win situation. And remember that in small communities, "we're all in it together."

> **Micropreneurs**
>
> In many of our small and rural communities, *micropreneurs*, or entrepreneurs with a small operation, are prevalent. Micropreneurs are less interested in growth and prefer the idea of keeping their business small—they may provide a service such as landscaping, babysitting, cleaning, or hairbraiding. At the Ferguson Municipal Public Library in Missouri, our Small Business and Employment Center is especially equipped to serve these micropreneurs with promotion, advertising, and basic equipment to help them get started. We have seen increased interest in micropreneurship as people want to develop an income stream they can depend on. Consider how you could support micropreneurs in your community—perhaps they need a space to have meetings or check their e-mail, software and printers to make flyers, or an online course on accounting?

Leveraging Existing Expertise, Services, and Resources

When it comes to supporting local businesses, the key for small public libraries is to focus on what they do best. Do you have a facility that provides a high-quality Wi-Fi connection? Do you have space to hold large or small group events? Small and rural libraries are experts at making the most of small spaces. How often has your library been asked if you can partner with this or that organization because you are centrally located, have a parking lot, and a willingness to host?

What programs are you already running that could advance entrepreneurship? As noted earlier, most public libraries provide computer help. Could one or two of your regular computer sessions be geared toward business needs? Additionally, new businesses need to publicize their offerings.

Can your librarians share information on how to write a press release? Social media marketing, graphic design, and Excel are all important business skills—and you may already provide instruction on these. Could the focus on how to use a particular computer program or online tool be connected to business needs?

One of the most underrated services that libraries provide is a safe space to make mistakes, to try out unfamiliar skills, and receive encouragement to just keep going. Starting a new career, job, or business is challenging, with many ups and downs. Sometimes the library and library staff are most useful when they act as a sounding board for someone trying to work out what to do next. Libraries are seen as places where smart people can provide reliable answers to anyone with a question. We need to use this expertise to support our entrepreneurs and our small business services partners.

Additionally, flexibility and open communication are key to good partnerships and good programs. Many small libraries have the advantage in this area since they are able to shift gears and adjust without creating too much organizational chaos. While working with the state-funded CareerCenter in its locality, the Topsham Public Library in Maine, for example, has been able to respond to challenges, scale quickly, and test out new things. The Topsham Public Library has also stepped up to meet emergent needs, such as providing a newly formed local advisory board on workforce development (of which the library is a member) with meeting space.

Tribal Libraries: Yakama Nation Library

Engaging people of the Yakama Nation in entrepreneurship is particularly challenging because the people of this region in Washington state are conflicted when aligning themselves with the concept of entrepreneurship itself. For centuries, Yakamas have experienced state and federal policies that were designed to separate them from their assets and sovereignty. A deep subconscious resentment towards industry is the consequence of generations of injustice.

On the surface, the people of our ancestral lands understand entrepreneurship at its core as the activity of building businesses or taking risk in order to make profit. But the systems and principles of entrepreneurship remain a foreign concept for many people of the Yakama Nation. In building businesses on the Yakama Reservation, the entanglements of capitalism fundamentally conflict with our traditional values, as they favor the individual instead of kin and the community. First and foremost, the concept of accumulating and preserving individual wealth (what we consider the driving motivation of entrepreneurship) as we understand it today has not been a cultural value within traditional circles. Culturally, the people of these lands accumulate wealth only to give it all away.

Consciously or unconsciously, the people of the Yakama Nation naturally conduct themselves in accordance with their traditional life-ways. The nearest teachings that Yakamas have concerning entrepreneurship are the stories of the crafty and industrious Spilyay (Coyote). Across numerous tales, Coyote and his foolhardy attempts to cheat or exploit the working class always end in failure and in turn emphasize the practical, communal, or natural orders.

Historically, the people of these lands would hunt, fish, gather, and trade for everything they needed to live. Services, expertise, and craftsmanship were exchanged for goods or recognition. The negotiations in these ancient exchanges were subjective in comparison to the objective dollar. Nevertheless, trades were rarely unequal.

These ancient systems were communal. In the times before colonization, survival wasn't realized through the wealth, might, or intellect of the individual: the concepts of private land ownership and private wealth run counter to our traditional life-ways. Instead, survival was realized through the collective identity of the tribe or band. Lateral support is woven into the social fabric of indigenous society. These ancient traditions and life-ways serve as the source code for replicating our indigenous culture for future generations.

Therefore, when Yakamas begin their journey into entrepreneurship, they are typically skeptical. We are constantly seeking to define entrepreneurship through our own cultural values and traditions, and to lift up our community and our indigenous practices through the lens of entrepreneurship training and upskilling.

The Yakama Nation Library Business Maker Space

Located near the Yakama Nation tribal headquarters, the Yakama Nation Library (YNL) has been the primary resource that tribal members utilize for accessing information and technology. Academic research is conducted there. Cultural revitalization happens there. Fundamentally, YNL has been the central hub precisely because of its open-source and self-determined format. Elsewhere, the community works through bureaucratic employment—educational, legal, and social service systems that cause frustration and aren't responsive to or aligned with the community's needs. The library is the sole haven for creativity and for designing a self-determined trajectory.

YNL provides internet connectivity and a central meeting space for many living in remote areas of the reservation. Even with the internet in place, however, the community relies on open-air markets, yard sales, pow wows, and other community events for business and trade exchanges. People routinely buy, sell, and trade at the library either in person or online by accessing public computers and Wi-Fi.

YNL developed a Business Maker Space to respond to the needs of local entrepreneurs and makers. This allows the library to support entrepreneurs in making, selling, and trading their goods and services, while also contributing to the economic resilience and vitality of the entire community.

After the closure of the Yakama Nation's printing press in the early 1990s, community members were left to figure out printing independently. People took it upon themselves to become familiar with both digital and pre-press technologies to mass-produce their flyers, T-shirts, and other products. Flyers and announcements are a key marketing tool for community members to engage in business and entrepreneurship. These flyers might promote fundraisers, craft sales, services, giveaways, and ceremonies.

Since the 2000s another cultural shift has occurred, and widespread emphasis is now placed on using computers and technology in education and the workplace. Consequently, the library became the learning hub for business and technology education when it started offering marketable business skills, including word-processing and spreadsheet operation with certificate programs that would eventually evolve into endorsements from Microsoft directly.

The 2010s through the present day have marked the most recent evolution in cultivating business skills in our community. In this period, in addition to physical flyers for outreach and promotion, interest in social media and graphic design has grown. Today the community is increasing their knowledge and skills to leverage the internet and social media to their own advantage. In tandem with social media campaigns and digital marketing, business owners, craftspeople, fishers, hunters, and contractors are utilizing the print services and design software that the Yakama Nation Library currently offers.

In order to bolster the indigenous economy first, YNL entered its most recent phase in the business technology revolution by offering the Yakama Nation Library Maker Space and developing the Yakama Small Business Network. The library's maker space was imagined as a place for Yakama small businesses to access the internet, technology, and software needed for managing and marketing their business online. The maker space also provides access to printers and equipment for making business cards and announcements, and for graphic design. The savvy library staff who maintain the maker space provide support in accessing online classes and programs for writing business plans and proposals for grants and loans. The maker space staff also update and facilitate the Yakama Small Business Network.

Both the network and the maker space are intended to be leveraged by indigenous entrepreneurs looking to practice business in culturally relevant and traditional ways. The maker space, therefore, is designed to promote creative entrepreneurs and traditional ways of life in our community: weavers, fishers, and hunters, for example. Our library program is intentional about holistically supporting the reemergence of traditional life-ways through the lens of entrepreneurship.

Small and Rural Libraries Build Business

Keeping an entrepreneurial mindset will help you stay on track and adapt to changes, something rural and small librarians already know how to do. Whether it's partnering with other groups, repurposing your resources, or just dipping your toes in the water, small business initiatives are possible at your library. Taking the resources available to you and applying them to your community's needs and culture creates an opportunity to innovate and dynamically address challenges. In addition, knowing your patrons' names, learning about their businesses, and keeping up with your tight-knit community will allow you to create lifelong learners and advocates for your library.

NOTE

1. Institute of Museum and Library Services, "Rural Libraries across America Continue to Expand Programs and Resources," news release, October 1, 2020, www.imls.gov/news/rural-libraries-across-america-continue-expand-programs-and-resources.

Identifying Stakeholders, Building Partnerships, Finding Funding, and Sustaining It All

Julie M. Brophy, Lori Hench, Karly Feinberg, Diane Luccy, Sheldon Burke, Danielle Milton, Stacey Goddard, Atlas Logan, Adam Pitts, and Christopher Bourret

This chapter discusses the essential strategies and core components of any strong library business program or service. To ensure community support and lasting sustainability, consider your stakeholders from the start and build in plans to assess, adapt, and evolve dynamic programs tailored to your library's local circumstances.

Identifying Stakeholders

It's important to know who the stakeholders are in your community so that you can provide small business programs and services that complement, not compete, with the players already present in the entrepreneurial ecosystem. This approach helps grow the library's positive impact and supports the idea that libraries are connectors in the community. But who are the stakeholders in your community? And why are they important?

Who Are Our Stakeholders?

Stakeholders help an organization meet its strategic objectives by contributing their experience and perspective to the mission and vision of the organization. In other words, your stakeholders are those individuals or groups that have an interest in your library's business programs and services. Whether internal or external, these stakeholders have a vested interest in supporting the economic ecosystem of your community. You need to know who they are to have their support and ensure the success of your small business initiatives. The stakeholders in your specific community can generally be grouped into five categories:

Elected officials: Whether it's the mayor, city or county council members, or other representatives, it's critical to get your local elected officials on board. These stakeholders can provide financial and promotional support. Reach out and offer to make presentations about the resources offered by your public library.

Library leadership: These may include administrators, members of the library board of trustees, and your Friends and Foundation board. Leadership support is crucial to success. Do you need additional staff? Resources? Funding? Leadership can help you with these important needs.

Community members and other potential participants: Don't forget to consider hosting focus groups and community conversations to find out what the community wants or needs, not what you think is needed. Once you create small business programs and services, you'll need community members to attend, actively participate, and be inspired by what they experience.

Funders: We'll expand on this critical group in a later section of this chapter, but establishing stable, reliable funding is critical for the ongoing success and sustainability of any program. Consider reaching out to local banks, foundations, and nonprofit organizations, as well as local, state, and federal agencies for grants and other funding opportunities.

Partner organizations: It should be a high priority for you to collaborate with the small business organizations and agencies in your local community. Read more about this in the "Building Partnerships" section below.

Once you've identified your stakeholders and done your background work, you'll be better situated to bring your small business programs to fruition and make a positive economic impact on your community.

How Do You Identify the Stakeholders Relevant to Your Program?

One way to identify stakeholders relevant to your library's small business initiative is to conduct an environmental scan. The scan will identify existing resources, services, and programs that serve small business owners in the community, as well as track trends in the internal and external environment. The results from your environmental scan will help you make the best decisions about what programs and services to offer, when to offer them, and to whom. Remember that we don't compete, we complement. We want to be diligent about not duplicating services and efficiently allocating limited resources.

There are a number of different tools that you can use to do the environmental scan and related analysis. Some common ones include SWOT and PESTLE. Once you have figured out who the stakeholders are, you can also consider which of them needs to be involved at what level, and what issues they may bring with them. You probably know a lot more about your stakeholders and the economic environment than you think.

For each stakeholder or stakeholder group, you will want to define who they are and what role they play in your work; determine strategies to make your case for public libraries as an integral part of economic success in your community; and know when and what you will be asking of them. In the process of "selling" the role of the public library to stakeholders, be prepared to share small business success stories and feedback from surveys,

---

Identifying Stakeholders for Your Library's Small Business Program

Here are a few questions to ask yourself:

1. Does the stakeholder have a fundamental impact on your organization's performance?
2. Can you clearly identify what you want from the stakeholder?
3. Is this relationship dynamic? Do you want it to grow or to be sustained?
4. Can you exist without or easily replace the stakeholder?

focus groups, small business coaching appointments, and other small business-related services in order to illustrate your value.

Building Partnerships

Your library may already have established partnerships, or you may have identified possible new partners in the process of identifying stakeholders. The idea of cultivating, formalizing, and maintaining partnerships can seem daunting and time-consuming. However, partnerships enable you to offer a greater depth and breadth of expertise and services to your patrons. Partnerships help share the workload and address capacity issues. Partnerships can create stronger and more cohesive business communities, helping to ensure individuals get the referrals they need. And if you're new to business programming, partnerships can connect you to the very people you are trying to reach with your efforts.

Devising a program outline or curriculum for your small business initiative is a good starting point for exploring new partnerships. Knowing what topics you need covered makes it easier to narrow down whom to approach and how to frame your request. Take stock of the agencies and institutions in your community. Are there groups you've worked with in the past that you think would be helpful to work with again? As you think of active groups in your community, are you aware of what services these groups offer? Researching local agencies and institutions will help you focus your time and energy on the potential partners that are the best fit for you.

Types of Partners

Possible partners come in all shapes and sizes—ranging from nonprofit groups to local companies, to governmental agencies, and more. What partnerships will work best for you depends on various factors, including geography and the scope of your project. A few examples of potential partners for library small-business initiatives include:

> Chambers of Commerce. Your local chamber of commerce is a great place to start when you're looking at potential partners. The chamber is already working with businesses in your area and has likely already gathered information on what resources and support business owners ask for the most. This data could augment

any needs assessment or survey information you've collected or are planning to collect. Chamber meetings are a wonderful opportunity to spread the word about what library services you have to offer business owners and their employees. Whether you're giving your library's "elevator speech" during a meeting, or sharing that information in one-on-one conversations, you're letting chamber members know what the library can do for them. Some chambers offer meeting sponsorships which allow the sponsor more "floor time" to talk about their organization and services. If your budget allows, consider sponsoring a chamber meeting to gain a larger platform for what you'd like to share with that audience.

Your local SCORE chapter. The Service Core of Retired Executives (SCORE) has an established reputation for providing industry-specific mentoring to aspiring small business owners and entrepreneurs. SCORE also presents workshops on a variety of small business topics. Reach out to your local SCORE chapter to learn more about what services are available and to let them know what you can offer their clients. SCORE volunteers may not be aware of the business research help the library can provide, and may send clients to you for assistance with things like sizing their market or identifying possible locations for their business. For some communities, the closest SCORE chapter may be an hour or more away—but don't let that discourage you. Many SCORE chapters provide online workshops, and will happily offer mentoring help via Zoom, e-mail, or telephone. SCORE's national website offers some free webinars, but be aware that your local chapter may charge registration fees as part of their operating costs. If your budget allows, consider whether you could offer SCORE presenters an honorarium or other stipend so that the workshops they present will be free for your patrons.

Community-based social justice organizations. Seek out organizations and clubs that serve underrepresented populations in your service area. Is there a Hispanic merchants association group that meets regularly, or a women's center that offers entrepreneurial classes, or an LGBTQIA+ business alliance in your community? Think about how the services your library offers could complement those organizations. Underrepresented populations may not be thinking about the library as a resource, so meeting them where they are is a critical first step. Among the Libraries Build Business cohort, those libraries' partners have included women's business centers, BIPOC business associations, immigrant-serving language programs, and more. Your local nonprofits and community-based organizations will have the expertise to connect with underrepresented entrepreneurs in a culturally responsive manner.

Local credit unions, banks, or other lending institutions. Remember that aspiring small business owners and entrepreneurs usually have one thing in common: at some point they all need funding. Introducing yourself to local bank and credit union staff (perhaps at a chamber meeting) will get you on their radar as a place to refer clients who might need to do a bit more homework before they are ready to apply for a loan. Cultivating a relationship with your local credit union or bank might lead to other opportunities as well, such as being able to provide programs on financial literacy at your library. While this isn't necessarily business programming, it can help individuals get on the right path to achieving their dream of business ownership.

Business improvement districts (BIDs), business alliances, and visitors bureaus. The primary goal of local BIDs, Main Street associations, and similar alliances is to cultivate greater economic prosperity in their communities by bringing in businesses and setting those businesses up for success. For this reason, they'll be interested in investing in local entrepreneurs that want to launch a business. Find out what promotions and events these organizations are hosting, and whether they'd be interested in sponsoring an event for the library, offering a class or workshop, or networking.

Marketing Your Library Program to Potential Partners

Broward County Library

A *coworking space* is an office space that is used by people from different companies (or other organizations) to share the cost of office space, equipment, and other infrastructure. There are approximately fifteen coworking spaces within five miles of the Broward County Main Library in Florida. Yet, the library's free coworking space—Creation Station Business—thrives in this competitive ecosystem. The secret to our success? Establishing partnerships with many of these spaces and bringing value to their customers and businesses. For instance, the library can share business resources such as databases, patent and trademark information, and educational classes. This is advantageous for the library in that we have access to a new audience, and advantageous for the coworking space in that they can enhance their customer offerings at no additional cost. Only once have we been rebuffed in trying to establish a partnership (by a for-profit coworking space that saw the library as a competitor). While librarians may be shy to form partnerships for this reason or others, know that libraries have a lot to offer potential partners, even for-profit companies.

Libraries' primary strength lies in leveraging their established public reputation. For many, libraries hold a special place in their heart. In 1984, the newly opened eight-story Broward County Main Library seemed like an anomaly in a barren downtown. Since then, Fort Lauderdale, Florida, has ballooned into a thriving metropolis. While the city grew, the library served the community's needs, librarians hosted programs, library managers established community ties, and library staff interacted with hundreds of small business owners on their lunch breaks at nearby restaurants. The library is part of the social and cultural fabric of Fort Lauderdale. Because of these community ties, libraries are trusted spaces where people can learn, study, or meet with neighbors. Compare this to nonprofits and for-profit groups, where the public may be more skeptical of their aims and goals. Partnering with the library benefits these organizations in reaching the public, and the library in stretching its budgets to reach its goals.

For example, one of our partners, General Assembly, is a for-profit, private educational organization with over thirty campuses worldwide that was looking to grow its operations and establish itself in Broward County. A large organization such as General Assembly could buy office space and pay for a marketing campaign, but instead of spending its budget on establishing itself, General Assembly chose to work with an established community anchor as a free way to gain access to the Broward market. After all, who better to work with in Broward County than the Broward County Main Library, one of the oldest institutions in downtown Fort Lauderdale?

Strategies to Build Partner Relationships

Once potential partners have been identified, the next step is to develop relationships with them. Start small: ask a potential partner to meet for coffee so you can learn about their organization. Start attending community organizations' meetings and listening to the discussions. Often, just listening to their needs will lead to an opportunity for the library to assist them. Learning about the potential partner prior to working with them is important. Research what they are working on, the services they provide, and what their goals are. By attending the meetings, you will begin to develop the necessary trust between the organization and your library. At first you may get a questioning response similar to "the library is here?" This will eventually turn into "the library is here!" as your relationship progresses. Once you've developed a relationship with community organizations, making an ask of a partner, whether it's for a grant or a deeper collaboration, is going to be much easier because you already have a relationship in place.

When your library and a partner have agreed to work together on a project or in an ongoing way, it is important to define what each partner's role will be and how much time they should expect to commit. This can range anywhere from a partner offering a one-time presentation at the library, to committing to teaching a recurring workshop series, to the library offering a partner ongoing access to its meeting space or resources. If you are struggling to find partners, incentives can go a long way. Remember, a partnership is a reciprocal, mutually beneficial relationship, so try to brainstorm some ways your library can support your partner's organization. Offering guest speakers an honorarium is a nice gesture, too, if you have the resources to do so.

Formalizing Your Partnership

Three of the most intimidating words to hear when working with partners might be Memorandum of Understanding (MOU), or Memorandum of Agreement (MOA). Regardless of what you call them, MOUs and MOAs don't need to be scary. Instead, they can provide a framework for any partnership because they clarify the roles, responsibilities, and expectations of both parties.

MOUs can help avoid misunderstandings and other communication errors, especially now that many meetings are held virtually. MOUs clearly define the responsibilities of each partner and spell out the goals and outcomes of the project. Having an MOU in place provides important continuity if key players on either side of the partnership change; it contains all the details necessary to bring a new person up to speed and prevents someone new from coming in and changing agreed-upon terms.

That's not to say that MOUs aren't a lot of work, especially if you or your potential partner have a formal process for creating and executing MOUs. A governmental agency, for example, may require their legal department to review and approve any MOU, which could take weeks, or longer. If you think you'll need an MOU with your partner, start the discussion sooner rather than later so you have plenty of time to complete the process.

Depending on the size of your organization and that of your partner(s), there may not be a need for a formal MOU. At the very least, though, consider spelling out roles and responsibilities in an e-mail or document so that both partners can refer to it as needed. As time passes, people don't remember what was said or agreed upon, so having a written record of who is doing what is very important to the success of your partnership.

Examples of Successful Partnerships

Some partnerships don't work out despite our best efforts. Yet, in many cases partnerships can prove even more fruitful than you had originally hoped. Let's explore some examples of thriving partnerships that have benefited the library, the partner, and the community.

Spokane County Library District, Washington

The Spokane County Library District has had a long-standing partnership with a local credit union. The credit union presents monthly workshops at library branches on a variety of topics, including budgeting, saving for retirement, and preventing identity theft. The credit union surprised the library during their 2019 Season of Giving by donating $1,000 to each of the library's 11 locations.

Richland Library, South Carolina

With the help of a Libraries Build Business grant, Richland Library established FastTrac for Female Entrepreneurs, a series of ten classes that provide critical resources for women to grow and develop their small businesses. Before getting started, the library reached out to Midlands Technical

College, the Women's Business Center at Benedict College, and the City of Columbia Office of Business Opportunities to determine their level of interest in collaborating on this program series. Each partner agency made a commitment to the project and contributed different skills, including social media and outreach, facilitating and hosting individual programs in the series, and managing registration and follow-up. Richland Library's strengths were complemented by the strengths of the other organizations involved, resulting in a successful program series. You don't have to do the important work alone—collaboration is the key to success.

Gwinnett County Public Library, Georgia

The work of the Gwinnett County Public Library (GCPL) with the formerly incarcerated started as a partnership with the Greater Gwinnett Reentry Alliance (GGRA), a coalition of social service providers, government agencies, and community members that support the reentry population. In 2019, the library gave a closed-circuit television presentation on library resources to inmates at the Gwinnett County Jail and hosted more than forty small business programs featuring partners such as SmallBiz Ally, SCORE, the Latin American Association, and the University of Georgia's Small Business Development Center. With this framework in place, GCPL was ideally positioned to connect justice-involved individuals with small business resources. GCPL applied for a Libraries Build Business grant to fund its New Start Entrepreneurship Incubator (NSEI), an entrepreneur development program tailored to the needs of formerly incarcerated individuals. The library's original partnerships have evolved to support the NSEI program in a myriad of ways, with partners serving as presenters at monthly in-person meetings, providing ongoing mentors to program participants, and more.

Leveraging Funding Opportunities

Funding is an ongoing challenge that presents numerous barriers for the average library. For some programs or initiatives, it may be necessary to seek additional funding beyond the library's operational budget. Successful grant-seeking requires a significant up-front investment in time and capacity-building. These investments involve data collection, developing systems of evaluation, creating boilerplate language or copy to describe your programs and their impact, developing budgets for programs, and meeting other basic requirements set by most grant funders. Having a good narrative story of a program participant is a powerful tool in attracting funders, too. Making these investments does require effort and time, but it has the potential to pay dividends in terms of the ability to access grant funding and support that might otherwise be left on the table.

Make the case to your administration or board to invest in development and grant-seeking and to persist in these efforts, recognizing that success will entail some amount of learning and trial and error. If sufficient funding isn't available to hire a dedicated grant writer, a consultant can help you get the foundations in place and start the process. This will entail delving into the details of your work—the who, what, when, and why of what you're doing, who you're serving, the greater need it's addressing, and its impact, as well as research to identify well-aligned prospective grantors.

When seeking funding, keep in mind local and regional businesses that are likely to focus their grants on priorities like workforce and business development, which entrepreneurship is a natural part of. Banking institutions are generally a great fit and can be a valuable partner in supporting small business programs on many levels. In addition to grant opportunities, many businesses are happy to provide volunteer resources and in-kind contributions to your programs that can be highly useful to those you serve, such as leading workshops focused on financial literacy and small business financing.

Making Use of Partnerships, Data, and Feedback

If your library currently lacks the capacity to do grant-writing on your own, consider leveraging partnerships. The use of library spaces, research databases, and the ability to market programs to library visitors are valuable additions for partners. Partner agencies can be quite willing to bring the library in as a subcontractor on grants or initiatives, which can help provide monetary resources for your programming, equipment, or other needs. As mentioned earlier, creating Memorandums of Understanding can help set clear terms for the partners' expectations, responsibilities, and deliverables that will benefit both parties.

Basic data collection about your library's impact in the community can go a long way to facilitating funding and other support. Quotes, personal experiences, and any kind of evidence of direct impact on those you've already served are some of the most powerful content you can collect and include in your own proposals or when cultivating partnerships. A mix of quantitative and qualitative outcomes is a great way to tackle funders' evaluation requirements, and surveys are highly effective tools for collecting evidence of impact on your audience. The Providence Public Library in Rhode Island, for example, started capturing program feedback to share with funders and now has a wealth of data illustrating the library's impact—largely through the use of a post-program survey.

Remember, persistence is key in the pursuit of funding—build this expectation into your timeline and don't get discouraged. If you submit a proposal that ends up being declined, ask for feedback whenever possible. This is valuable because you will often get specific input like "your expected numbers served seem low for your budget request," or "your need data wasn't substantial enough or didn't convey enough urgency," so you can take actionable steps to improve these in the future. You can also continually research and uncover new funding prospects where you can potentially reuse your proposal content. Make sure that none of your groundwork is wasted.

Sustaining Your Investment

Whether it's your overall business services and initiatives or one particular continuing program, sustainability encompasses both keeping it going and keeping it relevant. While funding is generally considered a crucial element of sustainability, other factors also influence the ongoing success of your small business efforts. Your library's ability to maintain its partnerships, funding, programs, educational content, and business reference services requires regular assessment, evaluation, and responsiveness to provide effective support to your business community.

Engaging Staff and Planning for Change

Do you have staff who have time allotted to prioritize this work and who are knowledgeable about business reference service? Consider creating a team of employees who are interested in serving the business community, and create opportunities for them to access training, share resources, and participate in programming while networking and learning from each other. The skills these employees gain will benefit your community's entrepreneurs, and as an added bonus, these core employees will model their skills for other staff, too.

Turnover happens. Expect and prepare for changes to your business-interest staff by engaging in succession planning for both staff and for your programs and services. As an ongoing practice, encourage other staff to familiarize themselves with your business services and participate in programs. For programs, establish a framework which includes a planning and implementation timeline and keep it accessible in a shared location, making it easier for a new person to implement the events. Keep a list of established partner organizations, associations, and presenters with contact information. These practices ensure that changes in your own staff won't derail your library's progress, and they allow for a more seamless transition.

Keeping and Deepening Partnerships

As touched on earlier in this chapter, forming partnerships is a great way to combine resources to attain a shared goal. Partnerships allow your library to extend its reach to encompass that of your partner's reach and tap into their particular expertise. Partnerships can be great for programs because they allow your library to provide information and services you wouldn't be able to provide otherwise. And oftentimes partners will agree to hold these programs for free (or for a nominal fee). Partnerships lend themselves to sustainability because the effort and resources are contributed from a larger group, meaning that the work is more easily funded and supported. Forming partnerships and collaborating with outside organizations will ultimately lead to a more unified and supportive entrepreneurial ecosystem in your area.

Learn about the Community's Needs and Target Your Programs to Meet Them

When it comes to initiating and sustaining small business programs, it is important to identify specific needs you want to meet and audiences you want to reach—such as veterans, formerly incarcerated individuals, immigrant communities, etc., or aspiring entrepreneurs who don't have a business yet, or new businesses, creative businesses, tech businesses, and so on.

Identify programs and delivery methods that will allow you to meet the needs in your community, and then make these programs relevant and accessible to the groups you identified. The Baltimore County Public Library, for example, received a lot of questions about starting nonprofits. As a result, the library developed a two-part nonprofit academy to satisfy this informational need. Additionally, aim to find ways to alleviate barriers (such as tech divides, language and literacy challenges, etc.) in order to make your programs and resources accessible to as many people as possible.

Using Assessment to Stay Relevant

Establishing a consistent method to solicit feedback can provide your library with the information it needs to evaluate its programs and services in a non-biased manner. Consider creating a brief general questionnaire which not only gathers feedback on current programs or services, but also includes input on topics of interest for future events, and then use that information to tweak your current services and develop new ones.

Even successful initiatives will falter and lose relevance if they don't evolve. Both internal and external factors can prompt change. How many public libraries were regularly providing virtual programming and services prior to the COVID-19 pandemic, as opposed to now? The Baltimore County Public Library's Entrepreneur Academy started as an in-person program, offered in one branch and accommodating about twenty-five students. In the wake of the pandemic, it's now being offered via Zoom, hosts 100 or more students per cohort, and includes attendees from across Maryland; an optional co-learning session is offered to allow for informal shared learning, interaction, and networking.

Advocacy and Buy-In

Be an advocate for your small business initiatives. Get the word out through marketing and promotional efforts on your library's website, social media outlets, and print publications. Encourage your program participants to share their experiences and recommend the library to their business colleagues. Visit business associations, chambers of commerce, and other organizations that are active in the entrepreneur ecosystem. Finally, document and share your successes with stakeholders.

All of this helps to create buy-in—that is, other groups now recognize your library's efforts as a valued, relevant part of the small business ecosystem. Buy-in from small businesses and entrepreneurs means they'll look to you for education and resources. Buy-in from partners makes them eager to collaborate with you. Buy-in from your own administration and funders means you'll be able to count on underwriting and support to sustain, expand, and promote your work.

Setting Up for Success

In sum, to ensure that your small business efforts are a success, it is key to identify stakeholders, build partnerships, find funding, and sustain your initiatives despite changing needs and circumstances. While this may seem overwhelming when looked at together, breaking these steps into bite-size components can help make this work manageable for libraries of all sizes. This foundational work will lead to relevant and enriching programs for your community.

Equity, Diversity, and Inclusion in Library Entrepreneurship Programs

Adriana McCleer, Madeleine Ildefonso, LaKesha Kimbrough, and Michael Sekaquaptewa

The Libraries Build Business initiative defined equity, diversity, and inclusion (EDI) principles in library entrepreneurship programs as "a commitment to providing programming, resources, and other supports for small businesses and entrepreneurs from underrepresented groups and low-income communities in culturally responsive, impactful ways." This includes taking a strengths-based approach to integrating our library services and supports in our local contexts and listening to the needs and interests of those in our community, lifting up and prioritizing the voices of disenfranchised community members, and orienting ourselves toward social justice.

In learning and growing together, the Libraries Build Business cohort tried many ideas, tools, and approaches to advance EDI in their small business and entrepreneurship programs. We shared our experiences with each other and discussed theoretical concepts and frameworks. We explored how these concepts and frameworks can be used in library practice to advance EDI and build holistic and engaging library programs for and with our communities. We hope that what we've learned along the way can help you do the same.

Our framework is continually being refined in conversations with each other as peers and practitioners and within our communities. The framework also revealed limitations and areas in which we could become more responsive and inclusive in our outreach and programming efforts. In this spirit, we engage in a cycle of action and reflection, continuously examining our work, collaborating with peers and our patrons and customers, and finding channels to be more inclusive, thus broadening our understanding and scope.

The Libraries Build Business Initiative's Commitment to Equity, Diversity, and Inclusion

Our nation has systems of power and injustice that have developed and maintained significant disparities that limit equity of access to business and entrepreneurship resources and support, thereby limiting the business success of Black, Indigenous, people of color, immigrants, women, those in the justice system, veterans, low-income, and other marginalized individuals and groups.

The National Community Reinvestment Coalition reports that "there are tremendous gaps in black and Hispanic business ownership relative to their population size [in the United States]," and there is "a troubling pattern of disinvestment, discouragement and inequitable treatment for black and Hispanic-owned businesses."[1] Other barriers include limited access to mentors and role models, limited financial literacy, lack of access to funding, and exclusion from social and business networks. Recognizing these disparities, the American Library Association established Libraries Build Business with the intent to support the creation and evaluation of library-led entrepreneurship models that would help low-income and underrepresented entrepreneurs start and grow small businesses.

By providing access to business information resources, financial resources, and business training, as well as connections and networks, public libraries can create a bridge that advances equity for marginalized community members, supports diversity in small business and entrepreneurship, and prioritizes inclusion. Among other things, libraries can reach out to underrepresented communities, work closely with community partners, prioritize representation, channel capital to low-income and underrepresented communities, listen deeply to lived experiences and the business visions of community members, and serve as advocates for equity, diversity, and inclusion.

Integrating EDI Principles into Our Work

The libraries in the Libraries Build Business cohort worked collaboratively on EDI principles in order to better integrate those practices and values into our small business programs and services. As a cohort we engaged in the following topics: (1) shared terms and understanding; (2) exploring and understanding historical context; (3) cultural humility as a tool for healthy engagement; and (4) a framework of healing-centered engagement. The cohort examined these themes and frameworks with the goal of creating and maintaining equitable ways of being and engaging; fostering safe spaces; and adopting equitable ways of honoring lived experiences in our professional and personal realms. The following subsections summarize these topics, with considerations for reflecting and integrating these ideas into library work.

Shared Terms and Understanding

We engaged in conversations to think about the importance of the language we use, why we use it, and how we use it. This practice required us to acknowledge that the words we use can, and often do, have different meanings to different people or groups. When we are embarking upon a journey that involves multiple stakeholders, it is important to have a shared understanding of words. For example, in starting a program for formerly incarcerated individuals, the Gwinnett County Public Library in Georgia considered a variety of terms to use to discuss their program with stakeholders, avoid stigma, and promote inclusion and belonging. Together, we learned how words and symbols help us make meaning of the world around us. They connect us, allow us to share ideas, and build community. We also reflected on how language can be used either for harm, or to help heal and repair. Having shared meanings for terms enables us to talk about our work in cohesive ways, helps us set shared goals, and when reflecting upon and evaluating our work, helps us collectively celebrate wins. What are some of the terms that you, your team, and your community use in your work? How might having a shared understanding of these support your projects?

Understanding Historical Context

Knowing the history of our land, city, or region, and what systems and cultures have impacted our lives, and the lives of those with and for whom we work and serve, helps us in several ways. When we understand historical events and the ways in which they have shaped and continue to shape our lives, we are better able to work for long-term, equitable solutions. With this lens we might explore, for example, how housing codes have impacted not only where people could live and work, but also how public services and institutions were funded, and how these historical decisions impact the present day. Or we might explore who has historically had access to services in communities (e.g., transit stations, grocery stores), the quality of these services, and if access was restricted—when was it fully granted? What might you learn about economic and small business development as you explore and learn about your area? How might your discoveries influence program design?

Using Cultural Humility as a Tool for Healthy Engagement
The framework of cultural humility, which has its roots in the medical field, has given us the opportunity to learn how self-reflection, addressing power imbalances, and developing mutually beneficial relationships can help libraries to create and maintain equitable spaces and programs. Applying these three components of the cultural humility framework influences its fourth component, structural change—change that impacts the fabric of our organizations. More specifically, we learned that:

- **Critical self-reflection** helps us to stay aware of our biases and interrupt them when we might be acting on them. A practice of self-reflection can help us understand our behaviors and patterns and help us reclaim parts of our narrative that felt incomplete or suppressed. Through this practice, we are able to connect to and with ourselves and others in meaningful ways.
- **Power imbalances** often happen in spaces where "power over" rather than "power with" is upheld, and when we fail to remember that all parties bring valuable knowledge to the relationship/partnership. We can address power imbalances by naming them, engaging in healthy listening, looking for authentic ways to share power and partner with others, and by being as transparent as possible. When we do these things, we create the conditions for trust and relationships to be strengthened, as well as for collective ownership and belonging to take place.
- **Mutually beneficial relationships** are those that enrich and serve all parties; each person gives and receives, and in some

way benefits from the relationship. This can look different for each member of the partnership, and this is okay. When we do not create the conditions for mutually beneficial relationships, we set ourselves up for power imbalances, which can lead to oppressive spaces that perpetuate harm. Mutually beneficial relationships support the growth of all involved and aid in the creation of nurturing, healing spaces. Some of the ways we might create such relationships are by recognizing the importance of cultivating trust, respect, and safety, and the fact that these take time to build.

When we engage in a practice of reflection (both as individuals and organizations); become aware of, name, and address power imbalances; and develop and sustain mutually beneficial relationships, we help create the conditions for structural change. How can we do this practically in library work? This might involve exploring your library's policies and procedures. Are they perpetuating bias? Is the language your organization uses deficit-based or "coded" to cover up oppression and systemic inequities? It might also involve exploring your library's guiding principles, revising them, and using them to make decisions that honor a commitment to justice, equity, diversity, inclusion, and belonging. In sum, through collective reflection, we can come to understand the roots of injustice and inequity. This allows us to look deeper than individual change and transformation and reimagine structures that would allow for systems-level change. We can take practical steps to move this work forward by examining the power structures within our organizations and communities.

Using Healing-Centered Engagement as a Tool for Healthy Engagement
Healing-centered engagement (HCE), a term coined by Shawn Ginwright, is a framework that has its origin and roots in the field of youth development. It is a robust framework that is applicable to many contexts, including library spaces. This framework is asset-driven and is a tiered approach. This means that individual transformation influences interpersonal connections, which, in turn, positively impact the larger culture of our institutions and communities. There are five principles of HCE that help nurture equitable spaces and strengthen relationships. As you read about these five principles (below), consider: how do you envision they might deepen your own library's work?

Culture: Healing-centered engagement involves building a healthy identity and sense of belonging. We acknowledged our own cultural and racial identities and reflected on what this means for how we show up in our work, allowing us to do the same for members of our communities.

Agency: This is a reminder to us that feeling like we have some power and control over our lives can provide us with hope and help us remember that we are more than the worst thing that has happened to us. We can nurture others' agency by listening to them and by providing opportunities and ways to create change.

Relationships: These foster a sense of belonging, which helps us to feel seen and valued. We develop healthy relationships with care, commitment, and intention. We can model healthy vulnerability, be consistent, and remember that we do not need to have all the answers.

Meaning: In this framework, "meaning" means exploring who we are and what purpose we are meant to serve. Having clarity about our meaning in life and in our work can help us feel purposeful and connected. Discovering and working from our meaning involves gaining a deeper understanding of ourselves. We can aid in healthy meaning-making by creating room for many voices to be heard, creating ways for individuals to take part in identifying and enacting solutions, and finding ways to help foster the passions of those with whom we work and serve.

Aspirations: These help us to imagine life beyond oppression and to set clear goals toward which we can work, both personally and collectively. Having aspirations and an aspirational mindset can help us imagine new solutions to old or familiar problems and can generate a feeling of optimism about the future. We can ask, "What if?" and encourage imaginative thinking.

This framework can help libraries and library workers embrace equity and belonging by centering humanity and relationship-building in our work. Building successful entrepreneurship programs isn't simply about business practices and skill-building—libraries must inspire confidence and agency by building people-centered practices of dignity and respect. For this reason, successful business programs often include time for networking and relationship-building, wraparound services, and needs assessments to understand the best times and locations to hold programs.

Engaging authentically and intentionally in the work of equity, diversity, inclusion, and belonging asks us to commit to interrupting, dismantling, and reconstructing systems that have been designed to create privilege through othering. Libraries can do this in a variety of ways. These frameworks and conversations provide us with a foundation to enrich our professional practices and advance the work of EDI in our library small business and entrepreneurship programs and beyond.

Shifting Paradigms: Entrepreneurs and the Purpose of Entrepreneurship

When we incorporate equitable and inclusive practices in our small business programming, how we view entrepreneurship and how we measure success naturally shifts. Entrepreneurship in the United States has traditionally been a career path reserved for middle-class white men who share the goal of building individual profits, wealth, and prestige. Many of our resources, networks, and business organizations are designed with this population and this outcome in mind. But as the small business ecosystem diversifies, lifting up the talents and expertise of underrepresented entrepreneurs, we demonstrate that entrepreneurship can be practiced from a variety of perspectives and offer a range of community benefits.

Entrepreneurship can be a vital path to economic stability for individuals from many backgrounds and with different lived experiences. It can also help to build a strong local economy that is responsive to the community and customers. In this way, entrepreneurship can be viewed as a form of mutual aid: when entrepreneurs from the community offer goods and services that reflect the needs of their neighbors and customers, a healthy and sustainable economy is built. Small business owners are valued for what they offer, and their customers, by shopping with them or engaging their services, help these businesses grow and thrive.

This mutually beneficial balance is a critical component of building strong, vital communities and is the goal of equitable and inclusive business practices. The libraries in the Libraries Build Business cohort engaged with these ideas and considered how developing good relationships and exploring power balances are key to creating spaces and programs that are vital and inclusive. In the Yakama Nation, for example, the goal of the library's Business Maker Space program is to support local entrepreneurs in ways that acknowledge and include traditional, ancient life-ways. To be culturally responsive and uphold local values, the Yakama Nation Library had to define entrepreneurship through an indigenous lens, with the purpose of helping the indigenous economy to sustain itself and flourish. The Business Maker Space program uplifts Yakama cultural values, including resiliency and self-determination. Equitable business practices that prioritize trade, community wealth, and community vitality are highlighted, in a reflection of their importance to the Yakama Nation.

Broadening Our Understanding of Entrepreneurship

Yakama tribal member Delores Moore saw a need in her community for high-quality portrait photography. Seniors at the local high school needed to submit head shots and portraits for graduation ceremonies and other announcements; however, not everyone could afford professional photography.

Therefore, in order to serve her community and those close to her, Moore took it upon herself to learn the fundamentals of photography, editing, and printing images in order to meet the needs of the community. Her skills and talents have become an asset to the community, and Moore demonstrated her cultural commitment to that community.

Photography and portraiture are not Moore's full-time job. She is also a dispatcher for the Yakama Nation Fire Management. This situation is common among other artists and makers for the tribe; they may practice two or more careers simultaneously.

While there is not a quantifiable dollar amount that Moore invests in the tribe, there is a metaphorical one. The value of Moore's investment may return later in life when she calls upon the tribe for assistance, or when one of the families she has helped recognizes her ceremonially.

Engaging Accessibly, Equitably, and Authentically

Building accessible, equitable, inclusive library programs and services that are responsive to your local community requires listening and refining your strategies and models to fit the local context. Learning and integrating principles and frameworks such as cultural humility or healing-centered engagement can help. Investing in relationship development and collaboration are critical steps, and focusing on community needs is vital to success. Library small business programs that provide patrons with the tools to help them reach self-identified goals contribute to both confidence and community relationships. Asking people what would be most useful to them takes time and may not be scalable—veterans, for example, may have very specific needs that are different from the needs of others in the community. Still, the deep impact this practice can have makes it worth the effort.

Evaluating Resources and Sharing Knowledge

As part of our EDI work, the Libraries Build Business cohort evaluated the existing business support resources that we could leverage for our programs. We recognized that many how-to books and resources that deal with market research, patents, and stocks focus on only a few segments of the business sector and may not be relevant or responsive to the needs of underrepresented business owners. The cohort libraries identified new resources and developed strategic partnerships to support EDI goals. For example, in Los Angeles, the library is working with a vendor, Cell-Ed, to build resources that resonate with ESL and immigrant audiences and can give them more agency over their entrepreneurship. In Appleton, Wisconsin, the library initiated a partnership with the ColorBold Business Association, with the intention of supporting entrepreneurs of color with tailored resources, support, and networking opportunities. Seeking vendors and partners that share your vision and commitment to equity and inclusion is critical to providing high-quality support to small business owners in your community.

As we engage in building and implementing equitable services in our libraries, we can also demonstrate principles of EDI in our professional practice by sharing resources and strategies to support other library workers and, ultimately, advance the goals of small business owners across the country. The LBB cohort shared their findings with library workers across the nation through traditional channels, such as publications and library conference presentations and mixers. But in order to eliminate financial and professional status barriers to accessing these findings, the cohort also shared its findings in free, publicly accessible platforms (e.g., Instagram Live, YouTube clips, webinars) and created a virtual community to connect library workers who are interested in small business.

Transformational Practices

The framework of cultural humility recognizes that identifying power imbalances is a key step in moving toward equitable practices, spaces, and structural change. As municipal institutions, libraries hold power through their processes, policies, access, and funding. Libraries can help to transform communities by collaborating with them. While the library houses many experts and much expertise, we can't move forward unless we step back and let the community lead. Libraries need to consider the balance of institutional and community labor. For example, in any given project, consider how your library is advancing economic equity by sharing funding with community contributors in the form of grants, honoraria, or stipends. It is also important to keep in mind that the community itself is not a commodity, and that the library must prioritize listening and shared learning to build trust. Investing in relationships and building agency can help move projects from transactional to transformational.

As information professionals, librarians are deeply invested in being accurate, prepared, and thorough when providing resources and assistance. But this is not enough: to engage authentically, libraries must prioritize community perspectives. For example, immigrants come to the United States with many different levels of education, literacy, and English language fluency. They often have no other option but to build a small business based on instinct and hustle, operating outside of regulations and without the help of basic resources and supports. Their biggest asset is their community—not the library. To meet the goal of supporting immigrant populations, it's essential for library staff and institutions to be open and humble. We must be open to listening deeply, finding resources that may be untraditional, and embracing the role of learners, rather than experts. A business librarian may have a wonderful range of knowledge and tools, but focusing attention on this may actually create additional barriers. De-centering institutional resources and library expertise can be challenging, especially when institutions want to make use of their existing resources, but again, to be effective we must ask: are those resources truly meeting patrons' needs?

Cultivating a Sense of Belonging

Libraries can foster belonging and inclusion by providing space to build relationships and personal and professional agency. At the Appleton Public Library in Wisconsin, the library intentionally cultivated belonging with a

BIPOC entrepreneur storytelling series. Creating platforms for traditionally marginalized individuals to share their lived experiences as small business owners broadens the entrepreneurial ecosystem, contradicts stereotypes, and deepens our understanding of small businesses' struggles and successes. Library workers should acknowledge their individual and institutional biases to advance equity and inclusion through such efforts. For example, we can challenge institutional biases and advance equity by providing opportunities for collaborative decision-making and platforms for individuals to share their story. Listening to and learning from someone's story is a privilege, and no one is entitled to know another's story or capitalize on people's identities or lived experiences. Libraries should consider who benefits from storytelling, take care in building trust with potential storytellers, and offer compensation to storytellers to advance economic equity and inclusion in such efforts.

Responding to Trauma

When we as libraries are learning from communities or asking communities for information, keep in mind that we are generating programming and ideas from their lived experiences—and their trauma. Be sure to connect with partners who can offer relevant support. Trauma-informed programming as a part of regular library programming is a step towards building trust and rapport and genuinely considering and honoring the experiences of individuals.

Furthermore, the framework of healing-centered engagement encourages us as libraries to recognize individuals as whole selves (i.e., not only entrepreneurs), and this has the potential to transform the community. For many underrepresented small business owners and entrepreneurs, the first step in a library business program may not involve jumping into business topics and "how-to's." Libraries may first need to address barriers, trauma, and healing. For example, at the Los Angeles Public Library, in partnership with Cell-Ed, the Healing Justice Transformative Leadership Institute, and city street vendors, Cell-Ed units were developed to provide community and personal safety and healing strategies and resources. At the Gwinnett County Public Library in Georgia, the New Start Entrepreneurship Initiative connects individuals returning from jail or prison with a staff social worker as they move through the entrepreneurship program. The social worker ensures that participants are connected to social services, and addresses any concerns that lie beyond the business content of the program.

Continuing the Work

The Libraries Build Business cohort designed library business and entrepreneurship programs that center the experiences of low-income and underrepresented individuals to explore and highlight how public libraries can collaborate and serve their interests. The initiative prioritizes authentic engagement and inclusion in program design and evaluation. All libraries can continue to advance these goals and integrate social justice, EDI principles, and the frameworks of healing and belonging into their work, acknowledging that there is always space to continue to grow and improve, alongside the community.

NOTE

1. Amber Lee, Bruce Mitchell, and Anneliese Lederer, in cooperation with Jerome Williams, Sterling Bone, and Glenn Christensen, "Disinvestment, Discouragement, and Inequity in Small Business Lending," National Community Reinvestment Coalition, https://ncrc.org/disinvestment.

Specialized Library Supports for Entrepreneurs

Ryan Metheny, Andrea Levandowski, Sara Brown,
Tony Orengo, Nathaniel Burnard, Marra Honeywell,
Julie M. Brophy, Rachael Svoboda, and Brandon West

In this chapter, we'll showcase innovative examples of entrepreneurship programs from various library types beyond public libraries and adult-focused programming. This chapter features the work of the New Jersey State Library, the LA Law Library, examples from academic library collaborations, and youth entrepreneurship programs from the Orange County Library System in Florida and the Allen County Public Library in Indiana. These case studies are meant to highlight additional approaches to fostering an entrepreneurial mindset and inspire partnerships between different types of libraries—with the goal of addressing the needs of local business owners and entrepreneurs holistically and strategically.

How Can Libraries Work Together to Support Entrepreneurship?

Libraries are uniquely placed to meet a variety of entrepreneurial support needs and are typically flexible enough to adapt to changing situations rapidly when necessary. Beyond public libraries, other types of libraries and library organizations also have resources, services, and expertise to offer in support of small business and entrepreneurship initiatives. Additionally, it is not only adults who can benefit from entrepreneurship programs, and it is not only profit that drives entrepreneurs. In this chapter, we make a case for inspiring youth with entrepreneurship training, building statewide library networks to share business resources and grow professional capacity, and leveraging the specialized business resources at law and academic libraries.

As illustrated in this chapter, by working with other types of libraries, institutions, and library networks, public libraries can expand and strengthen their support for small business development, bringing greater benefit to their communities. By working together, libraries can better bridge social, generational, and economic divides to provide opportunities and ensure that entrepreneurship is not just for the privileged. When there is a local demand for it, libraries should also expand their definition of entrepreneurship to include applying entrepreneurial principles to address social justice issues and build enterprises that explicitly work to meet community needs and foster empowerment. Libraries champion equity, diversity, and inclusion in community spaces, and they can bring this approach to their business programs, too. Furthermore, library entrepreneurship programs can foster agency and creativity in youth and entrepreneurs-to-be, and can advance library ideals of information-sharing and democracy in at-risk or underrepresented communities.

Statewide Professional Development: The New Jersey State Library

The New Jersey State Library has championed the entrepreneurship and business development work that public libraries do for well over a decade. The state library has developed various business-focused initiatives over the years, but the consistent message is that libraries are drivers of local economies and have the ability to positively impact community development. The guiding principles that have steered the New Jersey State Library's work are:

- Strong and engaged libraries are reflections of communities where people want to live and work.
- Libraries are investments in and for members of the community.
- Community economic development is a library issue.
- Business services at public libraries promote social equity, including livable wages and financial security for community members.

While these are not radical ideas, they are important points that would interest most potential partners and key stakeholders, not to mention librarians who may question what they have to offer or who may incorrectly consider business services to be the antithesis of library ideals.

The New Jersey State Library fosters business and entrepreneurship in the state by supporting the work of public libraries with resources as well as partnership and professional development opportunities. First, by providing statewide databases, including those relevant to business information needs, the state library ensures that every public library in New Jersey is able to offer something to its business community. Next, the state library works to build partnerships relevant to business services at a statewide level with an eye to creating opportunities for connection at the regional and local levels. Specifically, the state library communicates with agencies and organizations such as the New Jersey Business Action Center, the New Jersey Economic Development Authority, the UCEDC (a nonprofit economic development corporation), and other organizations to enable the sharing of relevant information through libraries to their business communities. Lastly, the New Jersey State Library builds capacity among library staff to help them better assist business owners and entrepreneurs.

The state library's professional development offerings benefit both dedicated business services staff as well as library staff working in other areas (such as reference or adult services) whose work may nonetheless intersect with business and entrepreneurship. While professional development related to supporting local businesses can include instruction on the basics of business librarianship and business research skills, it also involves more general learning opportunities, such as the marketing and promotion of library services, building partnerships, and conducting community needs assessment. Importantly, the New Jersey State Library recognizes that everyone has something to share and that library staff learn best from each other. Therefore, the state library works to bring together a network of colleagues and peers from across New Jersey who can share resources, ideas, and model program ideas for one another.

Specifically, after identifying a gap in professional support for economic development among library associations and statewide organizations in general, the New Jersey State Library launched the NJLibsGrowBiz Committee in 2017. During the committee's meetings, library staff from around the state have the opportunity to hear from guest speakers on business-related topics, providing librarians with an opportunity to learn together and form partnerships with other business support groups. Meeting participants are then encouraged to share updates, questions, successes, and failures from their own libraries in a collegial environment. The New Jersey State Library has also hosted the NJLibsGrowBiz Summit, a full-day workshop devoted to economic development in libraries. The summit was held in-person in 2018 and virtually in 2020. Both summits included keynote speakers, breakout sessions, and networking with business support nonprofits and governmental agencies.

State library agencies across the United States support local libraries in developing initiatives to promote workforce development, business development, and entrepreneurship. These state-level efforts can help to ensure that the work of individual libraries is seen as a cohesive whole—illustrating the value that libraries bring to the economic success and vibrancy of their communities. Public libraries should be made aware of the business and entrepreneurship resources available to them through their state library agencies, including any related services, such as training and marketing materials, that could assist them in business programming.

Additionally, state library agencies should ask library staff about their needs when it comes to business and entrepreneurship services. State libraries support the development of local libraries and often have the ability to dedicate resources for these purposes. State library staff members can help identify common needs and typical roadblocks to then consider possible solutions. Beyond prioritizing business development and entrepreneurship services through professional development, state library agencies are also uniquely positioned to maintain awareness of trends, initiatives, and funding at the federal or state level that may provide additional resources to the libraries they serve. Finally, as best practices emerge in local communities that would bring value to other locations, state library agencies can become champions of that work to stakeholders and the library field as a whole.

Get Legal Support for Your Business Services: LA Law Library

The process of starting a business, and many aspects of maintaining and growing that business, involve the law. Incorporating a business, obtaining permits and licenses, formalizing arrangements with business partners through a contract, protecting a trademark or other intellectual property: all of these are legal issues a business owner may need to navigate. To that end, public law libraries can prove a vital resource for entrepreneurs and serve as a valuable partner for public libraries that want to expand their services for business owners.

Every state has at least one publicly accessible law library, and many larger states, including California and Texas, have a system of county law libraries that are specifically dedicated to serving the general public's legal information needs. Law libraries have many resources an entrepreneur could benefit from. These include self-help books and databases on business and legal topics; access to codes, cases, and regulations that govern the legal issues a business may encounter; and, perhaps most importantly, helpful reference librarians with specific expertise in finding the answers to legal questions and referring patrons to legal resources.

The relationship between the Los Angeles Public Library (LAPL) and its local law library counterpart, the LA Law Library, illustrates how these two types of libraries can partner to ensure that their collective resources serve entrepreneurs more effectively than either one could alone. The LAPL Central Library's Business and Economics Department often refers patrons with legal questions to the LA Law Library's main branch a few blocks away; and the LA Law Library likewise refers patrons with market research or general business acumen needs to LAPL for access to its collection of invaluable databases and print material. LA Law Library reference librarians also frequently take calls from public librarians who are assisting patrons with legal issues, to help them in interpreting legal issues and finding the best resource.

This partnership deepened in recent years when the LA Law Library began to expand its programming to include classes and workshops on legal topics for entrepreneurs. This programming has grown into a twice-yearly business series, "Starting & Growing a Business: Legal and Financial Knowledge You Need to Succeed," sponsored by a local bank. LAPL provides vital support by referring patrons to the series and helping to spread the word about it. Librarians at LAPL appreciate having a resource like the business series to which they can send patrons with business-related legal issues, and patrons who attend the series at the LA Law Library learn about the resources offered by the Business and Economics Department at LAPL. No doubt, similar partnership opportunities between public and law libraries exist throughout the country.

Tap into Central Hubs of Innovation and Learning: Academic Libraries

University and community college libraries support both academic entrepreneurship initiatives and community-based initiatives as they keep up with twenty-first-century skill development, resources, and technology. Universities and community colleges are vital centers of activity both locally and in their state—supporting economic development, fostering intellectual curiosity, and developing a skilled workforce. More and more, their goal is to serve as a community resource and embed themselves and their students in the local context, offering interdisciplinary information access and research support.

There is a growing field of entrepreneurship activity on many college and university campuses—including technology commercialization centers, start-up incubators, pitch competitions, and makerspaces—which may serve active students, continuing education students, and the community at large. Providing small business support is a concrete way that academic institutions can support their local communities. In Baltimore County in Maryland, for instance, the Community College of Baltimore County has a Center for Business Innovation, while Towson University has an initiative called StarTUp at the Armory that provides a coworking space and a business incubator.

These centers of industry, technology, and innovation are exceptional resources that academic librarians can leverage to support the campus community and the larger surrounding community or region. Among other things, academic libraries provide access to databases and key data on target industries and demographics, as well as expert research help. Many also offer innovative and collaborative physical spaces where business-minded campus community members can develop and nurture ideas. They can also be a source of valuable support to public library-led small business programs.

When higher education libraries and institutions share their resources and expertise with public libraries, businesses benefit. For example, in Kansas one of the key components of Cultivate Indy, the Independence Public Library's small business lab project, was to introduce their patrons to the tools and resources available at the local community college's makerspace.

Additionally, Fab Lab ICC (at Independence Community College) and the Independence Public Library (IPL) partnered to create a mini-makerspace at the public library's small business lab. Fab Lab ICC provided guidance on what equipment to purchase and has been instrumental in training public library staff on how to use and teach each piece of equipment. Now IPL patrons have access to a 3D printer, a laser engraver, and two types of large-format printers/plotters for prototyping and developing ideas. When public libraries partner with community colleges, they also gain access to subject matter experts in business, technology, and more. Among other things, the collaboration between Fab Lab ICC and IPL has led to free and reduced-cost small business training for public library staff, which has, in turn, helped them to better assist community members.

Academic libraries and their staff can also offer critical technical support for public libraries' business initiatives. For example, a key component of the Wyoming Library to Business (WL2B) initiative—headed by the Laramie County Library System—was made possible due to a partnership with an IT librarian from the University of Wyoming. Supported by a Libraries Build Business grant, WL2B helped expand business outreach services by providing one-on-one consultations with business owners in the Laramie County Library System's rural branches. The project also led to the creation of a video production studio for use by libraries from all across the state. The university IT librarian acted as the brains behind the video production studio—creating an equipment list, leading installation and troubleshooting, and providing research support during the initiative's rollout. As the field of entrepreneurship grows, there will be many opportunities for collaboration and resource-sharing between academic and public libraries with a common goal of strengthening economic development and opportunity.

Still, despite similar interests and goals, working with academic institutions can be challenging for public libraries. Academic institutions have a different service model that is focused on the university's goals. Additionally, at some institutions—community colleges in particular—instructors are paid to teach, not take on extra projects, and so they may have only limited (or no) extra time and capacity. In any case, understanding the business outreach goals of community colleges and universities can be key to effectively collaborating with these institutions as a public library. For public libraries that want to work with local higher education institutions, a good starting point is to find a like-minded individual at the potential partner institution with whom to begin a dialogue. With an internal champion on board, it can be easier to move the partnership forward to develop an important and mutually beneficial business service, resource, or program.

The Entrepreneurial Mindset: Youth Entrepreneurship Programs

Entrepreneurial programs for youth lay the foundation for economic empowerment by teaching young people the skills they need to become and think like entrepreneurs at an early age. These programs foster creativity and innovation, develop agency and confidence, and inspire the next generation's entrepreneurs and small business owners—helping to ensure thriving communities for years to come. Additionally, as community hubs, libraries can address socioeconomic barriers by providing equal access to resources and learning opportunities. Youth entrepreneurial programs in libraries help level the playing field among young people by facilitating access to technology (computers, Wi-Fi, prototyping tools, etc.), business mentors, and community connections. Read on to learn more from two inspiring library-led youth entrepreneurship programs.

BizKids Club: Orange County Library System

In 2019, the Orange County (FL) Board of County Commissioners commissioned the services of FOREFRONT, an independent Florida-based consulting, research, and advisory firm, to provide recommendations for the utilization of $20 million in new funding earmarked for children's programs and services in Orange County. FOREFRONT published a final report outlining focus areas for services targeted at the areas of juvenile prevention/diversion, mental and physical health, early childhood education/care, and child/student homelessness. The report recommended that programming to address these focus areas be primarily targeted in nine zip codes in underserved communities throughout Orange County. In response to FOREFRONT's final report, the Orange County government introduced the Citizens' Review Panel (CRP) Fund Distribution Process to distribute funding to 501(c)(3) health and human service nonprofit organizations in Orange County that offer children's services.

The Orange County Library System (OCLS) applied for and was awarded a portion of the earmarked funds for its newly developed BizKids Club, which provides programming on entrepreneurship and financial innovation for youth. With the CRP funding, the OCLS aims to introduce underrepresented youth to the worlds of business and entrepreneurship. The BizKids Club is offered at seven libraries located in the targeted zip codes, including the Orlando Public Library, the system's main hub, as well as the Fairview Shores, Hiawassee, North Orange, South Trail, Southeast, and Washington Park branches. To expand the program's reach, the OCLS reached out to community centers, public and charter schools, Boys & Girls Clubs, after-school programs, faith-based organizations, mentorship groups, and apartment complexes to partner to offer BizKids Club. The programs facilitated off-site were just as successful and surpassed the attendance of programs facilitated in library locations.

Specifically, the BizKids Club introduces underserved youth, ages 9–14, to the worlds of business and entrepreneurship. During eight two-hour instructor-led sessions, students are guided through a series of fun, hands-on activities and memorable role-playing exercises. The club's curriculum is designed to help students develop the skills and tools needed to successfully brainstorm and define a business idea, create a business plan, design marketing materials, and pitch their business ideas to others. Participants learn to use Microsoft Word, Excel, and PowerPoint to create flyers, business presentations, and budget and inventory spreadsheets.

The BizKids Club includes an important mentorship component. Instructors and volunteer mentors from various entrepreneurial and business backgrounds meet with students at intervals during the club. They serve as guides who listen, encourage, and suggest resources to participants. In addition to instruction and mentorship, laptops, Wi-Fi, nutritious snacks, and transportation options are provided to help reduce the barriers for youth who often face challenges related to living in high-poverty households. Additionally, each participant is provided with up to $100 worth of supplies to develop their products or services. Upon completing the eight-session club, students can participate in a one-day marketplace where they debut their products, pitch their services, and test marketing strategies. The marketplace offers participants an opportunity to see their business idea come to life—an accomplishment to inspire them to continue pursuing their goals and dreams, and believe in themselves and all they can achieve with hard work and dedication. The program's ultimate goal is to help youth become more aware of the opportunities that exist around them and gain confidence in their ability to creatively problem-solve and tackle challenges.

In sum, when starting a business program for youth in underrepresented communities, it can be useful to partner with community stakeholders that offer services to young people. This approach can help libraries reach youth who may not otherwise enter through the doors of their facilities. Additionally, it is critical to address practical barriers that might prevent youth from participating by providing transportation, technology, meals, and so on. Finally, take care to develop a curriculum that sparks enthusiasm and lets students know that entrepreneurship and economic opportunity are open to them regardless of socioeconomic status.

Team Read: Allen County Public Library

The Allen County Public Library (ACPL) in Indiana has partnered with the Northeast Indiana Innovation Center (NIIC), a nationally recognized and well-established entrepreneurial incubator, since 2018. Since that time, the partnership has grown from patron and service referrals, to sharing expertise and training opportunities, to engaging in collaborative programs and marketing. In 2021 the partnership between the ACPL and the NIIC expanded further to support Team Read, a teen employment program operated through the library's summer learning initiative.

In a typical year, Team Read employs up to forty teens as "reading rolemodels" in its outreach to sites across the county. Team Read teens gain work experience, receive college and career planning support, and learn about brain development and trauma-informed care. In 2020 the program was canceled due to the COVID-19 pandemic, but it was reimagined in 2021 with public health measures still in place at outreach sites. Eighteen teens were hired to work at their neighborhood library locations. The teens gathered together twice each week for virtual outreach programming and expanded trainings. The 2021 program included more community partner involvement and life/job skill instruction than in past years, including the addition of an entrepreneurial track led by the NIIC. This was a mutually beneficial expansion: the NIIC had been looking to expand its outreach to youth and teens, and the library had a ready group of teenage summer staff.

As part of the program, the library and the NIIC designed a series of speaker visits highlighting different areas of entrepreneurship and future opportunities for the teens. While the initial plan was to use the NIIC's existing curriculum to introduce traditional concepts of entrepreneurship and work through scheduled activities with the group, it quickly became apparent that the teens had a different viewpoint on what entrepreneurship was all about. As a result, the library and the NIIC pivoted to meet their needs.

Ultimately, the teens divided into groups to develop business concepts to present. Each group worked on a concept that revolved around some form of social entrepreneurship: ideas for businesses that would meet a community need. Among this group of teens there was almost no interest in money and profit, but tremendous energy for using entrepreneurship in the service of community activism and change. The teens clearly expressed interest in fostering community arts and supporting diversity and social justice. While this was not the expected direction, it was important to follow the teens' lead and interests.

Given the teens' departure from what might be considered a traditional entrepreneurial focus of looking to maximize profit in favor of nonprofit development, the NIIC connected teens with social entrepreneurship mentors. Entrepreneurs-in-residence with relevant experiences were invited to share their stories and engage in conversations with the teens to illustrate how entrepreneurial thinking coincided with social justice and economic empowerment. One entrepreneur shared her story of founding a business in India that hired only women in one severely disadvantaged neighborhood, and how that business and its employees worked to impact the neighborhood through practices of fair trade and equitable employment. Another shared her experience working with kiva.org, a nonprofit that issues crowd-funded microloans to women and new entrepreneurs in underserved areas in nations around the world. Finally, a conversation was facilitated with the director of the NIIC's Women's Business Center, who talked about how the NIIC works to coach and aid women entrepreneurs of all ages and backgrounds.

This collaboration laid the foundation for future programs co-led by the library and the NIIC and opened up doors for exploring social entrepreneurship more thoroughly, a concept which resonated deeply with many youth and teens. The entrepreneurship program met the goals of both partners by exposing the teen participants to opportunities for personal growth, introducing them to ways of applying entrepreneurial thought to real-world challenges, and providing them with specific tools and concepts to actualize their dreams. A key lesson for other libraries illustrated in this initiative was the importance of looking to existing partnerships for possible win-win ways to building on existing programming. Another takeaway is the importance of responding to the program participants' interests and being willing to explore new avenues for and expanded definitions of entrepreneurship.

Putting It All Together

Partnerships and networking are essential to providing high-quality services to your community. Beyond the community business partners you read about in chapter 2, consider reaching out to community colleges and academic institutions in your area, your state library and state's law library, and schools. Be creative with how you define entrepreneurship training, and try to broaden your idea of who an entrepreneur is and what they'll need. Don't underestimate the value of having a network of peers to share resources and ideas with, either. As you read the case studies in this chapter, we hope you were inspired with new approaches, ways to collaborate, and promising ways to strengthen ties to colleagues who are also doing this work.

PART II
Case Studies from the Field

Small Business and Entrepreneurship Programs in Public Libraries

PROGRAM 1

Supporting the Local Economy

Developing Business and Job Seeker Services from Scratch

BUSINESS AND JOB SEEKER SERVICES, ADDISON (IL) PUBLIC LIBRARY

Lesley Cyrier and Emily Glimco

Setting the Stage

Addison, Illinois, a suburb of Chicago, is situated in a thriving commercial and industrial sector in DuPage County. Our community is home to the fourth-largest manufacturing park in Illinois, one that boasts 20 percent of all manufacturing operations in DuPage County, and is also home to a large number of restaurants, making for a unique and diverse business community.

Upon hiring a business services specialist, a role that focuses on working with businesses, entrepreneurs, and community job seekers while actively representing the library in the community, business and job seeker services at the Addison Public Library have grown quickly and organically. We began with traditional library business services: one-on-one appointments, business library cards, and the promotion of our collections and databases, spaces, and programs. Since then, we've developed a number of additional initiatives to support our local economy.

Service Area

- Suburban
- Medium, less than 99,000 population

Goals and Impact

As our community grows—the Chicago Metropolitan Agency for Planning expects the number of jobs in Addison to increase by 38 percent, or 8,600 jobs, by the year 2030—we know that it is extremely important to connect with both our local businesses and with community members seeking employment, thus building a foundation that will support the local economy for years to come. With this in mind, the Addison Public Library identified "supporting the community's economic wellness by providing education opportunities and business resources" as one of the top priorities in our 2017–2020 strategic vision. Additionally, local businesses contribute a substantial portion of the revenue we use to operate the library through the commercial and industrial property taxes they pay, demonstrating their significance to our community and further bolstering our rationale for supporting them.

As we gradually became a recognized part of the Addison business community through a consistent presence and through the relationships we built up at local chamber of commerce meetings, Kiwanis meetings, and other community events, we also continued to expand and reimagine our business services. Our traditional core services and programs continue to be the heart of what we offer, but special events and series also provide incredible impact and publicity for those core services, as do the business and individual stories that make the Addison community special. The impact these job seeker and business services have had on our community over the past two years has not gone unnoticed. The Addison community won the 2020–2021 Robert Wood Johnson Foundation Culture of Health Prize, and the library's services in bolstering the economic health of our community was a feature of our award submission.

Getting Started

Networking with other librarians doing similar work is a great way to get guidance and peer feedback as you develop your library's business and job seeker services and align them with your community's needs. Get to know your community and what makes it unique by showing up at every meeting, job fair, and networking event you can. Before you go, develop a strong working knowledge of all your library has to offer, from databases and collections to meeting rooms and programs. Being present in the community will raise the public's awareness of the library's offerings, especially those for local businesses and job seekers, and over time the community will come to see the library as an invaluable community asset.

Key Resources
Our library brought the following key resources to its initiatives:

- **Zoom** for virtual programs
- **Basic supplies** like pens, notepads, and folders
- **Printed materials**, including flyers and marketing material

Key Partners
Addison's local chamber of commerce and industry is a great partner for promoting our events and services to local businesses. We regularly work with local area nonprofits like the Goodwill Workforce Connection Center, the College of DuPage Career Services Center, Ray Graham Association, NAMI DuPage, the People's Resource Center, and WorkNet DuPage to develop materials for our New Job Toolkits and to host programs at the library.

Budget
A $2,000 Libraries Lead with Digital Skills grant funded our Getting Addison Back to Work series, paying for presenter fees and promotional materials as well as the first 100 New Job Toolkits. Any other costs for programs or additional New Job Toolkits were paid from the library's annual operating budget. You don't need a substantial budget to develop similar services for your library; the most important part is allocating staff time.

Implementing the Nuts and Bolts

As part of our efforts to develop a full-service, one-stop shop for local businesses and job seekers, we developed three flagstone initiatives to complement the traditional services we offer.

- **Small Business Saturday**, an event supported by American Express. Eight local businesses were featured on Small Business Passports that were distributed by the businesses and the library. Anyone who visited the participating businesses earned

- a stamp on their passport, which could be turned in at the library once completed in exchange for an entry to win a gift card to a local business.
- **Getting Addison Back to Work program,** funded by a Libraries Lead with Digital Skills grant from the Public Library Association and Google. During this month-long series, participants attended online workshops that were a mix of Google-focused programs and essential job seeker-focused programs, such as "Resume Revamp" and "Finding a Job during Uncertain Times," as well as an overview of the many community partners we use as referral sources. Anyone who attended or watched all of the programs had the opportunity to earn a certificate.
- **The New Job Toolkits** are always on display on an endcap near our service desk. These folders include a tool on every step of the job search process, from resume templates and tips to interview advice and salary negotiation tips, created by community partners. These tools are an evergreen product that we can perpetually offer and adapt.

One simple tool that we created early on is our business needs assessment, which allows businesses to request services and let us know what they need from the library. The form covers basic contact information, when they would be most likely to attend programs, topics of interest, which library resources they would be interested in utilizing, and the opportunity to sign up for our business newsletter. The needs assessment can be completed either online or via a print handout distributed at chamber of commerce meetings and other relevant outreach events. We use the responses from the form to make educated decisions on program offerings, and as a tool to facilitate scheduling one-on-one appointments.

Promoting Your Program

Work closely with your library's marketing department if you have one. For example, our communications and marketing coordinator works closely with our business services specialist to promote our business and job seeker services to the community through a mix of print and digital marketing.

Our library's print newsletter has a dedicated section for business and job seeker programs, and we regularly create flyers that list relevant outreach events. Make sure your printed materials are eye-catching and well-designed. The business services postcard that we mail to new businesses in town was granted a 2020 PR Xchange Award Competition for its design and has proved to be another effective way to reach out.

As for digital marketing, we have a targeted e-mail newsletter called "Business Matters" that promotes our upcoming business workshops and relevant library services. We also regularly feature the businesses we partner with on social media to raise their profile in the community, thank them for working with us, and promote our core business and job seeker services as well.

AdvancedTech posing for library promotional picture
Photo courtesy of Addison Public Library

Overcoming Roadblocks and Challenges

Developing a business program is about developing relationships with your local businesses, your patrons, and community partners. This process is not a quick one. It may take six months to a year for chamber members to expect to see you at their meetings, for patrons to realize that the library offers job seeker and business services, and for you to have found and established a good working relationship with your community partners.

Finding Success with Outreach Partners

One of our most vocal community partners is AdvancedTech Cell Phone Repair, a business that used the Addison Public Library to determine whether to open their shop in Addison and then used our resources to get started. Since that initial interaction, AdvancedTech has promoted the library at every opportunity and is usually the first to sign up for new initiatives like Small Business Saturday. Look for stories like theirs to find dedicated partners to promote your library.

Staff Responsibilities

Our program requires a full-time business services specialist to oversee all our programs and services and connect with the business community. We also benefit from the support of the communications and marketing coordinator, our Guest Services team, and our Adult Services staff. While the success of the library's business and job seeker services is specifically tied to our business services specialist's work, it is the work of all the library staff that makes our services a success.

Tips, Tricks, and Advice

- To build your audience, you'll have to keep offering programs more than once, even if no one attends at first. Be prepared to revise, adapt, and adjust your programs, and don't give up. Your dedication to developing job seeker and business services will pay off with persistence, and when your partners and community members see that you aren't going anywhere, they'll be more likely to take the plunge and dive into your library's offerings.
- Developing a strong business and job seeker service at your library doesn't only involve building strong relationships with your community; it also involves building strong working relationships with your colleagues at the library. Our business services specialist and our communications and marketing coordinator worked closely from the start of each initiative launched at the library, from development to promotion. Additionally, those two positions worked hard to ensure that the staff in all departments knew about the latest happenings in our business and job seeker services to get buy-in.

PROGRAM 2

BIPOC Business Community and Connections

Small Business—Big Impact

APPLETON (WI) PUBLIC LIBRARY

Adriana McCleer and Yee Lee Vue

Setting the Stage

The "Small Business—Big Impact" (SB-BI) initiative at the Appleton Public Library (APL) supports business start-up, retention, and expansion efforts, specifically for Black, Indigenous, and people of color (BIPOC) and immigrants. The initiative has involved adding library staff, offering engagement and education programs, establishing coworking opportunities, and building community engagement.

The local nonprofit "FIT Oshkosh" and the University of Wisconsin Extension conducted a 2019 research study of Black business owners in northeast Wisconsin. Respondents expressed "feelings of isolation and lack of social connection with other business owners," and "most did not use formal business development services, in fear of rejection and intimidation." SB-BI was designed to support connection and belonging for BIPOC business owners and facilitate their access to business services and resources. For over twenty years, through the college's entrepreneur training program, APL has partnered with the Fox Valley Technical College to present business resources to entrepreneurs who are launching new businesses. Building on this experience, SB-BI expanded its programming to include library-led engagement opportunities that are specifically designed for and with BIPOC and immigrants.

Service Area

- Urban
- Medium, less than 99,000 population

Goals and Impact

The goal of SB-BI is to support small business start-up, retention, and expansion efforts for BIPOC and immigrants. SB-BI is an opportunity for the Appleton Public Library to serve as a connecting hub for entrepreneurs, agencies, and information resources in efforts to address racial and ethnic disparities in access to information. The 2010–2030 City of Appleton Comprehensive Plan established an objective to "support/partner with organizations pursuing programs for entrepreneurial development comprised of networking, financial assistance, training, and supportive services for all types of entrepreneurs" to "create the resources and culture in which entrepreneurial development is encouraged." In 2019, the city of Appleton affirmed local business retention and expansion as a top priority "because nine out of ten jobs created in the City are created by existing businesses expanding their operations or by local entrepreneurs starting businesses." The library, as a city department, had the opportunity to make connections across agencies, services, and community members to advance these goals with a specific focus on historically excluded and underserved populations.

Getting Started

Our library prioritizes community engagement and collaborations, so the first step to implement a program like SB-BI is to listen. Library staff learned more about BIPOC and immigrant business owners' needs, assets, and challenges through direct outreach and relationship-building, program participation, and working with partners. We started by meeting with community agencies and business owners to learn more about the current small business landscape. To do this, we held virtual or in-person group meetings and met one-on-one to learn about what business owners and entrepreneurs needed, wanted, and sought to contribute to the initiative.

Key Resources

The resources our library brought to the initiative included:

- The library's collection of business materials and online business resources
- Subscriptions to Zoom and Constant Contact
- Gift cards—incentives for focus group participation
- Library meeting space—for hosting coworking experiences
- Business owners—as speakers, consultants, recruitment support, and participants

Key Partners

- The ColorBold Business Association cosponsored business programs and provided technical assistance for SB-BI Academy participants.
- The Wisconsin Women's Business Initiative Corporation (WWBIC) cosponsored business programs and provided technical assistance for SB-BI Academy participants.
- The Wisconsin United Coalition of Mutual Assistance Association (WUCMAA) provided technical assistance for SB-BI Academy participants.
- CAP Services cosponsored business programs and provided technical assistance for SB-BI Academy participants.
- Venture Wisconsin provided video production and SB-BI promotion support.

Budget

APL budgeted $64,718 for the SB-BI initiative, which we funded through the Libraries Build Business grant. With this funding, we used about half for programming costs, entrepreneur storytelling programs, and a business consultant to design and present the SB-BI Academy. Funding was also used for marketing, participation incentives, personnel, and professional development. SB-BI provides financial compensation for local BIPOC and immigrants, and thus serve as a model for other community entities to advocate and budget for appropriate compensation for labor, specifically racial equity labor (e.g., translation, cultural awareness/sensitivity, target marketing).

Implementing the Nuts and Bolts

The SB-BI initiative creates space and opportunities for BIPOC and immigrant business owners to interact with each other, network, and share knowledge and experiences; and it provides support for business start-up, retention, and expansion. Our SB-BI team worked with a business consultant to design a four-month, eight-session Academy for business owners. The cohort participants increased their knowledge in critical foundational areas of a successful business such as target marketing, customer service, leadership, team-building, and financials. They benefited from a one-on-one consulting opportunity with the program facilitator. They received hands-on development of key strategies for sustaining and growing their business and technical knowledge from diverse experts in crucial areas of business development and management. Our community partners and library staff provided technical assistance to participants, as well as coworking space, resources, and engagement opportunities to continue building community and connections.

In addition to the Academy, we launched an entrepreneur storytelling series, "Stories and Strategies," that highlighted BIPOC and immigrant stories and strategies for starting a business. The library staff also offer multilingual instruction workshops on library online business resources in Spanish, Hmong, and English. The programs and coworking opportunities foster social connection and bridge access to community resources in a welcoming environment. Diverse ethnic and racial representation is central to this initiative, so BIPOC and immigrants benefit both as participants and as contracted consultants, instructors, and speakers.

As we plan our programming at APL, we hold learning conversations and survey small business owners and entrepreneurs. This informs and improves our business programs, collection, and services. We also use Project Outcome, a survey portal designed by the Public Library Association for outcome measurement and analysis, to create program-specific participant surveys. This survey provides qualitative and quantitative data about the participants' experiences. Library staff use a continuous improvement model to iterate our program and service offerings. The success of individual programs directly informs future library initiatives, with staff continuing to offer the programs that have the most impact.

HOW TO: Launch a BIPOC Entrepreneur Storytelling Series

An entrepreneur storytelling series is an opportunity to spotlight the creative, resilient individuals in your community who are innovating, creating jobs, and contributing to a dynamic local economy.

This series can focus on their journey to and through entrepreneurship, the strategies that facilitated success, and the failures that helped them learn and grow. A focus on spotlighting BIPOC entrepreneurs advances diversity, equity, and inclusion by lifting up marginalized voices and experiences. The following is a list of key actions to take in launching an entrepreneur storytelling series:

1. Search for program inspiration from other libraries and business organizations that are offering "entrepreneur storytelling." For example, we used a search engine with keywords such as "library AND entrepreneur storytelling" and "library AND small business stories."
2. Learn about the local BIPOC small business owners and entrepreneurs to identify those with unique products, business models, interesting paths to entrepreneurship, and innovative approaches to marketing their business who would have a story to share. Create a list of potential speakers.
3. Work with the speakers to create a program series that is as diverse as possible, keeping in mind race, ethnicity, gender, business industry, and topics of expertise.
4. Consider and discuss program format options and confirm whether there will be an active moderator interviewing the speaker, if the speaker will present independently, or some other format. For our programs, we built in time for program attendees to engage directly with the speakers—asking them questions, applauding their successes, and taking notes for their own business pursuits.
5. Promote your events to your small business community. Encourage the presenters to help with marketing and promotion by sharing material via their personal and business social media platforms.
6. Pay your speakers for their time and expertise. This demonstrates the value your institution places on the time and effort they are

investing in the program you're asking them to contribute to. If you are working with women and BIPOC, this compensation also advances equity for labor that is systemically undervalued and underpaid.
7. Follow up with the presenters to collect feedback on their experience and gauge their interest in participating in future opportunities.
8. Share your speakers' names in conversations with other community partners to heighten the visibility of BIPOC business owners and entrepreneurs.
9. Maintain relationships with your speakers beyond the contracted presentation. Champion their successes, stop in to say hello, and patronize their businesses when possible. Continued engagement and trust-building will help transform their interaction with the library from transaction to partnership.

Promoting Your Program

Our SB-BI team promoted the initiative through e-mail newsletter, social media, and word-of-mouth marketing strategies. Use an e-mail marketing service, such as Constant Contact, to build and maintain a curated e-mail list that is specific to small business and entrepreneurship. With this service, data such as open and click rates can help you analyze engagement and interest. For social media and other outreach, work with your library's marketing coordinator to create and post engaging social media content and develop press releases for major events or milestones. Our staff created short videos in Spanish and Hmong and shared them via social media. A press release can engage the local media, giving you further reach.

Overcoming Roadblocks and Challenges

Business owners must often carry many responsibilities, and their time is limited. While we hope to see high numbers of participants throughout all of our offerings, we know this is an ongoing challenge. Strategic efforts to increase participation utilize collaboration, targeted marketing, and short workshop series. Partnering with other agencies creates greater visibility for a program, and two agencies promoting a program will have a greater reach with potential participants. Highlight what value the library program or service offers business owners so they understand why it is worth their time to participate. Finally, if you intend to have a cumulative series of workshops, higher frequency over a short span may have higher attendance than a spread-out series over a longer span because there is a shorter time commitment.

Staff Responsibilities

We had two full-time staff—the community partnerships supervisor and the adult services and engagement librarian—manage, develop, and implement our SB-BI initiative. We hired a part-time bilingual library assistant to support engagement and outreach to the business community. This individual brought a range of experiences with business start-up and management and with nonprofit management. We contracted with a local business consultant to design and present the SB-BI Academy. This individual engaged the participating business owners in expert- and peer-learning opportunities for business retention and expansion.

Tips, Tricks, and Advice

- **Prioritize partnership and collaboration.** Research and listen to learn about how the local economic ecosystem is already thriving, and then identify the gaps. Who is missing from the picture? What opportunities are there to address inequities, specifically racial and ethnic disparities? With this assessment, lift up other agencies' expertise and resources without duplicating efforts. Work in partnership with other agencies to address the gaps in a connecting role.
- **Build relationships with BIPOC business owners and entrepreneurs.** Approach this work with a focus on relationships, with a specific focus on understanding and centering BIPOC and immigrant business owners. Participants have expertise and experience to share, so look for ways to open space for peer-sharing. Contract with your participants to serve as paid presenters or ambassadors for the library. Then stay in touch with them beyond the program and contract period to strengthen the relationship beyond a transaction.
- **Consider innovative approaches to access.** At APL, we offered Academy participants options for interpreter support, and

technology for participating in the program virtually. Library staff created an accessible application process that was brief, and we also offered an optional video submission to reduce the application barriers related to literacy and English proficiency. Consider what barriers your potential participants may face and then offer accessible options for participation.

- **Create a welcoming space.** The library has been a long-standing coworking space that offers business resources, but it may not have a reputation or consistent function as a hub of activity for business owners. Focus on creating a welcoming space where BIPOC and immigrant business owners receive consistently excellent service, programs, and networking opportunities that can foster connections between business owners.

PROGRAM 3

Taking Budding Entrepreneurs from Business Idea to Business Plan

The Entrepreneur Academy

BALTIMORE COUNTY (MD) PUBLIC LIBRARY

Julie M. Brophy

Setting the Stage

Business programs and assistance have been offered at the nineteen branches of the Baltimore County Public Library for many years, but in 2018 the Baltimore County Public Library, in a groundbreaking collaboration with the Enoch Pratt Free Library (Baltimore), pooled their resources, expertise, and creativity and launched a training curriculum called the Entrepreneur Academy, a seven-class series designed to provide the tools and support needed to start or grow a small business. The Entrepreneur Academy takes budding entrepreneurs from business idea to business plan, while demystifying and de-romanticizing the notion of working for yourself. The first cohorts, held concurrently in-person at branches of the Baltimore County Public and the Enoch Pratt Free libraries, consisted of 60 participants, 52 of whom finished the series entirely. To date more than 350 people have successfully completed the series through the Baltimore County Public Library.

Maryland is uniquely situated to withstand economic recession because of the "eds, feds, and meds" in the region. Despite this, about 43 percent of the Baltimore region's residents have jobs but live below the federal poverty line. Our two library systems came together with the shared understanding that entrepreneurship is a way for marginalized communities to not only survive but to thrive. The creation of the Entrepreneur Academy marked the start of the Baltimore County Public Library's more intentional work supporting small businesses in the Baltimore region.

Service Area

- Urban, Suburban, and Rural
- Very large, more than 500,000 population

Goals and Impact

When we began developing this series, reports from various sources indicated that by 2020 approximately 50 percent of the population would file a 1099 tax form. For some, this is an attempt to replace existing work and become their own boss. For others, it's necessary to "make ends meet" and to bridge the gap between what they earn in their current job and what they need to survive. Public libraries can meet this shifting demand and support aspiring entrepreneurs, building on the library's traditional role in in helping individuals find and secure jobs to creating businesses and future job creation.

The Baltimore County Public Library's mission is to provide opportunities for our customers to explore, learn, create, and connect. This mission continues with our business programs. The library acts as a convener of business owners, connecting individuals to resources, partners, and each other to ensure a more vibrant, connected, and prosperous Baltimore County; and this in turn helps us to realign our services to better meet the needs of the community today. The Entrepreneur Academy became the flagship small-business initiative of the Baltimore County Public Library, proving the efficacy and importance of business programs to our staff and prompting the creation of a variety of programs and services for small business based on community needs and trends.

Participants in our business programs have consistently provided positive feedback, along with suggestions for future programs. Survey results have shown increases in knowledge and access to resources, and the number of "familiar faces" we see at our business programs provides positive reinforcement for staff. In addition to increased participation in the business programs, we've seen an increase in use of the resources and services we promote, including our one-on-one assistance with a librarian, and the number of requests for presentations we receive from local business associations and chambers of commerce. Moreover, being able to talk about our work with small businesses and its resulting economic impact has been beneficial when talking with government officials and funders.

> **Non-Profit Academy**
>
> When we learned from some Entrepreneur Academy participants that they wanted to start a nonprofit organization, we arranged for a companion series: the Non-Profit Academy. The staff at the library reached out to several Maryland nonprofits, who worked with us to offer a two-part series on how to start and build a nonprofit. These introductory classes cover topics like mission planning, legal compliance, board governance, and ethics and fundraising, and thus share invaluable resources with which to build on the skills learned in the Entrepreneur Academy. Listening to what people want brought results: 187 people participated in the two series we've offered so far.

Getting Started

Before you develop your program, talk with stakeholders, survey potential program participants, and hold community focus groups. At our library, we wanted to make sure that what we were offering was what entrepreneurs really wanted and needed to learn. We received feedback from our partners—the small business experts—and analyzed the success of past small business programs and services. Consider designing a survey that gathers information from both budding entrepreneurs and those already on their journey to small business ownership. By including both groups, we were able to determine what they wanted to know, and looking back, what information they now realize would have been useful. Results from the surveys and focus groups helped formulate what would become the Entrepreneur Academy.

Key Resources

Subject matter experts, including library staff, are the instructors in the Entrepreneur Academy. A virtual meeting platform or meeting room space, tables and chairs for participants, and a projector and screen are needed for each class. For the library-led class, laptops/tablets are provided for instruction. Additionally, a staff member attends each class to act as host, answer any questions, facilitate networking, and provide additional learning opportunities.

Key Partners

The Entrepreneur Academy was made possible through our collaboration with the Enoch Pratt Free Library. Though we have different systems with different staffing structures, budgets, and governance, we've worked together to advance financial equity by supporting small businesses in the Baltimore region and beyond.

The Maryland Small Business Development Center and the CASH Campaign of Maryland both provided guidance in the creation of the Entrepreneur Academy series, and their staff act as subject matter experts instructing classes.

The Small Business Administration and the Maryland Department of Labor provided technical support as we created the series.

Budget

Subject matter experts/speakers are the primary expense for the Entrepreneur Academy, with the library providing in-kind support through staffing, space, and promotions. Hiring instructors, including library staff, who are experts in their fields enhances the value of the programs and brings value to both the program and the library. Approximately $3,000 is spent on each cohort of participants in the Entrepreneur Academy, with additional stipends for other programs provided between $100 and $300.

Implementing the Nuts and Bolts

Creating what became the Entrepreneur Academy started with asking the right questions of the right people. Before we developed the curriculum, we asked our partners what their customers needed, experienced business owners what they wished they'd known when they got started, and local chambers what they were offering, to ensure that we complemented, rather than competed, with other groups. This, along with our collaboration with key partners, led to the creation of the curriculum.

The Entrepreneur Academy is a seven-class series that provides information and resources so that participants have all the elements of a business plan. The topics covered include Introduction to Market Research and Business Strategies; Business Finances, Taxes, and Recordkeeping; Marketing your Business; and Developing Your Business Plan. In the third week of the series, a panel of experts, including an attorney, insurance agent, and banker, presents and answers questions, providing invaluable free advice to the very engaged participants. Because we're aware that this series is a long-term commitment, we ask participants to sign a commitment letter and provide regular feedback to us. We survey participants at the initial, midway, and final sessions of the Entrepreneur Academy. These brief surveys ask about their confidence and knowledge for starting a small business, and their access to resources. To date, each cohort has shown a steady increase in each category. (See figure 3.1.) Additionally, we ask for suggestions for improvement and additional classes, and this has driven many of our additional business program offerings.

The in-person sessions enable networking on the same night, but when the sessions are offered virtually, we provide a co-learning opportunity each week. This sixty-minute session is led by a librarian and provides opportunities for additional learning and networking. Library staff prepare a lesson but are flexible and allow participants to guide the learning.

HOW TO: Package Existing Services for the Business Community

As we developed our business services, we took stock of our library's existing resources and services that might be of interest to entrepreneurs in order to market them explicitly to our business community. We looked at the services we offered already and reimagined their use by and for our entrepreneurs. You may already have resources at your library that you could market to entrepreneurs, too.

Look at the resources you currently have available and how you can "repurpose" them to support your small business community. In our library's case, these resources included:

- **Study rooms:** We renamed our study rooms "free small conference rooms," and promoted them as ideal for small meetings or business calls.

Cohort 1—Spring 2019 (In-person)

	Confidence in Starting Biz			Knowledge of Starting Biz			Have Resources to Start Biz		
	Initial	Mid-way	Final	Initial	Mid-way	Final	Initial	Mid-way	Final
Number of Responses	20	28	27	20	28	27	20	28	27
Average Score (out of 5)	4.15	4.07	4.26	3.35	3.75	4.22	2.45	4.46	4.59

Cohort 2—Spring 2019 (In-person)

	Confidence in Starting Biz			Knowledge of Starting Biz			Have Resources to Start Biz		
	Initial	Mid-way	Final	Initial	Mid-way	Final	Initial	Mid-way	Final
Number of Responses	27	20	16	27	20	16	27	20	17
Average Score (out of 5)	3.63	3.75	4.19	2.70	3.70	4.06	2.56	4.55	4.76

Cohort 3—Fall 2019 (In-person)

	Confidence in Starting Biz			Knowledge of Starting Biz			Have Resources to Start Biz		
	Initial	Mid-way	Final	Initial	Mid-way	Final	Initial	Mid-way	Final
Number of Responses	30	19	24	30	20	24	30	20	24
Average Score (out of 5)	3.80	3.90	4.20	2.40	3.40	4.10	2.00	4.50	4.50

Cohort 4—Fall 2020 (Virtual)

	Confidence in Starting Biz			Knowledge of Starting Biz			Have Resources to Start Biz		
	Initial	Mid-way	Final	Initial	Mid-way	Final	Initial	Mid-way	Final
Number of Responses	69	49	43	69	48	43	69	49	43
Average Score (out of 5)	3.80	3.80	4.26	2.83	3.54	4.07	2.74	4.41	4.63

Cohort 5—Winter 2021 (Virtual)

	Confidence in Starting Biz			Knowledge of Starting Biz			Have Resources to Start Biz		
	Initial	Mid-way	Final	Initial	Mid-way	Final	Initial	Mid-way	Final
Number of Responses	147	113	96	147	113	96	147	113	96
Average Score (out of 5)	3.54	3.69	4.15	2.68	3.41	3.95	2.64	4.33	4.61

Figure 3.1 Survey results from cohorts of the Entrepreneur Academy, Baltimore County Public Library

Figure courtesy of Baltimore County Public Library

- **3D printing:** We promoted our 3D printing as a way to test a prototype.
- **My Librarian:** We promoted this service as My Librarian for Small Business, a one-on-one appointment with a librarian for in-depth research and referral assistance.
- **Chromebooks, hot spots, and Wi-Fi:** Our library technology was promoted as free tech support.
- **Databases and other services (e.g., Notary, Passports):** With the right marketing, databases for market research, notary services, and so on can be important elements in starting a business.

Strategically and intentionally market these and other services and resources to the business community through social media, your library website, and flyers and posters.

Promoting Your Program

In addition to traditional program promotion (e.g., social media, e-newsletters, library website, flyers), consider issuing a press release to reach traditional media outlets. Promotional e-mails and flyers can be sent to small business owners and entrepreneurs in the community, as well as government workforce departments, chambers of commerce, local business associations, and makerspaces and artisans' groups. This multipronged approach to promotion worked for us: we had 170 people express interest in joining the first set of cohorts alone, one in the county and one in the city. This promotional opportunity benefited the whole library: we captured a new audience not only for the Entrepreneur Academy but for our libraries.

Overcoming Roadblocks and Challenges

Our efforts to identify and secure partnerships were painstaking and time-consuming. However, the work done in the lead-up to creating the program has strengthened and grown our partnerships and enhanced the experience of participants. The Baltimore County Public Library has a staff of generalists—there are no dedicated age- or subject-experts. In order to ensure that the library was prepared to support the increase in both programming and information requests, we formed an Entrepreneur Engagement Group; this is a team of librarians and managers who provide one-on-one business-focused reference services, train staff, support programs, and promote our library's services and resources at events with business associations and chambers.

Staff Responsibilities

There are currently thirteen staff members in the Entrepreneur Engagement Group, with key staffers from the Adult and Community Engagement Department providing leadership and oversight of business programs. Through grant funding, we've hired a contractual small business consultant to help us identify gaps in our services and spot potential partner opportunities.

Tips, Tricks, and Advice

- **Success takes time.** Doing your due diligence in creating any program, finding the right partners and cultivating those relationships, and ensuring that the staff are engaged in the process will bring long-term success.
- **Offer networking whenever you can.** While it can be intimidating to library staff to host networking nights, the customers we see at these programs are looking for ways to connect with others. Some participants may find their local chamber or business association intimidating, so networking opportunities at the library can provide entry to a larger community.
- **Celebrate success.** For many of our participants, the commitment it takes to successfully complete a seven-week class is noteworthy. We've hosted celebratory events where we give a certificate of completion, invite a representative from the local chamber to speak, and congratulate everyone with light refreshments. While not everyone attends, many of our participants invite their family and friends to celebrate, thus building our community through networking and solidifying the library's place in the community.
- **Follow up with participants.** Many of the "graduates" of the program have appreciated this follow-up. We provide information on new resources, programs, and services through the library, as well as other resources available to

the community (e.g., loan programs). This is beneficial for participants, but also to the library, because it reminds them that the library is *always* there to help and support them whenever it can.

PROGRAM 4

Empowering New Businesses with a Business Plan Competition
PowerUP!

BROOKLYN (NY) PUBLIC LIBRARY

Maud Andrew and Arcola Robinson

Setting the Stage

The Brooklyn Public Library (BPL) was the first public library to create a business plan competition for its community. Our goal was to equip novices with the business skills and information they would need for success. Designed just for start-ups, PowerUP! offers classes, mentoring, and access to business information to aspiring entrepreneurs for free. The program was a direct response to the need to empower those with the least access to resources—individuals without personal knowledge or a family background of business ownership, let alone a business degree. Because the library is often the place where people start their exploration, PowerUP! was designed to move participants forward, providing support, structure, and know-how, as well as an incentive that is rarely available to new small businesses—free seed capital.

Over the years we have innovated with the concept to reach new audiences and improve outcomes. We have offered the classes in Haitian Kreyol, added a live pitch competition, offered the competition completely online during the pandemic, and recently developed the BKLYN Fashion Academy (BFA), which trains aspiring designers in their craft.

Service Area

- Urban
- Very large, more than 500,000 population

Goals and Impact

In creating PowerUP! BPL's Business & Career Center sought to make tangible the power of information and the value of the public library. The goal was to bring entrepreneurs into the library, introduce them to the array of tools we offer for free, and engage them in a meaningful way by offering a cash prize for completing the hard work of developing a business plan that is so essential to starting a successful business.

Each year the competition has attracted hundreds of participants, thereby growing our user base and validating the library's role among our economic development partners.

We have helped hundreds of businesses get started throughout the borough of Brooklyn; this has contributed not only to the economic well-being of individual entrepreneurs who have started businesses, hired employees, engaged vendors and supported their families, but to the economic vitality of each neighborhood. We have found that many participants, and not just those who have won awards, have ultimately gone into business equipped with the business knowledge they gained in the competition.

Getting Started

Take time to assess the resources you have to offer prospective entrepreneurs. Do you have committed staff, business databases, a business collection, on-site counseling, librarians with business knowledge, workshops for entrepreneurs, and space and technology? If you have a core set of services that businesses can leverage to ensure a successful launch, then the next step is to create a work or support group to gauge the level of interest within your community and to build enthusiasm. Our group was called the Success Council; it was composed of local economic development organizations, representatives from the chamber of commerce, business owners, teachers from local colleges, city agencies, and library supporters in general. Pitch the concept to your support group, emphasize the benefits to the community, to the library, and, importantly, to them. Explain how their involvement could bring them clients, expand their network, increase their visibility, and enhance the vitality of the local economy. Once you have buy-in, this group can help you refine your concept and outline the rules.

Key Resources
The resources our library brought to the initiative included:

- An in-depth collection of business plan, marketing, and DIY "how to start" business books
- LibGuides (for example, BPL's Business Plan and Ideation Guide)
- Interactive databases such as Bizminer, Cision, Gale Business: Plan Builder and Entrepreneurship, LinkedIn Learning, Mergent Intellect, Mintel Reports Academic, Reference Solutions, RKMA Consumer Market Research, SimplyAnalytics, and Statista
- Online sources of free, local information, such as the NYC Small Business Services and the NYC Department of City Planning's Population Fact Finder

Key Partners
The PowerUP! model relies extensively on the support of numerous community partners; their representatives teach the classes, mentor participants, offer workshops, and judge the business plans, at no cost. As a result, the competition has created an umbrella under which community-based organizations have come together to develop the local economy. The competition introduces entrepreneurs to the local ecosystem of business assistance providers. Our partners are able to build their clientele as they donate their expertise, which is essential to our competition. The partners include:

- Business Outreach Center's Women's Business Center
- Small Business Development Center at City University College of Technology
- SCORE NYC
- NYC Department of Small Business Services
- Local Development Corporation of East New York
- Church Avenue Merchants Block Association
- Start Small Think Big

- Brooklyn Chamber of Commerce
- Bedford Stuyvesant Restoration Corporation Business Services
- IMPACCT Brooklyn

Budget

The Brooklyn Public Library's business plan competition has two major expenses: the seed capital awarded to the winning plans, and the salaries of staff. BPL raises private funding to cover the prize money, and absorbs the cost for staff in its regular operating expenses. Outside of staff, the funding needed to operate the program is relatively small. The prizes need not be expensive; they can be a basket of services from local businesses, or apprenticeships, or publicity in the local press. BPL has found funding from banks that need to satisfy their federal CRA requirements; it is likely that banks in most towns have similar requirements. Several of our donations are in the $2,000 to $5,000 range. BPL raises $65,000 annually for PowerUP! of which $41,000 is devoted to cash awards.

Implementing the Nuts and Bolts

Over the course of five months, the competition's participants take classes in researching their business idea and market, creating a market strategy, developing a set of simple financials, writing a business plan, and meeting with a business coach. Additional, optional workshops are scheduled to build their understanding of doing business, including digital marketing/social media, website/e-commerce development, finding and leasing space, legal structures and liabilities, presenting and pitching, and finding financing. We offer opportunities to attend motivational panels with other start-ups and meet with pro-bono attorneys and financial coaches. Participants are given in-depth assistance in using library resources to develop a target market, track trends, and analyze their competition. On average, 60 to 80 participants submit a business plan, and the finalists make live presentations. Cash prizes ranging from $1,000 to $20,000 and a selection of services are awarded to the top eight plans.

Because there are no shortcuts to starting a business, participants can join the competition more than once. Whether they are awarded a prize or not, we remind them that the real win is to launch their business, and we are available to help them in every step of their journey.

82 PART II: CASE STUDIES FROM THE FIELD

Brooklyn PowerUp! 16th anniversary ceremony
Photograph by Gregg Richards

HOW TO: Run a Business Plan Competition

1. Bring together a working group of library staff, city agencies, business owners, and community partners. Create a calendar with key dates, and assign duties to the team or working group.
2. Find funders and donors to support the competition financially, including banks. Stakeholders may also offer in-kind services such as consulting, printing services, advertising, website design, and association memberships.
3. Start with marketing. Create a mailer and mailing list and have all partners support promotion efforts.
4. Hold an orientation/application period. Host sessions to explain the rules and the expectations for the competition. Interested parties

submit their applications online. All Brooklyn residents who wish to start a business in the borough are eligible for the competition.
5. Run business classes, take attendance, and gather feedback from participants. Identify a few experts from your working group who have the capacity to teach classes. In addition, rely on librarians to develop classes on how to use databases and do market research.
6. Provide mentoring and other supports. We require a minimum of one consultation with a mentor, and we encourage more. We also offer financial coaches to build money management skills and improve credit scores.
7. Give participants ample time to research and write their business plans after classes wrap up. Provide support to help and keep participants engaged, and offer them opportunities to meet with librarians, use library resources, and attend additional workshops.
8. Communicate regularly with participants. Offer them encouragement and reminders, especially about deadlines.
9. Identify judges. Though it is time-consuming work, judging is exciting and rewarding, and hearing start-ups pitched can be inspirational. After the business plans have been submitted, convene the judges to review the written plans and select the finalists.
10. The selected finalists then present their plans to a second panel of judges who select the top eight winners. These winners are then awarded cash prizes.
11. Host a culminating event that allows participants to interact with the community: this is where you hear their stories and their passion. Our ceremony includes a live pitch from some of the finalists. Invite all partners and the press.

Promoting Your Program

Diversify your outreach. We use the following methods to promote the competition: printed mailer, fliers and announcements at the library, the BPL website, an e-mail newsletter, community partners, and word of mouth.

Overcoming Roadblocks and Challenges

Initially the competition was a victim of its own success. We had more participants than we were equipped to handle, and we lacked both the staff and the technology that were needed. Many of today's tech solutions were not available eighteen years ago; we didn't have a software system to manage participants, which meant that plans were submitted in print and on CDs and they were copied and mailed to the judges. After the first year we were able to raise money for full-time staff, and eventually we subscribed to an online platform (Survey Monkey Apply). Serving the needs of so many diverse participants is a constant challenge; some have limited technology skills or lack practical experience, while others struggle with business concepts or with their personal finances.

Staff Responsibilities

Two individuals are dedicated to managing all Business & Career Center-related programs, including PowerUP! They are responsible for creating, calendaring, marketing, managing, and evaluating all workshops and events for our department. Each individual spends about 50 percent of their time managing the business plan competition and the fashion academy. All librarians in the Business & Career Center teach market research classes, offer database training, and meet participants through BPL's appointment-based research service, Book a Librarian. BPL's marketing and development departments also support the initiative.

The BKLYN Fashion Academy

Following the PowerUP! model, the BKLYN Fashion Academy (BFA) introduces participants to library resources and an array of business skills workshops to help them develop their fashion businesses, and the academy relies on local talent, academic institutions, and community organizations to teach and mentor designers.

Designers attend full-day intensive sessions where they learn advanced skills such as draping and fashion illustration. Industry insiders share essential industry-specific business practices and skills in intimate technical labs where instructors offer hands-on guidance. Since design can be personal, designers are matched with mentors to support their progress in the program. Throughout the program, the designers work to complete a themed mini-collection that portrays their range, talent, and individuality. The culmination of the program is a display of their collections at BPL's Runway Show, which is attended by industry professionals and the press.

Tips, Tricks, and Advice

- Smaller libraries can adapt portions of the model described here to create manageable programs of their own that will engage and educate entrepreneurs in their community. The possibilities include staging a pitch competition that offers free training and the opportunity to present to local banks and funders; creating training workshops around fashion, cooking, videography, or other business skills; and creating a competition for the best business idea in a local industry, with the prize-winner awarded an apprenticeship in a local business.
- Partnership opportunities exist in all towns; and business support organizations, city agencies, and community colleges can all lend their expertise. In smaller areas, libraries play a large role in the local culture, and their visibility may allow them to convene community partners and leverage their support; in return, libraries can offer these community partners access to their patrons and their space. Together they can work toward their shared goal of building the local economy.

PROGRAM 5

Built to Last
Built in Broward

BROWARD COUNTY (FL) LIBRARY

Sheldon Burke

Setting the Stage

"Built in Broward," the Broward County Library's entrepreneurship program, supports African Americans, Hispanic/Latinx, and lower-income Broward County residents to break through barriers to access and give them the tools they need to create their own freelance tech businesses. The Broward County Library's free coworking space, Creation Station Business; General Assembly Miami, a global leader in technology; and Black Valley Digital, a minority-owned education and marketing firm, have partnered to provide entrepreneurs with free access to tech workshops, business mentorship, and networking through cohorts of aspiring tech entrepreneurs and monthly industry events with local tech leaders.

The spark for Built in Broward began in 2019 at the Equity in Energy, Innovation, and Entrepreneurship Summit hosted by the city of Fort Lauderdale, Florida International University, and the U.S. Department of Energy (DOE). The summit formalized a relationship between the three to establish a global entrepreneurial resources center in Fort Lauderdale to catalyze the Florida innovation ecosystem and create a DOE technology-transfer center.

Service Area Size

- Urban
- Very large, more than 500,000 population

Goals and Impact

The Broward County Library recognized a clear community need for tech upskilling as our region transitions to a tech-centered economy. The library's aim was to address the barriers to underrepresented groups participating in the tech industry and building their own tech businesses; namely, lack of access to affordable tech education and lack of access to networks. We learned that only 1 percent of Black STEM graduates went on to create their own tech businesses. The project addressed this by working with General Assembly Miami to provide free access to tech workshops that typically cost $150–$250 per person, and free access to industry events with local tech leaders; as well as working with Black Valley Digital to provide business incubators to a cohort of aspiring tech entrepreneurs selected to work collaboratively through the twelve-week program that allowed participants to capitalize on their tech education.

Key Resources
The resources our library brought to the initiative include:

- **Zoom** for virtual workshops, virtual events, quarterly business incubators, and weekly partner meetings.
- **Slack** for communicating. One channel was solely for our grant partners, General Assembly, and Black Valley Digital. We had another channel for our quarterly business incubators.
- **Kajabi** for recordings of quarterly business incubators and instructor development sessions. We wanted to ensure that participants, many of whom work full-time jobs, could miss a week or two and still participate in our programs.
- **A landing page** for our project so there was a central place for learning about all of our events and signing up for workshops.

Key Partners
With our program's technology focus, we sought partners that could lead technology training and real-world introductions to the growing tech entrepreneurship community. With that in mind, our partners included:

- **General Assembly Miami**, which facilitated tech workshops and industry events. They also procured local talent, created promotional material, and disseminated it to our partners.

- **Black Valley Digital**, which facilitated our quarterly business incubators and our instructor development program, provided mentorship to participants of both, and created a video course for Broward County librarians for project sustainability.
- **Alliance of Entrepreneurial Resources (AERO)**, which promoted our workshops and events to their clients. The alliance comprises the Broward County Library, the Jim Moran Institute, Broward SCORE, Broward Economic and Small Business Development, the city of Fort Lauderdale, the Greater Fort Lauderdale Alliance, Hispanic Unity of Florida, Career Source Broward, the Urban League of Broward County, the Network for Teaching Entrepreneurship, and the Broward College Entrepreneurship Experience.

Budget

We budgeted $122,692 for our program, which we funded through the Libraries Build Business grant. Our budget included the costs of the business development incubators led by Black Valley Digital for each twelve-week cohort, including instructor fees; the cost of the tech workshops facilitated by General Assembly; and our video courses and other resources. For libraries interested in tech entrepreneurship programs, strong partners and equipment are critical to an effective program.

Implementing the Nuts and Bolts

Built in Broward has three components. First, we hosted workshops and industry events facilitated by General Assembly. The workshop topics selected for Built in Broward ranged from artificial intelligence to visual design. Each workshop highlighted General Assembly and Broward County Library resources, and a post-event survey was given at the end of each session.

The second component is our twelve-week cohort-model freelance business incubators. Black Valley Digital went through applications submitted through our landing page and selected twenty qualified applicants each quarter. These participants received weekly virtual training on various business development topics such as pricing your services, finding leads, taxes, forming contacts, and more. There were also open office hours with the instructor and coworking sessions throughout the week for accountability.

The final component is the instructor development program. Broward County librarians were trained to use the library's existing educational resources like LinkedIn Learning to learn new tech topics and translate them into programs. Participants met virtually weekly and communicated daily over Slack. At the end of the training program, the librarians presented a tech workshop program using the skills they had learned.

HOW TO: Promote Your Business Program and Connect with Your Community in Style

Planning a successful business program requires strong community engagement. Here are some steps to build strong partnerships, publicly announce your program, and engage your target audience.

1. Identify the target audience of your business program. Once you have identified your target audience, research local business organizations that work with your target audience.
2. Network! Your library may already have a partnership with some of these groups already. If that is the case, ask these existing partners if they have a lead for new business organizations that work with your target audience.
3. Send e-mails, request meetings, and start building relationships with these potential partners, letting them know what the library can offer. For Built in Broward, we specifically offered to place their logo on all promotional materials for our program. This is a free incentive that organizations love.
4. Planning and developing a project as large as Built in Broward is a big deal, so treat it like one. Kick your project off with a virtual lightning talk—a quick, round-table Q&A on a particular topic—with your community partners and stakeholders. A lightning talk generates buzz for your program and demonstrates the value of your program to your target audience.
5. Draft a press release, blog post, and other media message to share the big news about your program launch. Send these items to your partners and have them share through their social media channels

to stretch your library's reach and get the message directly to your target audience.
6. Develop the content and questions for your kickoff event. For our lightning talk, we focused on questions that highlighted the business and entrepreneur resources that attending groups offered the community, areas where we could break down silos in Broward's business ecosystem, and of course, we asked them about their hopes for Built in Broward, to bring the focus back to our program. A representative from your library should also be on the round-table panel to highlight and promote the library's resources.
7. Stay in regular communication with your partners and stakeholders. Follow up with partners, thanking them for their support, and continue to engage with them on a weekly basis to keep the momentum gained from your lightning-talk kickoff event.
8. Follow up with attendees with a call to action. Lead them to a landing page for your program or to your first business program event.
9. Most importantly, in the future, regular communication is key. Continue to engage with your partners. Send them social media templates for your events and ask them to promote them to their clients, who could become your target audience.

Promoting Your Program

Your library's existing outreach is a strong place to start outreach for the business program. The Broward County Library used its existing Creation Station Business and library newsletters, and the library's social media channels to promote our monthly workshops, events, and our application for the business incubator cohorts. Additionally, Creation Station Business drew upon its existing community partners, especially AERO, who promoted Built in Broward programs to their customers.

Partnerships are a great way to spread the word and extend your reach in the community. For example, we formed new partnerships with groups to reach nontraditional library users, such as the Alliance Partner Council, which is made up of representatives from all thirty-one cities that make up Broward County; the Venture Cafe, a networking and coworking space; the Broward Black Chamber of Commerce, a business group specifically focused on promoting Black entrepreneurs; the Alan Levan Institute; and General Provision, a local coworking space with access to a large Slack Channel of tech entrepreneurs.

Overcoming Roadblocks and Challenges

Having many partners confers many advantages, but it can also have some disadvantages. Specifically, it can be time-consuming to maintain these relationships while doing other aspects of your job. Strong, regular communication is critical to maintaining your partners' engagement and program attendance. This is not always easy with busy schedules, but we found it to be worth it. We recommend weekly communications or meetings with partners.

Staff Responsibilities

The Built in Broward project had one business librarian from Broward County Library's Creation Station Business as the project lead. This lead librarian met weekly with key partners, scheduled workshops and events, moderated or presented workshops and events, and promoted the workshops and events and cohort application periods to our community partners via the Creation Station Business newsletter. Two additional librarians served as backup for the project's administration.

Tips, Tricks, and Advice

- **Start establishing relationships in your community today.** The success of the Built in Broward project hinged on our having strong relationships in the community. Those relationships took time to form, so don't wait until you start implementing your programs to start forming partnerships. For instance, Creation Station Business met with AERO members every month for three years, cross-pollinating member resources with our respective customers and working annually on an AERO Business Expo.
- **Don't be afraid to reach out to "competitors."** Libraries enjoy a positive reputation in most communities, and many businesses know that we are just trying to help the community with no

strings attached. Use this to your advantage and reach out to private businesses that occupy a similar niche as you. For example, General Provision is a for-profit coworking space located just one block away from the Creation Station Business coworking space. And yet, General Provision has allowed us to do outreach at their location and promote the Built in Broward project to their customers.
- **Create a landing page.** A landing page is an effective tool to gain partners, promote your project, and document your successes.

PROGRAM 6

Rochester—Innovation Was Born Here

Business Insight Center

CENTRAL LIBRARY OF ROCHESTER AND MONROE COUNTY (NY)

Jennifer Byrnes

Setting the Stage

The city of Rochester in New York has long been known as a hub for innovation. It birthed Eastman Kodak, Xerox, and Bausch & Lomb and is also the place where optical light-emitting diodes (LED) were invented. You know that smartphone you love? You're welcome. Following in those footsteps, the Business Insight Center (BIC) is an innovative division of the Central Library of Rochester and Monroe County. The critical difference from other library departments is that the BIC does not have a reference desk. We are by appointment only, and our staff are subject specialists who don't work in any other departments. The BIC is also home to the Carlson Center for Intellectual Property, one of the U.S. Patent Office's six Patent and Trademark Resource Centers in New York state.[1]

We primarily serve the Greater Rochester and Finger Lakes region, a nine-county area which includes the urban area of Rochester as well as rural agricultural areas of the Finger Lakes, with approximately 1,200,000 residents.

Service Area

- Urban and Suburban
- Very Large, more than 500,000 population

Goals and Impact

Imagine this scenario: You started a tech company out of your parents' basement. You are finally gaining traction and are scheduled to make a pitch in front of investors. They will want to know the projected growth of that industry, who has market share, and who owns what intellectual property. So you do what you always do. You Google it. You find a report that is perfect, if you only had the $5,000 to pay for it. What do you do? You call the Business Insight Center. Market research reports, which range from $500 to $5,000, are cost-prohibitive for most start-ups, but the information included in these reports is vital. On average we save the community $2,000,000 a year in market research reports.

Imagine this scenario: You have created a logo for your fledgling business and you want to trademark it. Should you pay an intellectual property attorney $1,000 to see if there is anything similar to your logo? Or what if you are an aspiring inventor who doesn't have the funds to determine if what you have is patentable? What do you do? The Carlson Center for Intellectual Property provides prior art searches for patents and trademarks, as well as information on the filing process. Cost: free. The expert staff at the Carlson Center has completed the prior art searches, and you now need an attorney to determine if you can go ahead with your trademark application. Once again, this is pricey. For students and low-income clients, the Carlson Center subsidizes meetings with an intellectual property attorney. The attorney gives it the go-ahead and congrats, you now hold a U.S. trademark. But what about that pesky patent application? The Carlson Center facilitates meetings with a patent examiner to review your application prior to filing. Who's getting an office action because the application isn't filled out correctly? Not you! Rochester has been in the top ten of cities with the most patents since Eastman Kodak began, and we are proud to help continue this tradition.

Lastly, we have been nationally recognized for our efforts. We have received two Urban Libraries Council (ULC) innovation awards within four years. In 2016 we were named top innovator, and we received an honorable mention in 2020. The division head also serves on the ULC's Entrepreneurs and Small Businesses Action Team.

Getting Started

To get started on providing market research services to your patrons, the single best thing you can do is unchain yourself from the reference desk and get out there. Those who are busy running a business don't have time to come to you. Attend meetings and do outreach to connect your services to the entrepreneurs that need them and the partners that can promote them.

Key Resources

Our Business Center's go-to resources are IBISWorld, Frost & Sullivan, and PitchBook. IBISWorld contains comprehensive industry surveys on more than 700 industries. Frost & Sullivan has the pulse on emerging technology. PitchBook serves two functions: identifying venture capital firms, and researching start-ups that you won't find information on in other databases, because they are too young. Other tools in our toolbox include:

- **InnovationQ**: For prior art searching
- **Mergent Intellect**: For identifying businesses by NAICS or SIC code in specific geographic areas
- **Factiva**: For business literature
- **Statista**: For statistics on just about anything
- **LivePlan**: A platform that guides users in writing a business plan

Key Partners

Our key partners include the following:

- **The New York State Small Business Development Center**, which provides speakers for Business First Wednesday, our monthly program for current or aspiring small business owners.
- **The Rochester Institute of Technology**, which includes the following:
  - **RIT Venture Creations**, a technology business incubator that provides various services to early- and mid-seed stage start-ups to help them advance their businesses. We hold office hours on-site there monthly.
  - **The Simone Center for Innovation and Entrepreneurship**, which assists students with experiential learning associated with innovation and entrepreneurship. The manager of the

Carlson Center for Intellectual Property attends their team meetings.

- **The Commissary,** a collaborative community which provides shared kitchens, combined with food industry-specific business assistance to help aspiring entrepreneurs. The Business Center established a small appliance-lending library embedded in the Commissary with funds received from the Harold Hacker Foundation.
- **Nextcorp,** a nonprofit catalyst for entrepreneurship and innovation-based economic development. We hold on-site office hours there weekly.
- **Luminate,** a six-month intensive accelerator program for optics, photonics, and imaging companies. We assist the program's participants with market research and intellectual property.
- **The Syracuse University Innovation Law Center,** a unique, interdisciplinary experiential learning program for students interested in the commercial development of new technologies. We provide the law center with market research services and teach patent searching.

Budget

Our program budget includes staff salaries and materials. To supplement our budget, we have an annual endowment fund of $50,000. The vast majority of our materials budget goes to purchasing databases, approximately $75,000. One may balk at that amount, but database access is what our clients want; they are not clamoring for print or e-books. Our division has one full-time division head, two part-time librarians, and one part-time clerk.

Implementing the Nuts and Bolts

Our clients call or e-mail to set up one-on-one appointments. The BIC is a service, not a place per se, that does research, not ready reference. We do not measure door count because we are often off-site, meeting businesses where it is most convenient for them: their office. We do not measure the number of transactions; we measure how many hours of in-depth research we have conducted, on average fifty hours per month. A typical query usually requires a minimum half-hour interview with the client and then, depending on the level of complexity, one to three hours of in-depth research, the results of which are e-mailed to them. All research requests are unique, so we don't have a finished product, but we continue with ongoing relationships with all of our corporate clients.

We don't train our clients on the databases because that is neither our customer service model nor our value proposition, for two main reasons: first, our clients should spend their time running and growing their business, not looking for information. We are better and faster at doing this. And second, most people will not remember how to use a database effectively if they are only using it every six months. We save them time by doing the research for them, and money, because they aren't purchasing the reports themselves.

Promoting Your Program

Over the past five years we have evolved from Rochester's "best kept secret" to being an integral part of the area's entrepreneurial ecosystem. In the beginning it was just word of mouth. As our ability to do outreach grew, our initial strategy was, in short, showing up. We attended all the networking groups, resource fairs, and whichever podcast would have us. We never saw a microphone we wouldn't speak into. Once we started holding office hours at other locations, our service really took off. We could roam around, ask people what they were working on, and provide them with information on the spot. Later, as more grant funds became available, we used different tactics such as sponsoring a tech conference, paying to have a page in a special supplement on bouncing back from COVID, and inserting a flyer highlighting our resources in the *Rochester Business Journal*.

Overcoming Roadblocks and Challenges

There was a long learning curve for community partners such as SCORE to stop sending people to the Business Insight Center without an appointment. Many of the SCORE volunteers were used to a time when our division had double the staff and always had someone at the reference desk. Needless to say, many people came in asking for assistance and were told they needed to make an appointment. Once they understood that we did this so that they were guaranteed one-on-one time with an expert, they saw the value in it.

It may be challenging to find staff who are a good fit for these positions. The requisite skills include inquisitiveness, curiosity, and good instincts for ferreting out information. This is not something staff can dabble in; otherwise, they will not gain the necessary exposure needed to become subject specialists.

Staff Responsibilities

- Division head—responsible for budgetary decisions, programming, and establishing new partnerships.
- Carlson Center manager—responsible for prior art searches, community outreach to discuss services offered, and on-site visits. Participates in week-long annual trainings at the U.S. Patent Office headquarters in Alexandria, Virginia.
- Part-time librarian—responsible for collection development, and assists other team members with research requests. Attends U.S. Patent Office training.
- Clerk—responsible for monitoring budget expenditures, represents the division on program and exhibits teams, posts events to calendars, and keeps everyone else sane.

Tips, Tricks, and Advice

- Memorize your own value proposition. In our case, we save you:
  - Time—We do the research for you. We are better and faster at it and don't want the entrepreneur to spend valuable time trying to navigate databases they use infrequently.
  - Money—You're not spending thousands in market research reports. Go and buy your team pizza and beer instead.
- Sticker shock—our tools cost money. A lot. Think about which ones would be the most useful to you and then make adjustments in your other budget lines. Say it with me: I can cut my book and periodical budget.
- Don't be intimidated by business jargon. Learn some basic acronyms, such as M&A (mergers and acquisitions), IPO (initial public offering), B2B, B2C, and so on.

- Read. A lot.
  - The *Wall Street Journal*. It grows on you. I promise.
  - Your local business publication
- Follow the leader:
  - The BIC has a training manual that is literally four inches thick that covers all the things one needs to know to be effective in this type of position. Learn from the best—reach out to colleagues and other libraries, starting with us.

NOTE

1. Chester Carlson invented Xerography.

PROGRAM 7

The Entrepreneurial Mindset

Encore Entrepreneurs and Key Advanced Entrepreneurs

CUYAHOGA COUNTY (OH) PUBLIC LIBRARY

William Kelly

Setting the Stage

The Cuyahoga County Public Library in Ohio has long recognized the critical importance of workforce development as central to our mission. We created Cuyahoga Works, our career counseling and job readiness center, over forty years ago. Increasingly we discovered that entrepreneurship is a vital facet of the workforce ecosystem, and that the library could provide a much-needed service and fill existing gaps within that system. One gap we discovered was supporting retirees and others who are currently outside the workforce but who have entrepreneurial ambitions. We found the perfect partner in Encore Cleveland, and developed Encore Entrepreneurs, a six-week series to provide budding entrepreneurs with core concepts and foundational knowledge to begin the process.

From this first program, we evaluated, improved, and refined our offerings for the business community. We launched Key Advanced Entrepreneurs, a more advanced entrepreneurial series to build on the introductory program, in partnership with the Economic Community Development Institute and funded by the Key Foundation.

Service Area

- Suburban
- Large, less than 500,000 population

Goals and Impact

In our first year, over 450 graduates completed the Encore Entrepreneur series. Over 94 percent agreed that they were better prepared to create a business, and 83 percent learned skills to grow their existing business. The most valuable tools that attendees identified were conceptualizing their business idea, marketing, financing, legal, and business plan development. These outcomes remained consistent over the next five years.

As our entrepreneurial programming evolved, we recognized that we were filling another need in the community: serving minority women in the low-to-moderate income range, a goal shared by our partners. Over 90 percent of our attendees were women, and the majority were minority women. The Key Foundation grant provided for one $5,000 entrepreneur award each year, to be given to the participant who demonstrated the most drive and potential. Each of the first three winners was a minority woman.

Getting Started

Approach a new entrepreneur initiative with an entrepreneurial mindset of your own. At our library, we researched the market and identified a need. As information providers, we knew that the area's entrepreneurial ecosystem was rich with resources and organizations providing valuable and often specific niche services. We structured our program to fit within this framework, referring customers when appropriate, while striving to avoid providing redundant programming. Evaluating your area's ecosystem may entail an informal environmental scan or a gap analysis, but it may also be as simple as a brief community survey or even talking to partners about which services and programming are lacking.

Targeting the "Encore" population proved successful because this population often felt intimidated by the traditional start-up and launch spaces. The library provided a safe, communal, and collaborative space that is less intimidating to participants. Once we identified our niche, we sought funding and constantly innovated and adapted, growing our service as needs dictated. By continuously evaluating our work and regularly reviewing community needs, we were able to expand and grow our "business," becoming a vital component in the workforce development community.

Key Resources

The key resources for our program include:

- **Consultants** from whom we could learn the key aspects of starting a business and who would lead the series.
- **Community experts** to serve as speakers/instructors for specific sessions in the series.
- **The library's spaces.**
- **The library's resources and databases.** We had already subscribed to several business databases that customers/entrepreneurs could access for freeKey Partners.
- **The Cleveland Foundation** provided us with the initial funding, which also gave us the ability to learn along the way, and thus evaluate and continuously improve the service. Having the time to tweak the program after each iteration resulted in a more robust curriculum for attendees and a clearer picture of the next steps to take. Encore Cleveland was launched by the Cleveland Foundation to offer "meaningful opportunities for Greater Clevelanders who are retired or nearing retirement from their primary careers." Encore Entrepreneurs grew out of this mission.
- **The Economic Community Development Institute (ECDI)** works closely with the Small Business Administration and specializes in microloans, so they made an ideal partner for the library. Additionally, ECDI provided individualized coaching so that the program could focus on each individual's needs, and guidance relevant to a specific business or industry could be offered.
- **The Key Foundation** funded a second, more advanced entrepreneurial series.
- **The Burton D. Morgan Foundation** provided funding which allowed us to develop a staff-led model and move toward sustainability.

Budget

We budgeted $35,880 for the first year of Encore Entrepreneurs. This cost included hiring a consultant to develop the curriculum for the six-week series and identify instructors for each session, as well as the cost of contracting the instructors. We offered six series the first year. We were able to identify further efficiencies in subsequent years and successfully extended the grant for five additional years, eventually getting the cost down to less than $2,000 per series.

Libraries must constantly balance the community's need for various services with the realities of a finite budget. Undertaking a new initiative is often a leap of faith. We found incredible support in our philanthropic community. Ultimately, after years of fine-tuning the original six-week series, we were awarded a grant to modify the curriculum into a staff-led series, ensuring the continuation of the program as well as creating further value for our staff. Sustainability is a key factor when evaluating return on investment.

Implementing the Nuts and Bolts

The Cuyahoga County Public Library endeavors to be at the center of civic and cultural life and prioritizes leveraging the existing services and opportunities in our community. The key to success when initiating entrepreneur programming is understanding the existing workforce landscape, amplifying what is already working, and referring when appropriate. We played to our library's strengths by emphasizing the library's reputation as a trusted and safe environment that encourages the free exchange of ideas, providing open access to valuable information and services.

Our first program, Encore Entrepreneurs, provides core concepts such as business planning and business conceptualization. The successful launch of this program, and our continual evaluation of it, led us to tailor the series to attendees who had some basic understanding of entrepreneurship but needed a fuller understanding of core concepts as well as their real-world applications. Subsequently, we recognized the need for a more advanced series to complement the existing, introductory version, and so we developed the Key Advanced Entrepreneurs initiative.

The Key Advanced initiative offers a more robust curriculum focused on business calibration, fine-tuning the business plan, and preparing participants for the funding stage. Graduates of this series earn a certificate of completion that is intended to demonstrate to potential lenders their proficiency in running a business.

As we continued to learn, we used the existing framework of our introductory six-week series and worked with a consultant to design the Encore Entrepreneurs curriculum in collaboration with staff, leaning heavily on library databases and resources. This pivot to staff-led programming moves us toward our goal of sustainability.

Promoting Your Program

Lean on partners to help promote your business services. Each partner has its own network and constituents and can reach potential entrepreneurs who may not yet be library users. The library's market penetration is significant, with a heavily visited website and robust social media engagement. Our quarterly print program guide is distributed in our 27 library branches, and our marketing e-blast goes out to roughly 300,000 subscribers.

Overcoming Roadblocks and Challenges

Designing a one-size-fits-all entrepreneur series is challenging. Our goal was to design a foundational series that covered the core concepts of starting a business, but we perhaps underappreciated the myriad types of businesses, as well as the varied levels of experience each participant brought to the process. Grounding the series in core concepts undoubtedly appeared too elementary to some, while the speed at which the series was conducted likely left some attendees feeling left behind. We continually modified and adapted the curriculum and series design to address these issues, and thus provide clearer expectations and allow for a more comfortable pace. We learned by doing and ultimately designed separate entrepreneurial programming to meet the varied needs of our community. It is okay to fail. As Samuel Beckett said, "Try again. Fail again. Fail better."

Staff Responsibilities

Our six-week Encore Entrepreneur series was led by our consultant and other external experts. The staff's responsibilities included promoting the series in the community by word-of-mouth marketing and speaking to existing organizations such as chambers of commerce. Branch staff were also responsible for setting up the meeting spaces and preparing any needed technology.

Tips, Tricks, and Advice

- Be flexible, adaptable, and responsive. Be prepared to fill the community's needs and don't assume you already know what those might be.
- Evaluate and modify as you go along. Allow the programming and curriculum to be malleable. Community needs should shape the content. Meet customers where they are in terms of their knowledge and desired outcomes.
- Model the entrepreneurial mindset that is required for any new start-up. Like any business, be prepared to grow. Be an example of entrepreneurial success by never stagnating. Evolve.

PROGRAM 8

Becoming a Resource Hub
The Dallas B.R.A.I.N

DALLAS (TX) PUBLIC LIBRARY

Heather Lowe

Setting the Stage

Big cities work well for big business, but it's easy for the small business owner to get lost in the entrepreneurial landscape. Dallas is a diverse, expansive city, and connecting to local resources can be a confusing endeavor. In urban areas, a shortage of resources is often not the problem. To the contrary, there may be so many types of assistance, licensing, and funding that it's hard for business owners to discern what's credible and applicable to their business model. The Dallas Business Resource and Information Network (B.R.A.I.N.) was developed through a partnership between the Dallas Public Library and the Dallas Office of Economic Development to help small business owners cut down on the noise and find the right resource at the right time. Entrepreneurs can come to the Dallas B.R.A.I.N. in person or online to get help identifying the next steps for their business and the resources to get there. The B.R.A.I.N. consists of Office of Economic Development and Dallas Public Library staff who work with individuals, organize networking events, host educational opportunities, and maintain a database of up-to-date community resources. The collaboration brought the expertise of economists together with the library's reach into the community.

Service Area

- Urban
- Very Large, more than 500,000 population

Goals and Impact

The Dallas B.R.A.I.N.'s primary purpose is to make access to business resources and education more equitable, with a particular focus on small and micro business owners. The program promotes entrepreneurial literacy and access to resources for small businesses and aspiring entrepreneurs. The B.R.A.I.N. focuses its efforts on three main areas: educational opportunities, one-on-one planning sessions, and a resource database.

Getting Started

Talk to your economic development department—whether it's local, county, or regional—to see if there are opportunities to expose communities to business resources and training. A partnership may be as simple as becoming a vehicle to broaden public awareness of programs already provided to communities that are not traditionally tapped into these resources. Then, you can research existing organizations that have ready-made frameworks for supporting entrepreneurs, such as Techstars' Startup Week or the Etsy Entrepreneurship Program. Finally, do market research to pinpoint which industries are popular in your area and then tailor your programming to meet those needs. Now you'll be equipped with information and the support to make savvy decisions about what programs to offer.

Techstars Startup Week

Startup Week is a locally based, volunteer-led, week-long conference that brings together entrepreneurs, community partners, and business resources. More than 140 cities across the globe host their own Startup Weeks to celebrate and support their entrepreneurial community. The event originated with the start-up accelerator Techstars to encourage local networking and inspire budding business leaders. Startup Week includes learning tracks, networking events, and mentoring opportunities. Libraries can get involved by hosting events, working on the organizing team, and promoting the event to the community. Find an event near you or create an event in your community by visiting the Techstars website: www.techstars.com.

Key Resources

The key resources our library brought to the initiative can be duplicated by others:

- Market research databases: These provide the necessary tools for entrepreneurs to educate themselves and prepare for accelerators, micro-lending, and investment.
- Space: Modern libraries have ample meeting space and are generally conveniently located. Offering free space for meetings, networking events, and nonprofits can build the profile of the library as an entrepreneurial hub without intensive staff time.

Key Partners

Serving a diverse business community requires expertise, and this expertise doesn't always exist at the library. It's important to partner with organizations that can bolster the library's strengths with their business savvy and a strong reputation.

- Office of Economic Development: Partnering with the business experts in your city is a no-brainer. The local Office of Economic Development shares many of our library's municipal goals and has the industry know-how to give library programs credibility. And in turn, our library can help the Economic Development Office reach a wider audience of small business owners.
- Goldman Sachs: Our library's partnership with Goldman Sachs produced the Business Industry Group Forum, a monthly series that provided business owners with information about opportunities with the 10,000 Small Businesses program and the city of Dallas's Purchasing Department.
- Dallas Entrepreneur Center (DEC): The DEC is a Dallas 501(c)(3) organization that offers networking, coworking space, mentoring, and accelerator services to small businesses. The DEC held pitch competitions and monthly happy hours at Dallas's downtown Central Library.
- Service Corps of Retired Executives (SCORE): SCORE is a national nonprofit service organization that offers free and low-cost educational opportunities to help small business owners navigate the complexities of running a business.

Libraries make great locations for these seminars and workshops.
- **Veteran Women's Enterprise Center:** This Dallas-based center focuses on empowering female active-duty service members, veterans, reservists, and military spouses in their entrepreneurial pursuits through mentorship, education, and connection to funding. Veterans are eligible for special entrepreneurial support and funding, so don't forget to include these resources in your services.

Budget

We developed the Dallas B.R.A.I.N. partnership with no additional funds outside our normal operating budget, but we did allocate existing resources to the program. One full-time library associate position was earmarked for the project to work in coordination with Office of Economic Development staff. Business research databases were already a part of the library's regular e-materials budget, but they may be a cost to consider if your library doesn't already subscribe to them.

Implementing the Nuts and Bolts

After doing your research and talking to your local business development office, decide which elements your library should focus on first: educational opportunities, one-on-one assistance, or a resource database.

- **Educational opportunities:** The educational opportunities supported by our library include events like three rounds of the Etsy Craft Entrepreneurship Program, introductory forums on the 10,000 Small Businesses program, and a multi-week series on opening a food-related business. Seminars that focus on obtaining the correct permits and licenses are particularly popular among the small business crowd in Dallas. We also built our repertoire of opportunities by adding in programs by service providers like veterans' organizations and SCORE volunteers.
- **One-on-one assistance:** The Dallas Office of Economic Development and our library's staff developed an online and in-person intake process to assess each businessperson's

needs and goals. The staff suggest resources applicable to each client's situation and offer one-on-one listening sessions. In the one-on-one sessions, staff assist with business plans, market research, and talking through options for next steps. In the first year of the program over 2,500 people utilized these services. Sometimes the thing entrepreneurs need most is someone with whom they can talk things through. However, be careful not to give legal advice.

- **Community database:** The goal of the B.R.A.I.N.'s online database is to simplify and vet potential resources like funders, accelerators, and networking opportunities. Library staff work to keep the database on our partner organizations up-to-date. Selections on the database can be narrowed to meet the needs of the entrepreneur, thereby cutting out the time-consuming process of figuring out which organizations offer which services and who has reliable resources.

> **Etsy Craft Entrepreneurship Program**
>
> Etsy, the online craft store for handmade goods of all kinds, provides an advocacy program to help crafters build businesses from their wares. Etsy's Craft Entrepreneurship Program is a curriculum and logistical support for teaching local artisans the skills of running a business. The classes go over marketing, budgets, production, and photographing items. Instructors are selected from local entrepreneurs that use Etsy as their platform. The program is cohort-based, so not only do students get business know-how, but they also gain a supportive group of colleagues. You can apply to bring this program to your city at: https://advocacy.etsy.com.

Promoting Your Program

If libraries want to become hubs for their business community, they must become part of that community. This means staff should go to mixers for entrepreneurs, pitch deck contests (contests where entrepreneurs can fine tune their "pitch" and potentially win prizes or investment), and the local Small Business Administration office. If the people and organizations that help entrepreneurs get connected start to associate your library with solid business assistance, they will begin to refer clients to your resources.

Overcoming Roadblocks and Challenges

Entering into a long-term partnership with another government department has its benefits, but it also presents challenges. The initial push for the B.R.A.I.N. partnership was led by a particularly passionate Office of Economic Development staff member. When the founder retired and there were organizational changes in the Office of Economic Development, the B.R.A.I.N. became less of a priority for the department.

While our library and Economic Development staff still work closely together, the library has taken on the responsibility of day-to-day programming for the B.R.A.I.N. initiative. Partnerships help libraries branch beyond their expertise and staff, but libraries should also have a strong conception of the types of programs and supports that can be offered in-house should circumstances change for a partner.

Staff Responsibilities

Staff are the lifeblood of a resource center like the Dallas B.R.A.I.N. Staff build relationships with business owners, business developers, and entrepreneurs' organizations. The bulk of staff time in the beginning will be spent outside the library talking to business leaders, government liaisons, and business organizations like chambers of commerce. For the Dallas Public Library, we dedicated one full-time staff member, along with part of the time of several other Business & Technology Unit staff at the Central Library. The day-to-day duties of these staffers include maintaining the community resource database, meeting one-on-one with entrepreneurs to help them pinpoint their needs and next steps, and planning the library's programming. The staff also kept up a business blog and periodic newsletter to keep the business community aware of upcoming opportunities and programs.

Tips, Tricks, and Advice

- Many resources that are available to entrepreneurs have a high barrier to entry. A knowledge of business plans, market research, business structures, and much more is required before taking advantage of some free resources. Make sure to cover the basics for those who are unfamiliar with the business landscape.
- Libraries don't have to be business experts, but we can do what we do best—connect individuals with credible,

trustworthy resources and walk with them on their journey. Sometimes the most important thing small business owners need is the knowledge that they have an ally.
- Research existing organizations that have ready-made frameworks for supporting entrepreneurs. Using road-tested frameworks can help you avoid common mistakes. The name recognition of programs like Techstars and Etsy can also give your program's profile a boost.
- Keep statistics and outcomes. Make sure to use surveys as well as hard metrics to measure the effectiveness of your initiative. Documenting positive outcomes can be helpful when seeking outside funding.

PROGRAM 9

Pathway to Entrepreneurial Success
The Stamford Small Business Resource Center

FERGUSON LIBRARY (STAMFORD, CT)

Elizabeth Joseph

Setting the Stage

The Stamford Small Business Resource Center, formed by and in the Ferguson Library, is a network of public and private organizations, library resources, programs, and services for entrepreneurs, small business owners, and aspirants who are at various stages of business ideas and goals.

Our partners host programs, conduct counseling sessions, and extend referrals to other local agencies which can further assist the entrepreneur. Our network of partners includes funding agencies which in many instances provide crucial seed money for businesses to grow and thrive. We also offer courses and lectures from experts spanning a wide range of industry and experience perspectives. We have an "entrepreneur-in-residence" (EiR) service staffed by two experienced entrepreneurs who have unique expertise and contacts in the entrepreneurial space. In addition, we organize and present a monthly edition of Stamford 1 Million Cups, a program from the Kauffman Foundation where we spotlight the many entrepreneurs who use the library's small business services. The library also offers a functional coworking space, access to technology and equipment for all small business needs (including the fabrication of prototypes), print and social media marketing campaigns, and audio/video content.

Our network of partners, combined with the library's resources, ensure the viability and vitality of our local entrepreneurs and small business owners.

Service Area

- Urban and Suburban
- Large, less than 500,000 population

Goals and Impact

Our program is aimed primarily at minority and women-led business owners who often don't have access to services and programs that facilitate starting and growing a business. The goal of our program is to reduce and eradicate barriers that prevent entrepreneurs and small business owners from starting and growing their enterprise. The library has seen a remarkable demand for our services, with requests increasing each year. Our program went from serving a handful of entrepreneurs at its start a few years ago to now serving scores of entrepreneurs annually.

Getting Started

Before launching a small business program, it is crucial to create a program plan. This program plan will consist of an economic survey and analysis of the area's small business sector. It should also include the scope of the library's programs, services, and potential partnerships. The roles and responsibility of the partner agencies should be defined and specified. It is also important to list the benchmarks, goals, and outcomes of this project. Equally important is a marketing plan, which should be a major component of the program plan. Our plan also contains an equity, diversity, and inclusion statement along with steps to achieve it.

Key Resources

In addition to staff and strong partnerships, there are certain key elements that must be in place, and these resources should receive full financial commitment and support from library leadership. We found the following tools to be necessary to launch and grow our program:

- Active social media accounts and a website to advertise the program and engage the entrepreneurial community
- Printed materials, including a program calendar, resources brochure, posters, and so on
- Designated spaces in the library for meetings, programs, and collections
- Access to computers, Zoom accounts, audiovisual equipment, and small business services (copiers, fax, etc.)

Key Partners

Our community partners include the state's Small Business Administration (SBA) office and various arms of the SBA, including SCORE, the Small Business Development Center, and the Women's Business Development Center. These agencies provide counselors, presenters for various workshops, and experts in a variety of areas identified by the clients of our Small Business Resource Center. Our private partnerships include the Stamford Partnership, the Community Economic Development Fund, and Stamford Next, which offer further support by offering speakers and access to funding sources. We have also engaged our local chamber of commerce, which posts and promotes our events.

Budget

Our library launched the program with both LSTA (Library Services and Technology Act) grants and community foundation grants. We allocate between $70,000 and $75,000 annually for print and electronic resources, honorariums for our EIRs, presenters, and other program expenses (technology, publicity materials, etc.).

Implementing the Nuts and Bolts

The Stamford Small Business Resource Center began with multiple conversations and pledges from stakeholders. We continue to strengthen these relationships while building new bridges such as coworking spaces.

When a patron expresses interest in our program, we ask them to submit an intake form that inquires about their business stage, industry, and need.

We match them with one of our EiRs who, after meeting with the client, will send them back to the library staff for assistance with their research needs. The EiR lays out a road map with steps to advance to the next level. Clients who have advanced in their entrepreneurial journey are instructed to apply to a local business incubator. Clients who need additional help are directed to appropriate agencies and community services.

Our program also offers weekly lectures and workshops on a wide range of subjects such as intellectual property, opening a restaurant, team structure and dynamics, financial modeling, social media, and valuation. We also host a monthly networking session for participants in our resource center's programming.

Participants in our program are surveyed after six months to determine their progress and response to the EiR's recommendations. They are also asked to rate their satisfaction with the resource center's programs, services, and the EiR. After a year in the program, participants are interviewed once again. The information gathered from these sessions reveals the efficacy and value of our program. The library collects and tracks the data on these entrepreneurs and small business owners and their ventures to understand trends, gaps, and opportunities for the future.

Promoting Your Program

Create a marketing strategy that includes print and social media platforms and relies on partnerships and outreach. In addition to these outlets, we submit press releases to local English, Spanish, and Haitian/Creole newspaper outlets, and have our partners cross-disseminate our materials.

The program staff utilizes every opportunity to conduct outreach visits, participate in city-wide events, and present the library's Small Business Resource Center to community groups and agencies such as the Stamford Rotary Club, literacy organizations, local colleges, and entrepreneurial networks.

Overcoming Roadblocks and Challenges

Sometimes even the best-laid plans can go awry. It's often hard to coordinate everyone's schedule in terms of deadlines, so it's important to realize that partner organizations have their own projects and mandates and cannot be expected to adhere to our timelines. Frequent communication and advanced planning are a must for all parties involved.

There are instances when certain programs are not as well attended as anticipated. It's important to not be discouraged by occasional low turnout. If this begins to form a pattern, try to understand the reasons for this and find creative solutions to correct the issue. There should always be a human connection with those served by the program. Reach out to your clients and establish a trusting relationship with them at the outset so that all follow-ups will be understood as a method to identify issues and implement needed improvements in the program.

Staff Responsibilities

Our program requires an enthusiastic and motivated staff, including a project director who is charged with budgeting, program design, delivery, development, and evaluation. This individual also builds partnerships, conducts outreach, and is the spokesperson for the library's program. The project support staff assists with the logistics of programs, purchasing, the tracking of spending, the maintenance of client records, and feedback surveys and marketing.

Tips, Tricks, and Advice

Think about your program as a business start-up. Be fully aware of the economic landscape, your patrons, their pain points, and the fixes for those issues. Be prepared to pivot when circumstances dictate. Agility is key, so be quick to adapt to trends and modify your services when necessary.

Our experience has shown that the following areas must be addressed for short- and long-term success:

- **Know and understand the industry jargon** in order to effectively communicate requirements, share insights, and assist with solutions.
- **The sustainability of the project should be addressed** in the original program plan, but if situations change or there are variations in funding or staffing, deploy a contingency plan swiftly.
- **Think analytically and evaluate critically.** It is vital to ensure the longevity of your core services, programs, and staffing by being flexible and adaptable.

- Brand your program, just as you would any other venture of your library. Make it known to the audience at events and programs that the library is offering these programs. It is possible for the library to get lost in a large network and be overtaken by bigger partner agencies, so your library's brand should be reiterated at all programs and in all publicity materials.

PROGRAM 10

One-to-One Support for Micro-Entrepreneurs

Business Help at Your Library

FERGUSON (MO) MUNICIPAL PUBLIC LIBRARY

Taneesa R. Hall

Setting the Stage

The "Business Help at Your Library" program at the Ferguson Municipal Public Library helps businesses, entrepreneurs, and job seekers cross the digital divide. Our one-to-one consultation services help people get started legally and correctly. The library offers free, reliable, and stable internet access for entrepreneurs and job seekers. We also offer equipment, resources, and spaces that entrepreneurs and job seekers may not have access to otherwise. The library also provides digital literacy training and assistance for those who need it. By providing these services, the library facilitates needed skill-building to both those entering the workforce and those starting a small business.

There are many micro-entrepreneurs in our area who offer landscaping services, hair-braiding, and cleaning services by word of mouth. With our program and support, they can formally set up their business, do outreach to customers, and secure needed materials and supplies. Entrepreneurs are often setting up their business as a "side hustle" until they are financially stable enough to quit their part-time job and start working for themselves full-time. By providing one place where they can find the necessary forms, print them out, fill them out, get them notarized, and send them, we are saving our patrons valuable time, energy, and money because they won't have to seek out all of these things individually. Due to high poverty rates, poor digital literacy, and poor internet connectivity rates in the community, it is difficult for many members of the community to complete the necessary steps to start a business or even find a job in many cases. The library strives to be a one-stop shop for these endeavors.

Service Area

- Urban
- Small, less than 24,000 population

Goals and Impact

Our goal is to help small business owners get started with all the information and tools they need to set up their business correctly, ultimately helping them to build a foundation so their business can thrive. Additionally, the library helps existing businesses to find resources that will help them to expand their business and find qualified workers for their establishment. The library fosters this connection through our job seekers programs, wherein we help develop resumes and find careers for individuals seeking employment.

By offering free, reliable internet access we are closing the opportunity gap and creating an inclusive space for low-income aspiring entrepreneurs to connect, research, and develop their business ideas, and work on their business.

Getting Started

Get to know the existing resources for small business owners and entrepreneurs in your community, as well as the common barriers facing entrepreneurs who need these resources and services. To do this, we contacted the city planning department and other organizations nearby to find out what resources were being offered. We discovered that while there are many resources for entrepreneurs in the Ferguson metro area, transportation to the organizations in question is a problem. Because of the poverty rate in Ferguson, most people rely on public transit. Many people were opting to try to muddle through the start-up process themselves rather than try to get to distant areas where help was more readily available.

Key Resources

As a small library with a small staff, we utilized our space and equipment as our primary resources for the business community. We now provide a variety of services:

New Virtual Services

- **New databases** targeting entrepreneurs and business owners
- **"Virtual meeting kits"** that can be checked out from the library. Each kit consists of the following:
  - Laptop
  - Case
  - Headset with mic
  - Wireless Hotspot

In-Person Services

- **A meeting room** with an audio system, lectern, and board table and chairs
- **3D printer** to build prototypes
- **One-on-one training** on the databases, and guidance in using the local resources
- **Business resource packets**

Key Partners

Consult with your city planning manager for resources, advice, and contacts. We contacted the city planning manager in Ferguson, who provided advice and consultation during planning.

Budget

We received $16,000 from the Libraries Build Business grant. With this funding, we upgraded our conference room and purchased equipment and furniture, including a 3D printer, two years of a Gale business database package, and technology for three "virtual meeting kits" that contain a laptop, headset, wireless mouse, and a carrying case that can be checked out to patrons to complete paperwork or lead virtual meetings.

Implementing the Nuts and Bolts

Because we are a small library with a small staff, our program needed to be largely hands-off. We are a twelve-member staff operating out of a 10,000-square-foot building.

We track the number of handouts provided and the reference calls and reference interviews made in our business program. A program survey helps us determine the best strategies for engaging our patrons and the perceived quality and value of our services. This information is taken and used to make our program stronger and more streamlined to help more patrons and provide better services in the future.

HOW TO: Provide Business Services on a Shoestring

1. Set up a dedicated space for entrepreneurs to work, host meetings and events, and conduct interviews. You can refresh an existing conference space with new furniture and state-of-the-art technology.
2. Add new databases that are targeted specifically for entrepreneurs and small business owners. At Ferguson, we purchased the Gale Business Package, which includes Gale Business Plan, Gale Entrepreneur, and Gale Legal Forms. These databases are used to help guide entrepreneurs through the start-up process and to help them build a solid business plan to grow their business effectively.
3. Provide equipment and technology for virtual meetings. We purchased equipment for three virtual meeting kits that include a laptop and a headset for entrepreneurs to check out, and then use to complete paperwork or conduct interviews or other business meetings as needed.
4. Set up your space to provide for other business needs as well. Try asking your community what they need the most. We purchased a 3D printer because some of our entrepreneurs had ideas, but needed equipment to build a prototype that they could patent. We also have a fax machine, scanner, projector, copier, notary services, color printer, computers, and reliable internet service.

5. Offer ready-made materials for people to review on their own time. We put together packets to hand out to individuals seeking more information about job opportunities and building their own business from scratch. These handouts go in a prominent area of the library where they can be seen by library patrons easily and picked up as needed.
6. Offer one-to-one, customized consultations with a librarian. When a patron comes in and asks about our business program, our librarian sits down with them at a computer and walks them through all of the resources we have available, what equipment we have in the building to check out, and answers their questions.

Promoting Your Program

Get your staff and patrons involved in outreach. The Ferguson Municipal Public Library promotes its program largely through in-house flyers and signage. We also promote it through the local newspaper and through our partnership with the city of Ferguson.

Overcoming Roadblocks and Challenges

For a small library, working with a small budget and deciding where your money will make the most impact is a necessity. Staffing is also a challenge, with staff members all multitasking and filling multiple roles.

Staff Responsibilities

The business program here is run by the adult services librarian, who has many other duties, as befitting a librarian in a small library.

Tips, Tricks, and Advice

- Partnerships are key to stretching your budget and expanding your services. Working with existing providers (when they are available) can help reduce the amount of money you have to spend on your program and will also keep you both from duplicating your efforts.
- Time is a valuable resource for both staff and patrons. Patrons are more likely to commit to a small amount of effort than a large one. Taking a pamphlet and perusing it at their own leisure

or taking fifteen minutes to look at the available resources with a librarian is a small commitment. They can then choose to come back for more intensive help if they wish.

- **Be prepared and knowledgeable.** Take some time to familiarize yourself with your library's resources and equipment before you offer them to patrons. This will give patrons more confidence in the library and your resources.
- Keep detailed notes and documentation about your programs and services, and regularly check in with other staff at your library about the programs and services at meetings. If other staff need to fill in while you are away, or new staff are hired, it's important that they feel prepared and ready to deliver the program and support entrepreneurs.

PROGRAM 11

A New Start

Entrepreneurship for the
Formerly Incarcerated

**NEW START ENTREPRENEURSHIP INCUBATOR,
GWINNETT COUNTY (GA) PUBLIC LIBRARY**

Adam Pitts, Atlas Logan, Ronald M. Gauthier,
Ann Serrie, and Andrea Devereux

Setting the Stage

The New Start Entrepreneurship Incubator (NSEI) at the Gwinnett County Public Library (GCPL) in Georgia supports a growing but largely overlooked subset of aspirational entrepreneurs: the formerly incarcerated. Our initiative provides a business education through in-person classes, online coursework, and a robust network of mentors and community partners. The project stemmed from existing partnerships with small business and reentry organizations and coalesced around a common goal to serve this uniquely disadvantaged population.

In 2019, we hosted more than forty small business programs featuring partners such as Small Biz Ally, SCORE, the Latin American Association, and the University of Georgia's Small Business Development Center. In addition, the Greater Gwinnett Reentry Alliance (GGRA), a key NSEI partner, facilitated a closed-circuit television presentation on library resources to 2,100 inmates at the Gwinnett County Jail, one of the largest correctional centers in Georgia. With this framework in place, GCPL was ideally positioned to connect justice-involved individuals with small business resources through a tailored entrepreneur development program.

Service Area

- Suburban
- Very Large, more than 500,000 population

Goals and Impact

From a lack of affordable housing and adequate transportation to societal stigma and employment barriers, formerly incarcerated individuals face an array of challenges often referred to as a "second sentence." A criminal record precludes employment in many fields, particularly those that require an occupational license. In many cases, the available jobs are low-paying, offer few, if any, benefits, and are subject to wage inequalities that favor those without previous convictions. Individuals who cannot find stable housing or employment are more likely to recidivate than those who do, perpetuating a cycle that disproportionately affects communities of color. This impact is especially felt in Georgia, a state with one of the highest incarceration rates in the United States. For many, entrepreneurship is the only viable path to success. Small business programming for this population was a mostly unexplored aspect of library services until recently. While several libraries have offered outreach to inmates, we are aware of few entrepreneurship programs designed exclusively for our target audience.

NSEI provides the knowledge and support needed to start a small business. It assumes no prior experience and anticipates many of the hardships outlined above. With this project, our goal was to create a learning environment in which systemically marginalized individuals could become successful entrepreneurs. While NSEI outcomes are most visible at the individual level, our program has the potential to stimulate local economic development through job creation, increased tax revenue, and innovation. In theory, it should also reduce recidivism by providing an alternative to the so-called "revolving door" that results in nearly two-thirds of ex-inmates being reincarcerated within three years of release.

Getting Started

To start working with formerly incarcerated individuals, strong partnerships are essential. Our partnership with the Greater Gwinnett Reentry Alliance, a coalition of social service providers, government agencies, and community members that supports the reentry population, was the starting point in developing our programs and doing outreach about the available opportunities. Consider holding an event such as a resource fair with partners and government agencies. For example, we hosted one with the Georgia Department of Community Supervision, the Georgia Department of Labor, and other agencies. Leveraging community resources and having a local presence will lay the groundwork for program development.

Key Resources

Our key resources in launching the initiative included the following:

- **LinkedIn Learning:** This library resource provides over 16,000 online courses, including many on small business and entrepreneurship topics.
- **Entrepreneurial Mindset Academy:** This is a self-paced online course that helps aspiring entrepreneurs overcome the fears and obstacles associated with starting a business.
- **Brian Hamilton's Starter U:** This online, self-paced, small business course is designed to help anyone become a successful entrepreneur.

Key Partners

- **Greater Gwinnett Reentry Alliance (GGRA):** This is an essential partner, both in terms of attracting applicants and providing information and support to current participants. Their mission is to inform and educate the public about issues surrounding reentry and to broker opportunities for those seeking to successfully return to the community.
- **SCORE North Metro Atlanta:** This organization provides monthly subject matter experts and support in locating mentors for our program's participants.
- **SmallBiz Ally:** This group provides small business consultations, workshops, webinars, training sessions, and a small business toolbox of resources designed to help other entrepreneurs overcome challenges so that they can focus on moving their business forward.

- **ACE Women's Business Center:** This center is dedicated to empowering women, minorities, and low- to moderate-income entrepreneurs through financial education and training.
- **Local Business Mentors:** Our program relies on volunteer mentors from the business community. Our mentors have run their own businesses and can share the ups and downs, pitfalls, and strategies it takes to build and sustain a business. Most of the volunteers are from Gwinnett County, but due to the role being mostly via phone, e-mail, or virtual meetings, the mentors can live in other areas of metro Atlanta. Mentors are assigned based on their business backgrounds and the areas of interest of the students. One mentor may elect to take on more than one student.

Budget

We budgeted $128,000 for our program, which we funded through the Libraries Build Business grant. With this funding, we hired an outreach coordinator with a social services background to support our program participants with resources and wraparound services. We also purchased a cargo van to use for outreach to the jail and our nonprofit partners, as well as transportation for participants in some cases, a laptop cart with MacBook Air laptops, and wireless hotspots. Our community business mentors volunteered their time to our program.

Implementing the Nuts and Bolts

The NSEI program is offered in six-month cohorts consisting of 10–15 students, with monthly in-person classes. Guest speakers present on topics such as licensing, marketing, finance, and business plans. In addition to the meetings, students meet one-on-one with their mentors, complete online coursework asynchronously, and participate in optional library-led office hours. To remove technology barriers, students are provided with laptops and hotspots to borrow while enrolled in the course. An outreach coordinator is available to connect the students with community resources and other educational opportunities. We purchased a minivan for transporting supplies and taking field trips to off-site locations, such as the Gwinnett Entrepreneur Center. Finally, local donors host a "Shark Tank"-style funding opportunity called Launchpad at the end of each six-month course. Students who complete the course in good standing are eligible to pitch their business proposals to a judging panel to receive feedback and potentially obtain start-up capital.

Evaluation was integral to our process. We used surveys at the beginning and end of each six-month course to get a before-and-after snapshot of student development. We also gauged the success of the program based on the number of new businesses launched or in progress upon course completion. This data is being used to improve future NSEI courses and enhance our other small business programs.

Considering Financial Capital

While working with the first six-month cohort, we discovered that insufficient start-up capital was a major roadblock to success. Like other barriers, securing a business loan with a criminal record can be difficult or impossible. Launchpad addressed this problem by providing an opportunity to receive start-up capital, or seed money, with no strings attached. The public response to our project has been overwhelmingly positive, especially among local benefactors who support community initiatives. If your small business program needs additional support, consider reaching out to local donors.

HOW TO: Work with Formerly Incarcerated Individuals

Navigating life after incarceration is fraught with challenges, but there are a few things your program can do to foster an inclusive environment:

1. **Use people-first language:** Instead of "ex-offender" or "convicted felon," use "formerly incarcerated" or "justice-involved." This is especially important as you begin marketing your program.
2. **Don't generalize:** Formerly incarcerated people come from all walks of life and represent a spectrum of educational and occupational backgrounds.
3. **Be sensitive to privacy concerns:** Always ask permission before taking photos or videos, especially for public use.
4. **Make connections:** Check your area for reentry organizations such as GGRA. These organizations are a hub of community resources that can help connect you to your intended audience.

5. Offer wraparound services: A staff member who specializes in social work can identify potential barriers to success and provide support to students.

Promoting Your Program

To recruit formerly incarcerated individuals to your program, connect with your partners that specialize in reentry services. We shared information about our program through GGRA, the Gwinnett Parole Board, the Gwinnett Reentry Intervention Program, and the Gwinnett Sheriff's Office. Marketing campaigns should include a mix of online and paper materials. For example, our initial marketing included a tri-fold brochure distributed to all 15 GCPL branches and the surrounding community, and program information on the front page of our library's website. If you can, have past participants share feedback or recommend your program. To increase recruitment for the second cohort, we filmed a promotional video with one of our students from the first round of NSEI that was shared with partners, on social media and the website, and distributed to prospective students.

Overcoming Roadblocks and Challenges

Create opportunities for rapport and trust-building. Past trauma combined with a reentry system that often sets people up for failure can understandably result in distrust of institutions. To earn buy-in and confidence, be sensitive to each participant's unique situation, and try to address the specific needs of this population. Our NSEI outreach coordinator has been instrumental in providing support to students struggling with the aftereffects of incarceration. We have also been mindful of privacy concerns, especially with regard to photography.

Check for understanding regularly and build accountability into the design. We implemented an end-of-month evaluation to "unlock" the following month's content. These evaluations were an opportunity for us to monitor comprehension of the course content and confirm that participants were connecting with their mentor at least once a month, thus promoting accountability and commitment to the program as well as helping us improve it.

Staff Responsibilities

A team of five GCPL staff have been involved with the creation and facilitation of the NSEI program. Collaboratively, this team compiled the curriculum and secured guest speakers for the monthly meetings. Once we received our pool of applicants for each six-month course, our staff were responsible for contacting qualified candidates, conducting the interviews, and determining who would be accepted into the program. The NSEI team facilitated the monthly meetings and virtual support sessions for students. On top of these core tasks, key roles included:

- A volunteer coordinator, who works to find and match volunteer mentors with participants. When possible, every effort is given to match participants with mentors who have similar entrepreneurial pursuits and/or expertise.
- An outreach coordinator with a social services background, who provides expertise in supporting our participants in the program both with coursework and in overcoming some of the barriers associated with each of their unique situations, making connections to resources, partner organizations, and social services as needed. The coordinator supports programming and communicates with participants.

Tips, Tricks, and Advice

- **Create incentive.** Because NSEI is grant-funded, we have been able to offer special opportunities and giveaways to encourage enrollment and engagement. These include free books on entrepreneurship topics, a refurbished laptop to keep upon completing the course in good standing, and the Launchpad funding opportunity.
- **If you use a cohort model, over-enroll your program.** We over-enrolled our second cohort in anticipation of withdrawals, based on previous experience. You can expect people to drop out due to other commitments and demands.
- **Effective marketing:** Targeted marketing, both in-person and online, has been key to reaching our intended audience. We issued a press release, interviewed with local media, ran strategically placed Facebook ads, and sent promotional materials to organizations and agencies that work closely with justice-involved individuals.
- **Send reminders before each class.** This has been an effective and simple retention strategy.

PROGRAM 12

Cultivate Small Business with BeanStack

Cultivate Indy

INDEPENDENCE (KS) PUBLIC LIBRARY

Brandon West

Setting the Stage

Throughout the past five years, Independence, Kansas, with a population of just under 9,000 individuals, has been in the middle of an entrepreneurial renaissance. Our downtown storefronts began filling up with new boutiques, and there was a push to relocate existing businesses to downtown. The only thing missing was diversity in the business owners. The Independence Public Library (IPL) began working to empower and connect underrepresented entrepreneurs to local economic development organizations and resources in an open and welcoming environment to help build diversity, equity, and inclusion in our small business community.

Cultivate Indy is a two-part program featuring a new business lab and a self-paced small business course. The Cultivate Indy Small Business Lab provides state-of-the-art equipment, software, and tools to help entrepreneurs develop their small businesses and prototype products. The business course uses BeanStack as a platform to guide entrepreneurs through starting, launching, marketing, and growing their small business ideas.

Service Area Size

- Rural
- Very Small, less than 10,000 population

Goals and Impact

The Independence Public Library launched Cultivate Indy to ensure that everyone, regardless of race, economic status, education, sexuality, or gender identity, has access to the resources they need to launch and grow their small business or entrepreneurial endeavors.

In addition, IPL aims to create a diverse and inclusive business environment within our community that is equitable for all. Cultivate Indy started with a goal of helping entrepreneurs from underrepresented populations successfully launch their small businesses and providing those businesses with their first-year membership in our local chamber of commerce and Main Street. Through IPL's work, we have been able to break down barriers that underrepresented individuals faced by becoming a one-stop shop for small business resources and development. Our goal was not to replicate any local service, but to act as an entry point and funnel patrons to the entities that can best serve them when the patron is ready.

Getting Started

Look for partners that offer small business programming. For example, IPL began offering limited programs through the Small Business Development Center (e.g., tax preparation workshops for small business owners). Do a needs assessment to understand the local small business landscape and entities. We observed that our landscape lacked diversity, motivating us to understand the barriers.

With the nearest small business centers one to three hours away, IPL worked to curate a collection of resources from organizations such as SCORE, the Small Business Administration, and local and regional economic development entities. By assessing and curating existing resources, the library can serve as an entry point to the entrepreneurial community.

Key Resources

Our initiative used the following key resources:

- **Grow with Google:** This offers courses in small business development and job-seeking. These courses provide a slide deck and all the resources you need to present on various topics. In essence, they are prepackaged programs for you to use.

- **BeanStack:** This is a web-based platform that allows readers to participate in reading and activity challenges. For example, IPL used BeanStack to create an activity-based challenge that provided users with the resources they need to walk through starting a small business, from start to launch and beyond.
- **Computers:** We purchased game-quality Dell desktops and iMac pros. These computers afford our patrons access to the tools and resources they need to start their small businesses. In addition, these computers have the Adobe Creative Suite software, enabling entrepreneurs to build apps, design marketing materials, and more.
- **Databases:** IPL provides access to various EBSCO databases, including Hobbies and Crafts Reference Center, Small Business Reference Center, Business Source Premier, and Entrepreneurial Studies Source. On top of these resources that allow our participants to dig into their business ventures, we also provide the Ice House Entrepreneurship Program by EBSCO, which helps library users take an entrepreneurial mindset course that can help them adapt and thrive in a rapidly changing world.

Key Partners

Consider a variety of partners to support entrepreneurs in a rural community. These partners have provided our library with the guidance needed to set up our BeanStack challenge, and have been valuable in attracting local, state, and federal resources. Our partners include the following ones:

- **The Independence Chamber of Commerce** is the local economic development entity that represents and supports new entrepreneurs who are navigating local resources and state and federal aid.
- **Independence Main Street** is the local organization of Main Street America, an economic development entity for small-towns' downtowns. Main Street is instrumental in helping find brick-and-mortar locations for businesses and promoting local businesses.

- **FabLab ICC** is a makerspace at the Center for Innovation and Entrepreneurship on the campus of Independence Community College.
- **The Montgomery County Action Council** works to bring large employers to the area and help small businesses navigate the Small Business Administration's resources. The Action Council works with entrepreneurs to complete federal applications and provides assistance with business plan development.

Budget

We budgeted nearly $69,000 for our program from the Libraries Build Business grant. With this funding, we renovated our Small Business Lab and purchased high-quality equipment such as computers, printers, and software. We also purchased databases. Some funds were used to provide incentives to program participants, such as memberships in local business associations, such as the local chamber of commerce.

Implementing the Nuts and Bolts

Cultivate Indy is a two-part program. First, we built a Small Business Lab, which includes high-quality equipment and technology, such as gaming-quality Dell desktops and iMac Pros. Our computers are equipped with the Adobe Creative Cloud suite, thus giving patrons access to software for app-building, marketing, and editing. We developed a mini-makerspace in our Business Lab that features smaller versions of equipment used at our partner's makerspace, so patrons can prototype their products. The second part of our program is a self-paced, small business development program that uses BeanStack to walk patrons from concept to growth, with built-in incentives along the way. As patrons complete portions of the program, they earn memberships in organizations in our community, such as the FabLab, the chamber of commerce, and Main Street. These incentives further the patron's business and connect them with more resources and other local entrepreneurs.

Measurement and evaluation help us adjust our program to meet the needs of our participants. In addition to surveys, we have built-in check-ins associated with each badge in our self-paced program, to aid in evaluation.

The library uses information gained through surveys and interviews to improve the program and leverage that knowledge to acquire more funding through grants and other local resources.

HOW TO: Use BeanStack for Small Business Programming

BeanStack is a web-based app that allows you to create and track reading and activity challenges. While BeanStack is primarily used for reading challenges, IPL used the activity portion of the app to create a self-guided challenge that walks patrons through the process of starting their own small business. Here are the steps to creating your own Small Business Challenge on BeanStack:

1. As you're thinking about setting up your BeanStack platform, consider the goals of your business program to determine what measurable outcomes you want participants to experience. For Cultivate Indy, the desired result is for patrons to feel prepared to launch their own small business.
2. List all of the steps the patron needs to complete to achieve the desired outcome(s). For example, IPL has activities such as attending a program about design thinking; writing a business plan; and filing for local, state, and federal licenses built into our BeanStack program.
3. Organize and group similar actions. These groups will become badges, with each of the steps becoming an activity in BeanStack. For example, IPL has the following badges for its program: Development, Plan, Formation, Marketing, and Growth. As participants complete activities and move through the process you designed, they will earn badges.
4. Before you begin building your challenge in BeanStack, you will need to list any resources someone will need to complete each step. You will also need to determine how you are going to have patrons "complete" the activity. For example, will you use the honor system, or will patrons have to submit assignments to move to the next phase?
5. After organizing your program, you are then ready to build your challenge in BeanStack. You can create your own custom badges and upload them to BeanStack to fit your program, or you can use a variety of badge designs that are available on BeanStack. Be creative.

A Sample Badge in a BeanStack Challenge

Badge 2: Plan

The key to a successful business is having a plan. In this phase of the Cultivate Indy program, you will work to develop a business plan for your small business. In order to receive the "Plan" Badge, participants will move through the following steps:

The completion badge patrons receive when they have completed all stages of the Cultivate Indy course
IPL Cultivate Indy

1. Attend a Small Business Workshop (When completed, they receive a code)
   - Link to Calendar
2. Determine Your Business's Structure (Honor system)
   - Link to IRS Business Structures Website
3. Name Your Business (Text box)
4. Participate in an Online Discussion (Honor system)
   - Link to Discussion Board
5. Write Your Business Plan
   - Link to SBA Business Plan Guide
6. Submit Your Business Plan (Code)
   - Link to Google Form for Submission (Auto Response with code)
7. Meet with Library Staff for Progress Check (Code)
   - Invitation to schedule the appointment
8. Revise Your Business Plan with Feedback (Honor system)

IPL's program is called "Cultivate Indy," so we used the stages of plants' growth to design our badges.

6. Before launching your program, test it to make sure that everything works properly; this includes any points, links, raffles, and so on.
7. When you're ready to launch the program, change your challenge from "Draft" to "Published," and your challenge will go live. You can now promote the opportunity and encourage patrons to sign up.
8. When you launch your program, be sure to monitor patrons' progress. IPL's program is self-paced, and each badge has a check-in

activity that patrons are required to schedule. This format helps with accountability and helps IPL evaluate the effectiveness of the badge and the program.

Promoting Your Program

Take advantage of social media, local newspapers, and the library discussion list to get the word out, and connect with community institutions. In our small community, we were successful in reaching underrepresented populations by connecting with local churches. We asked that each of the churches post our flyer and reach out to any members they might know who could benefit from the services.

Overcoming Roadblocks and Challenges

For a small library, staff time can be a real challenge, with all staff wearing multiple hats. It takes a considerable amount of time and energy to launch a robust program and connect with your target audience. Taking the time is worth it, though, since it is helping to build your community's economic resilience.

Staff Responsibilities

IPL has a staff of five full-time and five part-time employees, with one full-time staff member working on our small business initiative. This project lead is in charge of implementing the program, managing and recruiting participants, and networking with other economic development entities, in addition to other functions within the library.

Tips, Tricks, and Advice

- For any rural library beginning its program, it should enter into partnerships with a Memorandum of Understanding (MOU) to ensure that both parties are aware of their roles and responsibilities. This MOU will clarify roles and expectations between the library and outside organizations and can alleviate any miscommunication down the road.
- The library is a connector that supports and partners with local organizations. In a partnership of common tools and resources, both partners can work toward the common aim of providing a pathway for underrepresented individuals to achieve their goals. When everything comes together, patrons succeed, and you hear comments such as, "I'm amazed at what resources are available in our community!"

PROGRAM 13

Build Your Business Brand through Community Engagement

Invest in Yourself

KING COUNTY (WA) LIBRARY SYSTEM

Audrey Barbakoff

Setting the Stage

Invest in Yourself is the branding that the King County Library System (KCLS) uses for its small business, career, and financial programs. A distinct brand makes it easier for our library to connect with entrepreneurs who otherwise might not think of the library as a resource for their businesses.

Building a voice that speaks to small business owners involves much more than just a clever name or graphic. All our decisions—from what programs and services to offer, to which social media platforms to use, to what promotional strategies to adopt—need to be informed by the communities we serve. We conducted an in-depth community assessment with an equity analysis, and then developed a framework that helps us make choices that reflect what really matters to our community.

Service Area

- Suburban, Urban, and Rural
- Very Large, more than 500,000 population

What Is a Community Assessment?

Community assessment is a systematic way of developing a picture of your community. It helps us step outside our own perspectives and assumptions. There are many ways to conduct a community assessment, but it's crucial to keep an asset-based perspective—to think of your community as having strengths and aspirations to share, rather than just needs to fill. The University of Kansas Community Tool Box (https://ctb.ku.edu/en) is an excellent resource for learning about different techniques of community assessment.

Goals and Impact

Based on our community assessment, KCLS identified four small business audiences where we could focus our efforts. They are immigrant and refugee micro-entrepreneurs; creative freelancers; new or expanding small food businesses; and building trades contractors. For each audience, we identified the key opportunities and challenges, the library's unique value proposition, and ways to measure success.

For example, we learned that immigrant and refugee micro-entrepreneurs can often be surprised by the American regulatory landscape. Therefore, one of the key metrics we defined was an increase in the program participants' awareness of how to navigate external factors affecting their business. This goal led to programs such as a bilingual Latinx Small Business Roundtable that brought together entrepreneurs and support programs, and an introduction to starting a small food business led by a local restaurant owner.

Overall, the mission of Invest in Yourself is to support a thriving, resilient, and equitable local economy. Because fair access to small business resources has been systematically denied to minoritized groups, the library can only achieve this goal if we apply a racial and social justice lens. We hold ourselves accountable not only by designing programs in partnership with communities and based on community knowledge, but also by looking at who feels welcome in our small business programs. For example, one of the library's core entrepreneurship class series, a partnership called Startup 425, has consistently attracted audiences that are majority BIPOC and more than two-thirds female-identifying. Our survey results indicate high levels of satisfaction with the content and support of this series.

Getting Started

Connect with your community. Who are the key players in your small business ecosystem? Take time to ask them about their goals, hopes, and needs. Just listen; try not to jump in with library-focused solutions. Specific programs, services, or messaging will come later, grown from the soil of community knowledge and relationships. End every conversation by asking who else you should talk to, so your network becomes larger and more diverse.

Key Resources

We have found key resources for our initiatives to include:

- **Staff time** for relationship-building and reflection
- **A culture of innovation and inclusivity,** in which staff members in all positions and from all lived experiences feel safe to express ideas, try new things, and communicate outside of silos
- **Coffee** (or tea, or wine; you get the idea). Help your partners feel welcome and relaxed when you talk with them. Try meeting in a coffee shop, or going to their preferred space, or even just proffering a warm mug in your meeting room.

Key Partners

Go beyond talking with your local chamber of commerce, downtown association, or Small Business Administration office. If you want to understand how to reach entrepreneurs who have not been served well by mainstream institutions, you need to go to them and build trust. Does your area have organizations that are focused on or led by underserved groups? If not, who are the individuals who are prominent in those communities? In addition to connecting with entrepreneurs, think about how you can help provide more equitable access to the resources they need. What are the culturally and linguistically appropriate financial institutions, and who are the legal experts in those communities? These can also be valuable partners. Consider creating an asset map to help you identify your partners. The University of Kansas Community Toolbox provides a good introduction to asset mapping.

Budget

The initial phases of community assessment and mapping, discussions, and determining your library's strategy do not have a direct cost. (But if you can rustle up some funding for it, buy your community partners a cup of coffee to thank them for their time and input.)

Once you have done this essential work, you can develop programs, services, and communications that fit your budget. KCLS used its existing staff and software to develop and promote Invest in Yourself. If you don't have community relations staff, you may want to hire out some of this work. We fund our programs and services through a mix of operating funds and grants. You can design programs at any price point, all the way down to zero (think about volunteers or partners as your presenters, or using a freely accessible curriculum). Remember that when you create programs with partners, you can also pool resources to limit expenses.

Implementing the Nuts and Bolts

1. **Do your homework.** At KCLS, we began our community assessment by researching community-created documents about the economy, like city plans and reports from regional economic boards. We looked at school district and census data to learn about our populations. We discovered that there were a few key sectors driving the economy in our area (like technology—this is Seattle, after all).
2. **Listen to people.** Next, we reached out to key stakeholders in each sector for semi-structured interviews. We made sure to seek out people with diverse lived experiences, so that what we heard wasn't skewed toward a single perspective.
3. **Put it together.** Finally, we took everything we had learned and identified specific audiences to focus our efforts on for a meaningful impact. For each population, we created a one-page profile that explained who they were, what they wanted to achieve, how the library could help, and how we could measure success in serving them. (We used Lean Canvas; you could use something else.)
4. **Check your privilege.** Although we considered DEI throughout the process, our last step was to conduct a final racial equity analysis of our recommendations. The purpose of this was to understand how

our programs and services could maximize benefits and minimize burdens for BIPOC and excluded groups. The city of Seattle's Race and Social Justice Initiative offers a helpful toolkit on how to do this.

5. **Start making things.** Now that you have a clear idea of whom you're serving and what they want, it's time to start creating programs, services, and communication tools. You don't have to have everything figured out up front—the important thing is to keep learning and building relationships. At KCLS, we ran and advertised programs for over a year before things coalesced into a clear brand. Once we had brought all our work together under the Invest in Yourself umbrella, we were able to launch a web page, events tag, social accounts, and an e-newsletter that cross-promote each other. You might have a good brand first and add programs or services later. There isn't just one way, because it's all based on your unique community.

6. **Keep listening, engaging, and iterating.** The idea here isn't to learn a bunch of stuff from your community, then run off and design your own programs and services in a dark closet. Community assessment gives you a chance to build relationships. Keep these relationships up and make more of them. Create your programs and services in partnerships that really share power, or better yet, join in on grassroots initiatives that started outside your organization. Some things you started with won't work out the way you hoped. Keep changing, keep growing, keep listening, and keep engaging.

Promoting Your Program

Because we had learned about our populations of focus and had developed ongoing relationships with them, we were able to select those communication channels that would be most effective in engaging them. Invest in Yourself has its own page on the KCLS website, a presence on Instagram and LinkedIn, and a monthly e-newsletter. In print, my favorite piece is a bright green business card that reads: "This card could save your small business more than $10,000." The card unfolds into a resource list of databases, books, programs, and services for entrepreneurs. The card's format allows it to be easily handed out at a networking event, where business owners are expecting to exchange cards. The very best promotion, though, is word of mouth. Working with partners means that other organizations will also promote your programs and services to their communities, helping you reach new audiences.

Overcoming Roadblocks and Challenges

Starting a new stream of services takes time. Building up the relationships that will eventually lead to a successful service takes even longer. It can be difficult for staff to spend the time to lay this groundwork, especially when there is likely to be no immediate resulting program or output. Get buy-in from library leaders who can support this use of staff time.

It can also be challenging to build relationships with people whose lived experiences are very different from those of library staff. You may not have existing connections and feel unsure how to develop new ones. Groups that have been disenfranchised may understandably be hesitant to work with the library. If you can, find mutual trusted contacts who can introduce you. When you do meet, listen fully, with respect and humility. Assume that the people impacted by a problem are in the best position to solve it. See your job not as providing ideas for others, but as providing library resources to amplify their work. In the same vein, do not ask for their emotional or intellectual labor without a commitment to support them in return.

Staff Responsibilities

We created a cross-functional team to lead Invest in Yourself. The team's staff were selected for their personal passion for the topic, as well as for a diversity of roles from throughout the organization. The group includes librarians, managers, selectors, paraprofessionals, and support staff. People can take on roles appropriate for their interests and jobs. For example, one subcommittee focuses on programming, and another manages social media. A collections librarian features business content in the catalog, and the human resources department helps with staff training.

Tips, Tricks, and Advice

- Measure success by outcomes and impact rather than outputs. If a program builds relationships with underserved communities or helps advance an important community goal, this can be

more important than attendance or the number of programs. Find a way to concretely express the value of relationships, so that you don't default back to the more easily measured but less meaningful outputs.
- **Be patient.** True knowledge and impact come from relationships, and relationships take trust, and trust takes time. Do not expect to immediately develop a concrete program.
- **Be led by your community.** Listen to them always, and hand power to them whenever you can. Know that you will make mistakes, so learn from these and do better next time. Don't give up.
- Did I mention **coffee?**

PROGRAM 14

Building Support for Rural Entrepreneurs

Wyoming Library to Business— A Statewide Initiative

LARAMIE COUNTY (WY) LIBRARY SYSTEM

Rachael Svoboda

Setting the Stage

Wyoming Library to Business (WL2B) is a statewide initiative to support library-to-business outreach in any of our state's twenty-three county public library systems. This statewide expansion is scaled from the Laramie County Library System's current Library to Business service, launched in 2012. WL2B focuses on assisting women-owned and rural businesses through (1) the curation of current Wyoming small business resources; (2) creation of the Wyoming Library to Business Network, a peer-to-peer librarian group dedicated to connecting communities with Wyoming business experts and programs; (3) expanding partnerships with local, state, and national economic development organizations; and (4) leveraging partnerships and funding to work in tandem to provide technology for public libraries to empower their local small businesses and entrepreneurs. The W2LB initiative provides high-quality equipment for business stations and video production studios for entrepreneurs to access in their local libraries.

Service Area

- Urban and Rural
- Medium, less than 99,000 population

Goals and Impact

With the decline of coal and mineral revenue, Wyoming is in desperate need of economic diversification. The governor-appointed Economically Needed Diversity Options for Wyoming (ENDOW) Executive Council concluded that part of the solution to diversify the state's economy is to foster communities that are supportive of entrepreneurs and start-up businesses through sufficient capital access and access to mentors and collaborative work spaces. WL2B intends to remove barriers in order to empower any Wyomingite who dreams of being an entrepreneur or owning a small business. WL2B provides access to free business resources, professional services, seed funding, and available capital programs to the rural Wyoming community at large.

By connecting individuals to a myriad of resources, WL2B helps grow businesses throughout the state. Wyoming continues to have one of the largest gender-wage disparities in the country, with women earning 80 cents per dollar in contrast to their male counterparts. In addition, Wyoming's population is 35 percent rural, and consists of only 5.8 people per square mile, according to the U.S. Census Bureau. Each of these populations faces distinct challenges in participating in the entrepreneurial and business community, necessitating WL2B's efforts to increase awareness of the resources available to all Wyoming residents, especially those who continue to be underserved by preexisting services.

While it will take some time to reach all corners of the state's counties, having a centralized hub of business resources dramatically improves the chances of reaching the underserved. The WL2B program is designed to complement and leverage the services provided by the national, state, and local economic development organizations. In Wyoming, the presence of a public library in each county makes for a strong delivery system.

Getting Started

To create a scalable statewide initiative, a staff person dedicated to business outreach can coordinate with various library systems, partners, and local decision-makers. Starting with your programming partners, try to understand how their efforts are impacting the rest of the state and then identify possible gaps in coverage. Next, present your current program at local library conferences to gauge the level of interest in it. Start planning for the statewide initiative with interested libraries. Provide an overview of library, community, region, and state resources that you've identified and curated to other librarians and partners.

Internally, look critically at the services that are already provided by you and your partners and then divide them into manageable pieces. Partnership programming is one of the easiest to replicate since it can involve minimal staff time and can be as easy as introducing your partner to another librarian. One-on-one consultations are the most staff-intensive type of programming and are best carried out by an individual with a business background or a strong understanding of available business resources.

Key Resources

Our library initiative included the following key resources:

- **The library web page and a LibGuide** on business resources
- **Video production studios** equipped with technology to create videos, podcasts, social media ads, and other recordings
- **Business stations:** These are dedicated portable stations with a webcam-enabled laptop so that entrepreneurs and small business owners can meet virtually with experts from across the state; each station includes a portable projector so that libraries can take full advantage of the online programs and webinars produced by economic development organizations

Key Partners

- **University of Wyoming, IT librarian:** We work closely with the IT librarian at the University of Wyoming to drive the project's development and continuously improve the video production studios.
- **Wyoming Women's Business Center:** This nonprofit has been instrumental in supporting and marketing the launch of the business stations, meeting with community stakeholders, and connecting with librarians.
- **Wyoming State Library:** Our collaboration with the state library began early, and its support has been key to bolstering the credibility of our initiative. The state library has been instrumental in scaling up our initiative by communicating

directly with each county library director, creating a web page on the state library's website, and providing tools (LibGuides, Niche Academy) as needed.
- **Wyoming Small Business Development Center Network:** The SBDC Network was able to use funds to provide a photo light box to every public library. A light box properly lights small merchandise items so as to provide professional-quality pictures taken with a cell phone or camera.
- **Small Business Administration, Wyoming Division:** This government agency has been key to the brainstorming and evaluation of the program as a whole. They provided programming, marketing events, and collaboration in identifying underserved communities and gaps in service.

Budget

Wyoming Library to Business received grant funds from the Libraries Build Business program. Our budget included funding for the video production studios and business stations. You'll need to consider both an equipment budget and a space modification budget for the studios. For a statewide initiative like WL2B, create a travel budget for the project manager using the current GSA guidelines.

The studio equipment budget and space modification will vary depending on the particular studio that is built. It is important to decide what works best for your library space and patrons. First, how portable or stationary will your production studio need to be? It is good to consider the target audience when making these decisions, as well as investigating the community for possible makerspaces that are already in existence.

Implementing the Nuts and Bolts

As part of this initiative, WL2B has three main focus areas to best support small business owners and successfully scale our offerings across the state:

1. Grassroots training and teaching for development and use of the video production studios and business stations, and further expansion of the Laramie County L2B services to libraries around the state.

2. Creation of the Wyoming Library to Business Network to share resources, troubleshoot challenges and obstacles, and learn about new business offerings in the state. The network provided a resource for librarians to ask questions, share resources (such as templates and talking points), and build a network of peers.
3. Grants to community partners that have a demonstrated ability to support and grow small businesses/entrepreneurs.

To understand the impact of this work and the needs of Wyoming entrepreneurs and business owners, we collected qualitative stories and conducted surveys to assist with quantitative data.

> **What Is a Video Production Studio?**
>
> Modeled from Penn State University's One Button Studios (onebutton.psu.edu), our typical video production space "drastically simplifies the video production workflow, eliminating several time-consuming steps. The end result is a studio experience that requires the bare minimum of time and effort while simultaneously providing a consistently high-quality result packaged on a thumb drive in a standard format video file."
> Each production studio can be used to:
>
> - Add green screen graphics for a social media ad.
> - Create your vlog or podcast.
> - Practice and critique your interview skills and your "pitch."
> - Produce a self-tape for auditions.
> - Record a public service announcement for your nonprofit.
> - Demonstrate or unveil your product.

HOW TO: Evaluate Your Space for a Video Production Studio

The WL2B project has built video production studios in libraries across the state. Follow the steps below to assess the space you will be using for the studio before you build it.

1. **Identify the space for the studio and inventory the required components such as lightning and electrical wiring.** The "sweet spot" identified by Penn State is an 8 × 10-foot room. The space can be modified if it is part of a bigger room. Additionally, the studio

spotlights should be 93–96 inches off the floor, so be sure to assess the ceiling height.
2. Consider the light sources that are currently in the room. If there are windows, you'll want to factor in blackout shades.
3. Look into the electrical and technical considerations. The studio spotlights will each need to be plugged in to their own outlets. Can this be completed to code in your building? Additionally, an accessible data port is needed to build the studio.
4. Consider how customers will use the space and how accessible it needs to be. Will the equipment for the studio be mounted on a cart or permanently installed in a cabinet? For example, you can either mount a green screen to a wall or get a portable version of one.
5. Remember, individuals will be creating recorded material in the studio. Are there HVAC noises or other uncontrollable noises in the space? You may need sound adsorption panels or a flexible sound-adsorption screen
6. After recording, individuals will want to review and edit their work. Locate space for computers for editing footage.
7. To optimize the studio's use, be sure that library staff are trained and available to help. Consider the procedures for "checking out" the space and receiving staff assistance.

Promoting Your Program

When building out your video production studios, have a launch event and invite local stakeholders and community members to it. WL2B has been promoted in each county upon the completion and launch of that county's business station and studio. The Wyoming Women's Business Center (WWBC) has taken the helm in providing promotional materials and social media pushes, while assisting the county libraries with press releases. The WWBC created handouts, flyers, posters, and Facebook posts specific to each county. In addition, they customized a thirty-minute presentation on small business marketing for each business-station launch event using the new projector.

Overcoming Roadblocks and Challenges

Clear communication with stakeholders, partners, and our growing community has been key to developing, implementing, and scaling the project. Our largest roadblocks could have been overcome by establishing two items at the beginning: (1) communicating with stakeholders on an assigned platform such as Slack (*not* e-mail); and (2) the use of a specific project management software or platform to keep the project's moving pieces from colliding. All projects should have identified and agreed-upon methods of communication including where, how often, and the expectations for response time. Doing this at the front end will avoid unnecessary stress and headaches.

Staff Responsibilities

This project included a full-time business services coordinator/project manager to plan and execute the initiative, including budget and stakeholder communication, and a part-time L2B specialist to oversee the current Laramie County L2B program and assist with research, evaluation of processes, and materials. The Laramie County Library System's staff contributions included an IT specialist, adult services staff, and a communications coordinator. Wyoming State Library staff including the state librarian, the library development manager, and a database instruction librarian, and marketing and outreach staff also expedited collaboration and the development of resources.

Tips, Tricks, and Advice

- Before the beginning of every studio construction project, always meet with the construction lead and their team to review the plan. Make sure that the plan is in writing and posted where everyone can refer to it. A decision-maker must be on-site to resolve unexpected issues that come up and make timely decisions.
- Finding the right communication platform for all stakeholders can be challenging and must fit the needs of the project and those involved. For any communication that requires a great deal of frequency and decision-making, using a collaboration platform such as Slack, Trello, MS Teams, or Asana is vital to the success of the project and the project manager's sanity.
  Be sure to set communication frequency expectations and acceptable response timing. Agree in advance on how to handle the disruptions that are sure to come.

- A positive attitude, persistence, and adaptability are absolutely essential for a project of this scope and size. Be prepared to be the cheerleader, coach, and center at any time, sometimes within the same conversation.
- Create the topics your program will cover based on feedback from participants, thus ensuring that the content is relevant to their needs. All communities are unique and may need different resources and approaches.

PROGRAM 15

Connect with Immigrant Entrepreneurs

Sea Un Vendedor Ambulante Exitoso/
Successful Street Vending

LOS ANGELES (CA) PUBLIC LIBRARY

Madeleine Ildefonso

Setting the Stage

The Sea Un Vendedor Ambulante Exitoso/Successful Street Vending program at the Los Angeles Public Library helps Angeleno street vendors to become successful business owners by providing accessible, microenterprise mobile learning modules in Spanish, English, and ELL via an educational technology called Cell-Ed. Cell-Ed, the chief product of a company of the same name, is a mobile micro-learning platform that delivers content via a flip phone or smartphone. Many libraries use Cell-Ed for their adult learners and adult literacy programs because its mobile platform is so accessible for busy adults.

The focus of this project is on supporting a recently formalized informal economy, that of street vendors. Street vending was recently legalized by the state of California and then by the city of Los Angeles in 2019. A 2015 study by the Economic Roundtable found that Los Angeles is home to approximately 50,000 street vendors and that they contribute $504 million annually to the local economy. Our work with street vendors builds on our library's existing business services and relationships. The Cell-Ed micro-entrepreneurship skills program aims to center the goals of vendors and provide them with a sense of agency and understanding in the processes that they are embarking on to become permitted and successful business owners in Los Angeles.

Service Area

- Urban
- Very Large, more than 500,000 population

Goals and Impact

The Business Department at the Central Library of the Los Angeles Public Library has offered workforce development programs and workshops to help small businesses for many years. This department has a long and robust tradition of connecting business owners and entrepreneurs with information, either through library resources like books and databases or through library nonprofit partners and workshops. Adjacent to these services are the library's immigration services. Through the course of our work in supporting immigrants and immigration services with other city departments and nonprofits, we learned that while the city has many resources to assist street vendors, the vendors might benefit from more preparation before they are referred to these services.

Our goal is to help street vendors become successful business owners by providing them with mobile, accessible content in Spanish, English, and ELL that will increase their business, financial, digital, and civic literacies.

Getting Started

With many community partners, it's important to establish a timeline that works for all parties in advance. We reached out to Cell-Ed, our community nonprofit partners, and the vendors to discuss content, workflow processes, vendor needs, and timelines. Through these partnerships, we identified particular topics that were of the most interest to street vendors. The vendors were really excited to interact, share, and learn from the programs. We also understood from our own data resources that it was important to specifically focus on economic mobility for immigrant populations.

Key Resources
The key resources for our initiative included the following:

- **Apple iPads** distributed to vendors for use in meetings and to evaluate Cell-Ed content
- **Keyboards** so that the iPads could be used like computers
- **Hotspots** for connectivity for vendors
- **Zoom licenses** so the library could host Zoom meetings

Key Partners

- **Cell-Ed:** The Cell-Ed technology tackles one of the world's most intractable problems: teaching adults the basic skills they need to better their lives, such as reading a child's homework, communicating with confidence, or dividing numbers. Learners simply listen to lessons on their flip phone or smartphone anywhere and anytime — no internet connection or costly data plan is needed. They text to demonstrate their understanding of the lesson, and can talk and text with Cell-Ed automated and live coaches on demand. Cell-Ed is our primary partner and content provider.
- **Community Power Collective (CPC):** This Los Angeles-based nonprofit focuses on advocating and organizing vendors to be successful business owners. The CPC leads our work with the vendors and helps us prioritize topics of interest.
- **Healing Justice Transformative Leadership Institute:** This is a nonprofit committed to building individual and collective healing, transformation, and liberation with a bilingual and bicultural lens that encompasses various modalities, including trauma-informed and healing justice approaches.
- **Vendor fellows:** The CPC helped to identify vendor leaders to both test products and provide feedback, and also to pilot in sharing widely to their networks.

Budget
We budgeted $85,000 from our Libraries Build Business grant and used additional library funding of $31,000 to supplement the grant. The library

funding was used to purchase additional Cell-Ed licenses and to develop additional content that we discovered in continuing conversations with the street vendors. The initial $85,000 budget covered most of the Cell-Ed package, including almost all of the learning units along with some learner licenses. Since Cell-Ed is already a vendor for the library, it was simple to supplement the budget with funding that needed to be reallocated at the close of the fiscal year. The additional library funding paid for the trauma support strategies with Thriving Communities units. We're also collaborating to help produce instructional videos on the permit and licensing process which we can embed on our website with another city contractor to augment the Cell-Ed resources we are building. We also budgeted for vendor fellowships and needed equipment.

Implementing the Nuts and Bolts

The Cell-Ed learning units we developed for Sea un Vendedor Ambulante Exitoso/Successful Street Vending cover financial literacy, digital literacy, and business basics like customer service, marketing, business taxes, and banking, as well as referrals for permit information and additional resources. The Cell-Ed micro-learning platform also features several units that support thriving and resilient communities and focuses on addressing trauma, personal safety, and support strategies. The Cell-Ed platform is complemented by an ecosystem of resources ranging from financial coaching to immigration remedies, additional language learning, and workshops on a range of topics like access to capital, cashless payment systems, and civic literacy.

Vendors are surveyed with regard to the content creation and use of the library and its services. Cell-Ed is able to provide reports with regard to usage and outcomes. The best measure of impact is when our library understands how our work product changed or helped a library user change their life circumstance (outcomes). We'll also be looking to capture this information either through Cell-Ed surveys or over-the-phone interviews.

HOW TO: Work with Street Vendors

1. Find a community partner who has already built trust with the community. Talk to stakeholders and attend public meetings—or

ask for meetings with potential partners to learn more about the community you want the library to work with, and then build those connections so as to be able to work directly with that community as well.
2. **Start small to build trust with either an organization or community.** What other ways can the library support the community that this organization is connected with? For example, we issued a large number of library e-cards for the vending community that works with one of our partners, and hosted virtual drop-ins and in-language assistance for library card services. You may need to start with smaller projects like this to build trust before moving forward with bigger projects. Let them know how the library can help.
3. **Listen deeply and be humble.** While a community partner may be able to represent the interests of a community, be sure to include the target audience in conversations about projects. Librarians like to be experts, but it's important to take a back seat and honor community members. They are the experts of their lived experiences. In our case, we created space for vendor fellows—paid consultants—to surface and test the program's content.
4. **If you are able to, pay the community members for their expertise and their time.** If a municipal entity is building from community expertise, it's important to be transparent. If you cannot pay, be sure to name and call out the community for their input and make sure that this is agreeable to them.
5. **Be flexible.** What the community wants may deviate from your project goals. Be prepared to adjust your plans to be more inclusive and to truly meet community needs.

Promoting Your Program

We know from previous successes in immigration services that word of mouth is a powerful tool for creating a buzz about our services. Be sure that your staff, partners, and community stakeholders are equipped with information to share.

We promote our business programs widely alongside our regular immigration services, business activities, and financial literacy. Cell-Ed presented its product to our staff and our wide circle of partners. The staff shared information about the program more widely from a dedicated web landing page which will surface learning pathways for vendors.

Overcoming Roadblocks and Challenges

When you are flexible and allow for project pivots based on community need, you may also need to be resourceful and creative about funding. Look for intersections with other programs and activities where there is budget stability to integrate a new project or a new approach to the library's work.

Staff Responsibilities

Our project was mostly coordinated by two full-time employees and several full-time bilingual staff members who report in different work units. The bilingual staff would attend vendor meetings or help to run drop-in or informational sessions with the vendors in Spanish. The project manager oversaw the timeline, budget, project content development, and partner relationships, and the second full-time staff member worked to support project development, meeting coordination, and project implementation. Because we're a large institution, other work units will support further work in this space like public relations, digital content, and any adjacent services that will involve a multi-staff effort.

Tips, Tricks, and Advice

- Be flexible and open-minded—don't be too invested in your idea. Let the community inform you of what's most important, and then start to build trust and services based on their needs— even if these don't align with the data or the library's goals. You'll get there once you build that trust.
- Integrate social services, adult education, and other types of programming and resources into your programs for small business owners. We understand from working with many immigrants that their needs are intersectional and that forms and processes which require fluency and literacy in language, bureaucracy, jargon, and codes may disempower them. Street vending is often the first step in their entrepreneurship path and one that many believe is the most accessible.

PROGRAM 16

Taking a Shot with SCORE

Entrepreneur Workshop Series

MACEDON (NY) PUBLIC LIBRARY

Stacey Wicksall

Setting the Stage

In 2014, the Macedon Public Library (MPL) in upstate New York sought to boost entrepreneurial innovation and promote economic stability and a thriving local community. With the mission of "connecting people and ideas" clearly in mind, the library began to consider ways it could help generate business within the town of Macedon and across the county. The Entrepreneur Workshop Series was born in 2015 thanks to a strong partnership with the Service Core of Retired Executives (SCORE).

Service Area

- Suburban, Rural
- Small, less than 24,000 population

Goals and Impact

The main goal of the Entrepreneur Workshop Series is to give community members the information, tools, and support they need to have a successful shot at building a small business. We offered the workshop series five times between 2015 and 2019. Altogether we hosted 37 participants, and nearly 30 percent of them went on to successfully launch a business.

Getting Started

The idea to focus on entrepreneurship came from understanding the economic needs in the community and the county at large. We connected with the Canal Connection Chamber of Commerce and the Wayne County Business Council. Once we became involved in meetings, the economic needs of the area become apparent.

We recommend engaging with your community and making contacts. Our community connections led us straight to SCORE. Our partnership with SCORE was a great fit for the library's mission and goal.

Key Resources

To support entrepreneurs going through our workshop series, we provided laptops and public computers, databases such as EBSCO Small Business Resources, and our meeting spaces.

Key Partners

SCORE is an organization composed of retired executives and active professionals who are willing to share their expertise with others interested in developing small businesses. No matter what industry someone wishes to enter, SCORE has a knowledgeable mentor ready to help.

Budget

A workshop series can be created with very little budget required if local professionals agree to volunteer their time to present. If SCORE is used, there is a cost to register. This cost can be paid by the attendee, or it may be subsidized by the library.

We received grant funding from a local legislator, a grant program through our library system, and our library's Friends group to support the development and maintenance of our program. With these funds, we added relevant books and media to our collection. We also purchased laptops and EBSCO's Small Business Resources database.

Implementing the Nuts and Bolts

Keep the following six tips in mind when implementing an entrepreneurial program:

1. Get involved with the business community by joining a local business council or chamber. Make sure to listen carefully to learn the unique strengths, weaknesses, opportunities, and threats that are present in your locale.
2. Reach out to SCORE or, if SCORE does not exist in your area, reach out to professionals who will be willing to present on the areas that novice entrepreneurs must know about. We recommend seeking a "B-A-I-L" team, which includes a banker, accountant, insurance agent, and a lawyer. If you belong to organizations such as the Rotary Club, Lions Club, the chamber of commerce, business council, or Toastmasters, it should not be difficult to recruit a highly qualified team. Volunteers for these presentations often enjoy sharing their professional information with new entrepreneurs and realize this is an opportunity to indirectly promote their own business too, since participants often seek out loans, accounting help, insurance, legal advice, and marketing assistance from presenters they respect and trust.
3. Encourage entrepreneurs to pair up with a mentor. SCORE or the Rotary Club may be helpful places to approach when looking for volunteer mentors.
4. Educate yourself by reaching out to business librarians at either an urban public library or an academic library. Ask them to acquaint you with the basics of business librarianship. Find out if they are able to share business research information through the use of premium databases they can access; for example, sharing insightful industry articles or sample business plans culled from a premium database can be very helpful. Oftentimes medium and small public libraries cannot afford databases, and having a relationship with a bigger library with business resources can be a lifesaver.
5. Present your resources and librarians' skills as part of the workshop series. Make sure that entrepreneurs understand the value which the library can provide when they create a business plan, strategic plan, SWOT analysis, marketing research, and a business pitch. Remember to highlight the technology you have to offer as well as the meeting space that can be used for business meetings.
6. Network and promote both the small business programs being offered and the amazing success stories that emerge. Doing

this helps the library to become a respected business resource, advertises new businesses, and grows the entrepreneurial spirit in your community.

Promoting Your Program

In order to ensure that people are aware of your program, we suggest the following:

- Advertise the program with catchy posts on social media accounts, press releases, e-mail discussion lists, and the library website.
- Ask to present at Rotary Clubs, business councils, chambers of commerce, and any other organizations that support or attract businesspeople in your area.
- Contact employment centers to let them know about the program. Some states offer programs for the unemployed to start small businesses. In our case, such a program did exist, and our entrepreneur workshops were an approved source of entrepreneurial training.
- Talk about it. Word of mouth is one of the best ways to promote any program. Make sure to spread the word when you're out and about. Ask staff to publicize the program to patrons as they wait for books to be checked out.

Overcoming Roadblocks and Challenges

Don't let your library's physical or fiscal size put limits on its entrepreneurial programming. By networking and building relationships with people in the business community and other stakeholders, you can find outstanding professionals who are willing to present and mentor others, as well as champions of your work. For example, let local representatives know about the library's mission to grow the economy with new small businesses. Politicians on both sides of the aisle want to support these sorts of endeavors and may help to promote your programming and even earmark funding for it.

Staff Responsibilities

Our library's staff were responsible for scheduling and promoting programming; presenting library resources; connecting with business librarians,

Meet Melinda, the Proprietor of Kitten Around Cat Boarding

Melinda Kelsey attended our Entrepreneur Workshop Series with her husband, Rob. She is now the proprietor of a highly successful cat boarding business located just a short walk away from the library. For Melinda, who had wanted to start a business for several years, the SCORE workshops at the Macedon Public Library were invaluable. "There is so much information you need to organize to start a business and be successful. We learned how to organize our plans and dreams and to make them functional. We developed a plan and broke down the steps to achieve what we wanted to do. Even now as we make plans for the future, we look back on our notes and take a step-by-step approach. A workshop series like this, with your peers to bounce ideas off of, mentors to guide you, and speakers to inspire you, is a great way to begin. Libraries are the perfect place to have a program like this."

Melinda Kelsey with a cat she is boarding

volunteers, and stakeholders; and providing reference and technology support. Having more than one staff member who can meet one-on-one with entrepreneurs is especially helpful in making this intensive help available on a daily basis. If this is not possible because of a very small staff, offer special, entrepreneur consultation hours at various times of the day throughout the week or schedule individual appointments.

Tips, Tricks, and Advice

- **Reach out to a business librarian and be ready to learn.** Before the commencement of the first workshop series, SCORE pointed us to the Rochester Public Library's Small Business Resource Center (SBRC). We received lots of guidance from the business librarians there by visiting the SBRC. We learned which databases would be most helpful for business plan research, which sites could be used to access business plan examples, how to find and use NAICS codes, how to use the

U.S. Census website for a myriad of useful information, and were recommended books to add to the collection for those delving into entrepreneurship. We also found out about patents and grant research. Since we had no previous business librarian experience, the time the Rochester Public Library business librarians spent with us was critical to acquiring the knowledge we needed to be able to help entrepreneurs. To this day, we have not been afraid to reach out to Rochester Public Library business librarians with questions that may flummox us.

- **Just as written research often means scouring many sources for information, so too does building an entrepreneurial program at the library.** Listen carefully, ask questions, and be open about your vision and goals for building business programming at the library. Talking to others who are already working on generating business will build a network of support and guide you to potential collaborators. It will also help you to refine your vision and develop a highly intentional plan for creating the entrepreneurial environment you want to cultivate at the library.
- **Keep an eye out for grant opportunities.** Look to library organizations at the local, state, and federal levels, government organizations, community endowment funds, and private foundations to assess if grant opportunities or requests for proposals exist. Grant writing is work, but it can really pay off. It's like the lottery; you'll never win a cent if you don't play. And unlike the lottery, your odds are much better.
- **Know your vision and be passionate and excited about it when you share it with . . . everyone.** Make sure to let people know how the library can help to build business, and share your vision with them. If you are excited about entrepreneurial programming, others are bound to catch your enthusiasm.

PROGRAM 17

Opening the Doors to Economic Success

The Miller Business Center

MIDDLE COUNTRY (NY) PUBLIC LIBRARY

Sophia Serlis-McPhillips and Elizabeth Malafi

Setting the Stage

The Middle Country Public Library (MCPL) is located in Suffolk County, Long Island, and serves an area of 61,000 residents. In 2004, a building expansion enabled the library to devote 5,000 square feet to develop the Miller Business Center, a regional resource serving business professionals, entrepreneurs, not-for-profits, and job seekers. The space includes business, law, literacy, and career collections; public computers; 3D printing; reading areas; a meeting room; two conference rooms; counseling and adult literacy offices; and a shared office utilized by our local partners. The Miller Center provides various educational programs and services for business professionals, business owners, women and minority entrepreneurs, and micro-entrepreneurs. These programs include our Women's EXPO, Strictly Business networking events, and regularly scheduled classes and workshops.

One of our flagship programs for small business owners and entrepreneurs at the Miller Center is the Women's EXPO. Library staff and business professionals saw that many women makers were having a hard time turning their creations into a business. They were passionate about making jewelry, specialty cookies, art, and more, but lacked the confidence and knowledge needed to take the next step into entrepreneurship. While the EXPO culminates in a large event bringing more than 80 women-owned businesses together with over 2,000 shoppers, its purpose is to help women entrepreneurs all year round.

Service Area

- Suburban
- Medium, less than 99,000 population

Goals and Impact

The goal of the Miller Business Center is to educate and prepare regional business owners and entrepreneurs for economic success. The Women's EXPO supports this goal by focusing on women business owners and entrepreneurs, providing support and a venue for women entrepreneurs to market their products, and serving as a vehicle to promote economic development and collaborations among women entrepreneurs and business professionals. Ultimately, the EXPO intends to strengthen the reach of Long Island women entrepreneurs.

The impact of the EXPO can be seen as the women entrepreneurs start and grow their businesses and connections. Many of the women connect and partner with other participants to package their products together. A success story is often one in which an entrepreneur no longer needs us; their business has become so successful that they don't attend our events anymore. Several of the women have gone on to open retail locations or to mass-produce items to sell wholesale to major retailers.

Getting Started

The first thing to do before you get started is to get the library's administration on board with promoting and offering programs and services to businesses. Put together a plan outlining the specifics, including sample programs and services, staffing, and an estimated budget. Most importantly, demonstrate how your proposal ties into the mission of your library.

Key Resources

The key resources for our initiative included:

- **Space:** Our 5,000-square-foot space hosts our physical collection, equipment, and programming and events.
- **Business databases:** Data Axle's Reference Solutions and FTSE Russell's First research are our favorites.

Key Partners

The Miller Business Center has partnered with various Long Island business support organizations to enrich the center's resources and services. We've highlighted our two most unique and successful partnerships:

- **The Greater Middle Country Chamber of Commerce and the Brookhaven Chambers of Commerce Coalition (BCCC):** For thirteen years, the Miller Center has partnered with the Greater Middle Country Chamber of Commerce and the BCCC to host the Strictly Business program. The purpose of Strictly Business is to network and build local businesses and promote chamber membership.
- **Hauppauge Industrial Association—Long Island (HIA-LI):** The HIA-LI supports one of the largest industrial parks in the United States and is an organization focused on providing a forum for business leaders to network, problem-solve, and collaborate on key business issues. In 1999, the Miller Center and the HIA-LI partnered to share business resources, creating an innovative public-private partnership. Librarians provide one-on-one business reference assistance to the HIA-LI's members and a portal to access the library's business databases. Our business librarians attend the HIA-LI's new member orientations, business luncheons, and annual trade show, and serve on various committees. Through this partnership, the Miller Center was able to reach beyond its local business community and become more regionally involved.

Budget

The budget for the Women's EXPO is approximately $20,000 and includes expenses for the day of the event as well as pre- and post-event activities. Our expenses consist of staff salaries, printing supplies, postage, marketing and promotional items, raffle supplies, program/speaker fees, workshop supplies, photography, and travel expenses. We solicit sponsorships through the library's Foundation to underwrite the costs of the EXPO.

Implementing the Nuts and Bolts

While planning an event like the Women's EXPO may seem daunting and outside your realm of possibilities, it doesn't have to be. The key is to make the event fit your capabilities. After two decades of planning the EXPO, we have a robust planning committee, more than 80 exhibitors, and more than 2,000 attendees. This is what fits our community, our budget, and our space. If you decide to have an event like this, start small. Start by reaching out to more women-owned businesses and finding out what they need to create, grow, and succeed. This will help you determine what programming and resources your library is able to contribute. Once you have established yourself in these spaces, consider hosting an event like the EXPO.

HOW TO: Host a Women's EXPO Event

1. **Organize the staff needed to plan and run an annual event.** The first thing to do is to create an in-house team with the expertise and enthusiasm needed to have a successful event. Dividing the work across a team eases the potential burdens on any one person.
2. **Identify partners.** Your key partners should be organizations and individuals who share the goals of your project. The Women's EXPO relies on a planning committee to run a successful event. The committee is made up of representatives from our sponsors, local business support organizations, and women entrepreneurs. This group brings diverse perspectives that we may not see. For the EXPO, we knew we wanted to create a committee that had connections with the local entrepreneurial community, could connect us with potential sponsors, and had the expertise to mentor participants.
3. **Pick a date.** The EXPO is held during the workweek, as our hope is that business professionals and entrepreneurs will see it as a business networking event. The event gives women the chance to connect in ways they might not be able do to over e-mail or at a traditional networking event. Seeing a business owner at work gives

other entrepreneurs and professionals the opportunity to ask more about their work, offer or solicit advice, and even talk about shared interests.
4. **Develop supportive programming leading up to the big event.** In keeping with the library's mission to educate, we offer programs to help entrepreneurs get ready for the event. The programs cover topics like branding, social media, and web design. In recent years, we have added a networking event to the programming line-up. This connects participants with local businesswomen who can provide mentorship. It also connects them with each other, creating a peer group of women entrepreneurs offering support and guidance as they begin, grow, and expand their businesses.
5. **Recruit women to participate in the educational programming and EXPO event.** For an event like the EXPO, it is important to expand your audience. We cast a wide net by speaking with local organizations that work with entrepreneurs, attending local events to meet women who are just starting out, and looking on sites like Etsy.
6. **Spread the word.** In order to attract attendees, the Miller Center sends Save-the-Date e-mails and weekly follow-ups before the event. We utilize some of our business databases to create lists of women executives in the area and send them event postcards. These postcards are designed in-house using Canva and are printed for a relatively low price.
7. **Build excitement in the community.** Shopping for items from local women-owned businesses is a draw. Getting these shoppers to the event is very important, since they provide the true test of the success of the hard work these women are doing. One of the reasons why our event attendance has continued to skyrocket is because of our attendees. They love the EXPO event and look forward to it each year. Many of them bring friends and make a day of it.

Promoting Your Program

Promotion of your program should be 24/7 part of what you do. Every interaction, meeting, or event that we attend is a way to continue spreading the word. For the Miller Business Center, we used the connections we made to create a robust e-mail list of local businesses. This list now boasts over 4,000 names, and we use MailChimp to send out monthly newsletters and event e-mails. Word of mouth has been crucial to our success in this area as well.

Overcoming Roadblocks and Challenges

When you begin your work with the business community, your biggest challenge may be making people understand why you are in the room. When we started, we received many surprised reactions: "A librarian? At the Chamber of Commerce meeting? Why?" Eventually, after many interactions, people began to understand what we were doing for the business community, and those exclamations of surprise turned into exclamations of recognition.

Staff Responsibilities

The Miller Center encompasses business, workforce development/career information, and literacy. The team consists of a coordinator and four full-time librarians. All these staffers have responsibilities outside of their work with the Miller Center. They are responsible for the center's daily activities, including research assistance, collection development, programming, marketing, and attending events and meetings. Full-time and part-time librarians are scheduled at the Miller Center reference desk after receiving training on business research and services. Three part-time career counselors provide career and college counseling and programs. The Literacy Team consists of one coordinator, two full-time librarians, and one literacy assistant. They are responsible for the adult literacy programs and collections, as well as providing literacy assistance.

Tips, Tricks, and Advice

- If you have committed to helping your business community, you are a business librarian. You don't need a business degree, only the drive to learn from and connect with businesses and entrepreneurs. If you've got that, congratulations, you can call yourself a business librarian.
- The size of your dedicated business space should not hinder your efforts to develop your business services. Every little bit of assistance and support can help. Every community is unique. Tailor your space to the needs of your community.

- Your most valuable work may be done outside of the library. Immerse yourself in the business community by attending events, workshops, and trade shows. Developing these relationships can be time-consuming, but it can also lead to rewarding partnerships.
- **Don't be afraid to ask for money from people you have interacted with.** They understand about the work you are doing. Sometimes their initial small donations will increase based on your credibility and success.
- With this and many programs, our biggest resource is staff. Getting them on board with new ideas and projects is key. If they believe in what you're asking them to do, they will be motivated to see it succeed. Plus, you just can't do it alone, and having help and input is invaluable. Use the connections and partnerships you have made in the business community. Enlist your supporters as volunteers when working on a big project.

PROGRAM 18

The MAGIC Touch

Management and Government Information Center

**PRINCE WILLIAM PUBLIC LIBRARIES
(WOODBRIDGE, VA)**

Katherine LaVallee and Eva Gunia

Setting the Stage

The Management and Government Information Center (MAGIC) is a special collection and information service for small business owners, entrepreneurs, and nonprofits located at the Chinn Park Library, one of the twelve library branches of Prince William Public Libraries (PWPL) in Virginia.

MAGIC was established in 1991 with the primary role of supporting the business community and government agencies in Prince William County, the city of Manassas, and Manassas Park. MAGIC has specialized staff and resources to help members of the community, including area businesses and nonprofits, to start or grow a business, retrieve industry information, seek grant funding, and access laws and regulations. We also provide programming to train entrepreneurs and nonprofits on how to search the Foundation Directory Online grant database to find grant-makers and potential funding opportunities. MAGIC supplies market research data to assist with revenue forecasting and to better assess the barriers to starting a business in any given industry, as well as information on the local competitive environment. These services have helped our local businesses plan strategically for what's ahead.

In 2017, PWPL was awarded a Capacity Building grant from the Potomac Health Foundation which enabled MAGIC to become part of the Funding

Information Network and gain access to the Foundation Directory Online grant database and its training for nonprofit businesses.

Service Area
Suburban and Rural
Large, less than 500,000 population

Goals and Impact

MAGIC's goal is to assist anyone in the community who is considering starting a new business or who wants to improve an established one. If they feel they need a little *magic* to answer their research questions, the business librarians at the Chinn Park Library are there to help. Our team focuses on helping small, local businesses that don't have the time, expertise, or resources to find the information they need to answer their business questions. We strive to offer programs that focus on building stronger small businesses with the digital skills courses offered by Grow with Google, as well as developing stronger nonprofit skills like proposal-writing and finding grants in collaboration with Candid and the Potomac Health Foundation.

Getting Started

To get started, start thinking about what professional products and services you can offer and how you plan to integrate them into the business community. When producing a professional product and offering it to the business community, the branding should be a priority.

MAGIC logo
Image courtesy of Prince William Public Libraries

Branding is important because it creates name recognition and helps build trust, so we recommend having a logo for your department and using it on various correspondence. We use templates with our department logo for the cover sheet and table of contents which we attach to our in-depth research projects, thus creating a standard look for the products we produce.

Focus on becoming embedded in the business community. Making connections with businesses through outreach will help build trust, value, and visibility for your department. We recommend reaching out to your area's chamber of commerce and local volunteer networks. For example, here in Prince William County we have Volunteer Prince William, a nonprofit organization of which other nonprofits are members. MAGIC did a presentation on the services we offer at their monthly meeting. As a result, we were able to network with more than forty nonprofits and set up one-on-one appointments with several of them that wanted to search for grants.

Key Resources

The key resources which our library brought to the initiative included:

- **Meeting space** for programs and one-on-one meetings with members of the business community, and WebEx or Zoom for virtual meetings, demonstrations of library resources, and programs
- **Staffing** for programs and experienced staff for doing research
- **The internet, Adobe Pro, Outlook Quick Parts, and Outlook Tasks** are essential for professional correspondence and managing projects when doing research
- **Tools** such as Adobe Pro, IBISWorld, A-Z Database or Reference USA, Gale Business Resources, Lexis Advance, and the Foundation Directory Online grant database

Key Partners

- **The Potomac Health Foundation** funded our access to the Foundation Directory Online grant database and its training for nonprofit businesses.
- **Candid** collaborated to offer programs focusing on developing stronger nonprofit skills like proposal-writing and finding grants.
- **Grow with Google** provides in-person and virtual programs for the business community, focusing on building stronger businesses with digital skills.

Budget

Annually we budget around $1,000 for swag promotional materials; our IBISWorld subscription is $2,295, and we set aside about $1,000 for chamber of commerce events and guest speakers. We received a grant from the Potomac Health Foundation to fund our subscription to the Foundation Directory Online grant database. The programs we offer through Candid and Grow with Google come at no cost to the library. If you cannot budget for a subscription to IBISWorld, industry information can be obtained from the U.S. Bureau of Labor Statistics, Gale Business Insight Essentials, A-Z Database, and Standard and Poor's Industry Surveys.

Implementing the Nuts and Bolts

MAGIC staff provides industry overviews, including market research, trends data, and competition analysis for the small businesses and entrepreneurs in our area, thus contributing research for their business plans. For example, we assisted a person who wanted to open a coffee shop in Manassas. We provided them with demographics to establish the community profile, a list of established coffee shops in the area to identify competition, and a list of potential customers in the area to prepare for target advertising.

MAGIC also created two types of "books to go" kits. The first of these, the Business Start-Up Kit, provides basic information needed to start a business. The kit includes business plans, a social media marketing guide, a legal guide, and a list of small business resources by Prince William County's Department of Economic Development. The Grant Resources Kit is tailored to nonprofits that need a one-stop source of information on nonprofit survival and on how to access the Foundation Directory Online grant database. The kit includes information and resources on grant-writing, digital fundraising, nonprofit marketing, and a nonprofit handbook.

HOW TO: Support Local Entrepreneurs with Research

1. Establish a webpage marketing your business resources and services. On the PWPL's website, we have created a web page to include small business information, legal links, and government information, so businesses can do their own research and get access to our grant database.
2. Create handouts listing your library's business resources and services. Our handout mentions that we assist businesses with information needs relating to demographics, company research,

industry data, mailing lists, market research, starting a business, laws and regulations, property assessments, state and local government, and grants.
3. Set up a process to manage and respond to requests for information. At PWPL, requests for information are managed by using Outlook Task, wherein a request or task is assigned to a MAGIC team member, deadlines are set, and projects are managed.
4. Add a branded auto reply to your mailbox. This helps show off your professionalism and communicates to your patrons that you have received their e-mail and you will get back to them as soon as possible.
5. Communicate the next steps and timelines to your customer. About 90 percent of the questions and requests for information that we receive arrive by e-mail or through our online Ask MAGIC Form. Questions are answered within forty-eight hours unless the question involves in-depth research, which is typically completed within three weeks.
6. Be prepared to conduct research using your library's databases and resources. At PWPL, information is compiled from IBIS World and the A-Z Database. When we have an in-depth research request, we work on it as a team, with each member taking a section or part of the question to answer, before combining and sending the result to the patron.
7. Standardize your offerings. For example, the industry overview we provide small business owners is a three-page packet of market research information that looks at the competition, the barriers to entering the market, and projected growth. We include a table of contents.
8. Rotate assignments to monitor the e-mail and answer questions that come in that day.

Promoting Your Program

Take advantage of all marketing platforms: flyers, social media, and outside advertisements (e.g., Grow with Google's calendar of events, the chamber of commerce calendar of events). MAGIC creates its own specialty flyer that lists all our upcoming programs for the business community.

Overcoming Roadblocks and Challenges

Our biggest roadblock thus far has been program attendance. We are currently working on increasing attendance by trying to use more social media outlets and reaching out to more business associations.

Staff Responsibilities

MAGIC has a research team of three—two librarians, and one library technician who can assist with answering patrons' questions. Programming duties are divided between the two librarians. If you do a lot of programming, you may want one person to be the designated programmer for the department. The MAGIC department also manages their own outreach.

Tips, Tricks, and Advice

- If you are hosting a virtual program, create a background for your WebEx or Zoom profile with your department's logo, which creates name recognition and helps build trust.
- **Collaboration is *vital*.** When it comes to any kind of research, each person's brain works differently. Make sure you take advantage of the different perspectives of your team members.

PROGRAM 19

Develop an ESOL for Business Owners Class

Small Business Hub

PROVIDENCE (RI) PUBLIC LIBRARY

Christopher Bourret

Setting the Stage

The Providence Public Library (PPL) in Rhode Island hosts a Small Business Hub, which offers help to local small business owners and budding entrepreneurs by providing classes, special programs, resources, and referral help. PPL has a long track record of business services, including our Small Business Workshops in partnership with SCORE RI, ongoing since 1999.

Our newly established Business Hub helps us reach out to more diverse audiences in the greater Providence area, with a year-long specialized English class for immigrant business owners, serving both budding entrepreneurs and students with an established enterprise in restaurant, retail, and cleaning services. Our Business Hub also offers an expanded collection of business databases and books, as well as on-call business reference help by our information services librarian/business expert. Additionally, we host entrepreneur activities in our new 3,000-square-foot Workshop, which provides services like professional head shots; business card and other self-service printing services; maker activities and classes for entrepreneurs in the local creative community; and special workshops on patents, trademarks, and financial literacy provided by partner agencies.

Service Area

- Urban
- Large, less than 500,000 population

Goals and Impact

Our overarching goal is to connect community members who are in need of support with the resources available in the greater small-business community. With regard to educational needs, we help build business skills for 120 people yearly in partnership with SCORE RI and provide additional business, financial, and informational workshops for the public based on community-identified needs. Our education programming, such as our ESOL for Entrepreneurs class, is intended to build a bridge to local immigrant communities. We continuously try to improve our services and better understand the needs of immigrant entrepreneurs, creative entrepreneurs, and other local business owners through this effort, with the goal of connecting them to community partners and resources. Finally, our makerspace supports business development, especially targeting Providence's creative community of artists and artisans.

Building on our long-running and popular eight-week Small Business Workshop series, as well as our community adult education ESOL and computer literacy programs, we realized an opportunity to expand and market our services at the library to create a deeper, more inclusive entrepreneurship community that builds on the many resources available in our state. Most existing small-business support programs in Rhode Island target entrepreneurs on the "higher end" of the pathway; our projects target entrepreneurs in the aspirational stage and help provide the education and support necessary to start them on an "on ramp," creating the forward momentum needed to achieve success. We saw an ongoing demand for these targeted services among students in our ESOL classes, which led to the development of our ESOL for Entrepreneurs course. Further discussion with community partners revealed that while there are ever-increasing community resources available for those wanting to start a business, they are nebulous and inaccessible to many, especially those facing language or other barriers.

Getting Started

At the Providence Public Library, we realized that there were no specific ESOL programs for immigrant business owners in the area. You may find a similar situation in your own service area. Therefore, you might have a willing audience of potential patrons you can reach. Where to start? First, research the local business community, reach out to your local chambers (we have a Hispanic chamber in Providence), advertise at local adult education and immigration service institutions, and walk in (and support) local businesses to meet potential clients. Once you have a list of interested people, conduct a needs assessment to ascertain needed classes and programs and the best times to host them. Then you can market your programs heavily and do outreach. With our partners, we connected with immigrant business owners, local artists and artisans, and others.

Have a dedicated place on your library's website for information on business programs and updates. We created a Small Business Hub page which highlights our classes, databases, collection resources, and contact information for inquiries. This page gave us a central location that we now use to connect with local partners and referrals from the community, and it helps get our name out in the business community more effectively.

Key Resources

The key resources our library brought to our initiatives included:

- Classroom spaces, which can accommodate sixty or more participants for the Small Business Workshop series with SCORE RI
- Laptops and hotspots for ESOL students to participate remotely
- Workshop area devices and "maker" equipment—printers, button-makers, sewing machines, a T-shirt press, a wood cutter, 3D printers, and computers with design software to support entrepreneurs with prototyping, promotion, graphic design, and more
- Databases like Bizminer and A-Z Database, which we promote during the Small Business Workshops and our ESOL classes

Key Partners

- SCORE RI provides confidential counseling to small businesses as a volunteer organization of working and retired business

owners, professionals, and executives with experience in all aspects of business management. They lend their expertise in teaching our Small Business Workshop series and mentoring participants.
- **The RI Hispanic Chamber of Commerce** represents, promotes, and empowers the growing Hispanic business community in Rhode Island. They were instrumental in helping advertise our classes.
- **The RI Department of State Business Services** division provides guest speakers, resources, further training opportunities, and advice for our participants. They are a great referral source for us.
- **The RI Small Business Development Center** at the University of Rhode Island provides free counseling services and information for start-ups. They've helped us with providing guest speakers and are a referral service for our patrons.

Budget

We budgeted $150,000 for our Small Business Hub programming, which we funded through the Libraries Build Business grant. This funding supports a full-time ESOL teacher, a full-time specialist from Information Services, and administrative time for three more staffers (from Education, Information Services, and Development), as well as funds for purchasing and managing databases and business collections.

Implementing the Nuts and Bolts

In partnership with SCORE RI, we offer a "starting a business" workshop series semi-annually. In these workshops, SCORE counselors present information and provide guidance on such topics as marketing, finance, networking, and writing a business plan, while the library offers guidance on navigating databases, researching, and information on other community resources.

We were looking to add an "on-ramp" for non-native speakers of English to our current services, and so we started to plan for our specialized ESOL class and additional offerings to the community at large. Based on surveying participants, these offerings have included workshops on Google Suite

Tools; how to sell on eBay; financial security workshops presented by local banks; and patents and trades workshops taught by local experts.

After each program, we request participant feedback and ask the question "What do you want to learn next?" We also conducted interviews with participants. Improving our evaluation of programs is a first step in confirming that our offerings are indeed helpful, and identifying what the next steps could be for our business programming.

HOW TO: Develop an ESOL for Business Owners Class

Our "ESOL for Business Owners" course was developed for adult immigrants who want to start or grow their own businesses. It is a year-long specialized English course that focuses on marketing, customer service, finances, and operations. Participants sharpen their English skills through class discussion, reading, and writing. These classes enable participants to improve their own and their employees' English skills in order to expand their markets, improve their access to business assistance resources, and help invigorate the local economy.

This class ensures that minority business owners have more equitable opportunities to utilize resources and be successful. Launching such a class involves the following steps:

1. First, conduct a survey with participants found through your area's adult education agencies, as well as with local businesses owners (we found a list by going through our databases) to help gauge interest, see what types of businesses students run or want to start, identify needs and potential class times, and give you an initial group of potential class participants for the program.
2. Search for an appropriate ESOL curriculum. Local adult education agencies or community colleges would be good places to reach out to for help in designing one. The curriculum should cover vocabulary, grammar, and other syntax that relates to and covers topics essential to all small businesses, including customer service, writing a business plan, licensing, and marketing.
3. Tailor the class to meet the needs of the identified learners. We decided to offer it to intermediate/advanced-level speakers and opened it up to both current business owners and potential

owners, but this type of class can be presented in many different ways. For example, it can be geared to a specific group of entrepreneurs (e.g., restaurant owners, day care providers) if that is your audience.
4. Stretch out your recruitment and be willing to invest a lot of time in scheduling a day and time for the class that works for entrepreneurs. You may start with a large group of interested participants, but the day, time, and the necessary commitment may reduce their availability. Given that, it's important to have wraparound services in place like guest speakers, field trips, drop-in tutoring time, and extra computer drop-in skill lessons.
5. Build camaraderie and rapport within the cohort by developing homework activities around practical issues of their own businesses, and by having students share their reflections in class.

Promoting Your Program

Word of mouth and walk-in traffic are ready-made avenues to recruit people. Additionally, visiting local adult education programs and partner organizations attracts participants. We also rely heavily on e-mail newsletters, digital flyers to partner agencies, social media posts, and exploring new avenues, like sub-Reddits.

Overcoming Roadblocks and Challenges

Transportation and connectivity issues can be barriers to attendance for some students. Offer both in-person and online versions of your classes if possible. You can reach a wider audience if you make it as convenient as possible for your students to attend.

Staff Responsibilities

We have two Education librarians and two Information Services librarians leading this project; a total of five FTE staff support the work of the Small Business Hub. The Education librarians oversee the ESOL class, and the Information Services librarians handle the SCORE workshops and special one-off workshops for the general public. We all collaborate on planning for new workshop offerings and Small Business Hub resources.

Tips, Tricks, and Advice

- Identify needs and gather supports as you go. You'll be able to bring in appropriate speakers and other services to your cohort of learners in response to circumstances. In our case, business owners wanted better computer skills, and we were able to get them into our Excel classes, and find partners who could talk about writing a business plan, starting a web page, and so on. Programs can start small and grow naturally. At first, our Small Business Workshop series was just four classes; but it has since grown to eight to cover additional topics.
- Doing research and outreach in local immigrant communities is key so that the information and services you offer are relevant to these patrons. It's great if you can find a wide range of partners, from organizations that serve immigrant communities on the business side, like a Hispanic chamber of commerce, to organizations that provide refugee services or adult education. This will help you reach a wide audience for an ESOL for Entrepreneurs class.
- Tailor your ESOL curriculum to meet the needs of your patrons. Building up the curriculum based on participants' interests ensures good participation and leads to positive outcomes. For example, a student who runs her own cleaning company benefited from role-playing how to navigate difficult situations with employees in English, in a way that helped her in a similar real-life situation.

PROGRAM 20

Entrepreneurs Launch and Grow

The Entrepreneurial Launch Pad

RICHLAND LIBRARY (COLUMBIA, SC)

Diane Luccy and Mary Kate Quillivan

Setting the Stage

The Entrepreneurial Launch Pad at Richland Library in South Carolina supports emerging businesses at every stage of their development, with a focus on assisting and encouraging minority and woman-owned businesses. This three-pronged approach provides (1) free access to entrepreneur-in-residence (EiR) experts, (2) customized learning and networking, and (3) the Entrepreneurial Library of Things (LoT).

The EiR program was developed in 2018 through a grant. In the first year, we were able to host three EiRs—businesspeople from our community—who met one-on-one with customers who needed help addressing their small business "pain points." Additionally, we offer an artist-in-residence (AiR), who meets with budding artists and creative entrepreneurs to guide them through the process of transforming their art into profits. Targeted programming, networking, and resources also address local business owners' challenges and growth opportunities by means of our growing LoT collection and by hosting the 1 Million Cups program.

Entrepreneurs from marginalized communities have shared with us that they face significant barriers, including a lack of mentors and technical expertise for business start-up. Our programming focuses on these areas as well as financial acumen, reliable resources, and the supportive networking necessary for a successful business. Hosting 1 Million Cups at our Main location has allowed us to keep abreast of the needs of our entrepreneurs, as does the customer feedback from our small business coaching and our targeted small business programs.

> **What Is 1 Million Cups?**
>
> The Ewing Marion Foundation developed 1 Million Cups (1MC) in 2012 as a free program designed to educate, engage, and inspire entrepreneurs around the United States. Since that time, 1MC has spread to more than 160 communities and over one million cups of coffee shared among budding entrepreneurs.
>
> 1MC helps to address barriers that stand in the way of entrepreneur success and is a great way to network with other like-minded small business owners to share resources and support one another at weekly virtual or in-person meetings.

Service Area

- Suburban
- Large, less than 500,000 population

Goals and Impact

The Entrepreneurial Launch Pad was created to reduce the barriers to accessing critical business resources and information. Through our own research and with evidence from local reports, including the Midlands Regional Competitiveness Report, we know that many entrepreneurs leave Columbia for larger markets, such as Atlanta and Charlotte.[1] By offering high-quality programming and related business resources, we hope to address some of the issues that often keep talented entrepreneurs from staying in our community. By investing in local entrepreneurs, we invest in the quality of life in our cities, county, and state.

Getting Started

To get started, begin reaching out to small business community partners in your area to conduct programming on timely topics. While this approach was helpful for our library, we realized that we needed to ramp up our efforts

What Is an EiR?

Richland Library's entrepreneurs-in-residence offer invaluable guidance to new entrepreneurs and budding start-ups through office hours and public programs—thus connecting budding entrepreneurs with peers who have successfully designed, launched, and managed their own new business venture. This helps build an ecosystem that sustains the development and growth of future entrepreneurs in the region.

The EiRs are seasoned community entrepreneurs with proven expertise, a record of accomplishments, and a mentor's heart. They share their real-life experiences to help overcome barriers that can persistently derail small businesses in the early stages of entrepreneurship and beyond.

A top priority of the EiR is to meet individually with entrepreneurs and business owners in one-on-one small-business coaching appointments and discuss the "pain points" they may be experiencing with their businesses and to explore possible solutions, such as marketing, finances, and when to hire employees.

Meet EiR Karen R. Jenkins

Here's one example. Former EiR Karen R. Jenkins is an established entrepreneur in the city of Columbia and beyond with a proven track record and a large following in the community. Karen is also a high-energy leader who collaborated on various successful small business programs, even before she was selected as an EiR by our library.

During her four-month residency, Karen collaborated with many of Richland Library's small business community partners to present high-interest programs on cybersecurity, financials, and trademarks, and she even conducted a small business book group.

Being able to offer the EiR service has proven to be a win-win for both Richland Library and the local community.

---

in this focus area.

With this objective in mind, the Richland Library applied for and was awarded the Google Columbia Impact Challenge Grant in 2018. The GCIC Grant provided us with the funding and the opportunity to create our entrepreneur-in-residence model. The Libraries Build Business grant, awarded to us in 2020, took our EiR service to the next level, while also allowing for the expansion of our Entrepreneurial LoT.

With a smaller budget, we recommend prioritizing one-to-one small business coaching. Using community feedback will help you determine what to include in a small pilot Library of Things collection. Be sure to check out the nonprofit organizations in your community for grant possibilities and potential partnerships for programming. Start small and pilot to determine the specific needs of your community.

Key Resources

The key resources for our initiative included:

- **Entrepreneur-in-residence office or meeting space:** The EiR needs physical space to work and to host meetings and workshops.
- **Entrepreneurial Library of Things:** This collection is a natural evolution of the library's lending model and an extension of the various makerspaces and studios that are available to customers inside our libraries. The LoT aims to reduce the barriers for entrepreneurs, creatives, and lifelong learners by providing access to high-quality equipment. LoT equipment can be reserved for up to one week, with one renewal per checkout period if there are no conflicting reservations. Examples of items that can be borrowed include a podcasting kit, a document camera with extender arm, a backdrop kit, a GorillaPod 3K PRO Rig, a Canon vlogging kit, and much more.
- Several virtual platforms and other resources, including the following:
  - **MyTurn software,** which is used to create the online LoT catalog on the Richland Library website
  - **Calendly software,** which is used by the EiR to schedule the small business coaching appointments

Key Partners

Strong and diverse partnerships are integral to creating a strong, resilient local economy; strengthening community cohesion; transforming educational outcomes for youth; and helping to break the cycle of poverty. With these goals in mind, we partnered with:

- **Benedict College Women's Business Center (WBC):** The WBC stimulates innovation and entrepreneurship in underserved

communities by supporting and growing women and minority-owned businesses.
- **Midlands Technical College:** This school collaborated on the Icehouse Entrepreneurial Training, a series of eight classes that provide the foundation for business start-up, using the example in the book *Who Owns the Icehouse? Eight Life Lessons from an Unlikely Entrepreneur* by Clifton Taulbert.
- **City of Columbia, Office of Business Opportunities, and Richland County, Office of Small Business Opportunities:** These agencies are committed to supporting initiatives that benefit small, minority, veteran, and women-owned businesses that are located in, or want to do business with, the city of Columbia or Richland County.
- **SC Small Business Development Centers (SBDC):** The mission of the SBDC is to advance South Carolina's economic development by helping entrepreneurs grow successful businesses.
- **Small Business Administration (SBA):** The SBA is an independent agency of the federal government that works to aid, counsel, assist, and protect the interests of small businesses, preserve free and competitive enterprise, and maintain and strengthen the overall economy of our nation.

When looking for partners in your community, seek out organizations that align with your goals. Check in with local business centers, colleges, and the local programs offered by your city government.

Budget

We budgeted $140,000 for our program, which we funded through the Libraries Build Business grant. With our funding we pay for our EiR residencies (three per year), programming supplies and speakers, and our LoT equipment.

For libraries that may not have access to grant funds, consider starting small and offering a collection of items that patrons can borrow, such as a podcasting kit and camera kit, and then slowly build your LoT. The EiR service could also be scaled slowly by including local small business experts who are willing to volunteer their time.

Implementing the Nuts and Bolts

Our EiRs have taken our small business services to the next level by facilitating customized learning and networking opportunities, including one-on-one small-business coaching appointments, targeted programming in their respective areas of expertise, entrepreneur book groups, small business focus groups, and through social media. Our weekly networking through 1 Million Cups has fostered a connected community of like-minded individuals, and the library's reservable meeting spaces are an invaluable resource for entrepreneurs.

After each program, we ask participants to complete an exit survey. We use this feedback from the EiRs and our program participants to enhance our services.

HOW TO: Create an EiR Program at Your Library

1. First, develop the EiR job description. In our case, we were looking for an active entrepreneur in the community, in business 3–5 years, with a demonstrated commitment to EDI, and a confident user of social media to fulfill a four-month residency (10 hours per week). Advertise the position on your library's website and on social media platforms.
2. Select candidates to interview. We asked interviewees to prepare a brief presentation on a timely small business topic. After the interviews, make your final selection(s), and then make an offer.
3. Work with your library's marketing department or PR team to promote the EiR and residency events.
4. Implement onboarding and software training for the new EiR.
5. Create and schedule events/programs over the residency period (at Richland, this is four months).
6. Facilitate the programs, record the events, and incorporate program exit surveys.
7. Send out a follow-up e-mail for each program to participants and include the recording.

8. Create meeting or office space so that the EiR can hold one-on-one appointments.
9. Periodically meet with the EiR to support and ensure successful outcomes. Set up a monthly check-in and a monthly report from the EiR to track the number of appointments scheduled, the number of customers assisted, types of businesses, and so on.
10. Send an end-of-residency EiR survey to participants to review and improve the experience.

Promoting Your Program

Keep your library website and social media updated with your programs and events and involve your EiR and other staff in spreading the word. Richland Library has an active Small Business and Entrepreneurs group on Facebook, a Richland Library Residents web page, a weekly e-blast that is e-mailed to over 800 recipients, and dedicated staff creating website posts that we use to promote our small business programs. In addition, our EiR promotes and recruits participants when conducting one-on-one small-business coaching appointments.

Overcoming Roadblocks and Challenges

Working with partners can be tricky. Remember, the small business services you are creating for the community are intended to complement, not compete, with the services provided by other local small business agencies and organizations.

Staff Responsibilities

Two co-managers are assisted by a Small Business team of six: staff from the Business and Careers and Arts and Media departments.

- The Business and Careers manager oversees the EiR service and manages small business programming.
- The Arts and Media manager oversees the Entrepreneurial LoT and its technology.
- The Small Business team explains and understands the grant process, assists the co-managers with aspects of the Libraries Build Business grant, and are trained to take the lead in any

future grant opportunity.

Tips, Tricks, and Advice

- **Helping customers learn, create, and share is critical.** All entrepreneurs are makers, and we are here to help them "make" in whatever way we can. Often, inexpensive resources and solutions can be found to meet your patrons' needs. However, some innovations, such as equipment and residencies, can be costly. We believe this cost is well worth the investment, though.
- **Stay connected.** Richland Library meets virtually each month with our small-business community partners to share small business resources, cross-promote programs and services, and collaborate on upcoming events.
- **Make it a top priority to become the "Small Business Information Hub"** in your community. Richland Library acts as a content developer/expert and an outreach vehicle, thereby enhancing and expanding efforts to serve the most vulnerable in Columbia and Richland County.
- **Scaling is crucial.** Don't think that you must begin your small business services in a major way. Begin with one small business-related service, be successful at it, and once it is established, build on that solid foundation.

NOTE

1. "2021 Midlands Regional Competitiveness Report," 2021, Engenuity SC, www.engenuitysc.com/competitiveness-report.

PROGRAM 21

Biz.ability Workshops
Tools to Empower You

ROUND ROCK (TX) PUBLIC LIBRARY

Geeta Halley

Setting the Stage

Small businesses significantly impact the Texas economy, representing 98.7 percent of all employers. This fact, combined with regular entrepreneurial-related questions from members of our community, prompted the Round Rock Public Library (RRPL) to begin offering free small business workshops to the public. These free, timely workshops are presented by recognized experts and practitioners and cover a variety of issues facing small business owners and entrepreneurs.

The topics that have been covered include finances, marketing, human resources, taxes, and strategic planning. We offer two Biz.ability workshop series a year, one in the spring and another in the fall. We have had up to 70 people per workshop, with an average of approximately 35.

Service Area

- Suburban
- Large, less than 500,000 population

Goals and Impact

The most difficult obstacles to starting a business include the process of conducting market research, defining a sales strategy, and securing the necessary funding. Members of the RRPL staff frequently receive questions from aspiring entrepreneurs, some examples of which are listed below:

- "I'm a landscaper and want to get some landscaping jobs. How do I go about that?"
- "I retired from Dell and would like to start a small business, but I don't know if it should be an LLC or a sole proprietorship. What's the difference?"
- "How do I find out the demographics for the zip codes I plan to service?"
- "I'd like to start a remodeling business, but don't know where to start. Can you help?"

These real-life questions from our library customers prompted us to start Biz.ability as a public service to residents who have an interest in starting their own business or those who already own a business but are looking to gain more knowledge.

Biz.ability Success: The Fades Barbershop

Tina Ward, the co-owner of Fades Barbershop in Round Rock, is a past participant in Biz.ability. She learned about the free workshops from a Facebook post, and once she attended she realized they were a game-changer. She attributes much of her barbershop's success to what she learned in the workshops. "This is a free resource for local business owners who may not have the knowledge of how to find this type of information," Ward said. "It is also amazing how it brings the small business community together in a way that builds an incredibly strong network."

Getting Started

First, connect with your local chamber of commerce, Small Business Administration office, Small Business Development Center, or economic development office. Attend their events so that you can network there and become a recognizable face. We attend the local chamber's Power Luncheon and other "mixer"-type events. These events are perfect opportunities to talk about your library resources with those at your table. These "mixer" events are also places to find speakers from your own community. Their staff make great workshop presenters. Banks are also great partners; they can give classes on loan applications and financing options. Start small by holding one workshop a month, and then grow the program as you get more comfortable with the process.

Key Resources
Our key resources for this initiative included:

- **Equipment:** Tables and chairs, meeting room
- **Technology:** Projector, screen, HDMI cable, and speaker laptop or library laptop
- **Project Outcome survey tool:** We use immediate and follow-up surveys to learn what Biz.ability attendees benefited from the most. Project Outcome is a free toolkit designed to help public libraries understand and share the impact of essential library services and programs by providing simple surveys and an easy-to-use process for measuring and analyzing outcomes. Project Outcome is managed by the Public Library Association.

Key Partners
Austin SCORE has a calendar of workshops they publish every month. They have great volunteer speakers with proven credentials. We go through their workshop listings and select the ones we know address a need identified by either a Project Outcome Survey or an attendee comment, or that involve a currently "hot" topic.

Our other partners include the Round Rock Chamber of Commerce, the city of Round Rock, the Small Business Administration, and the Small Business Development Center.

Budget
The Biz.ability series is sponsored by the Friends of the Round Rock Public Library. As of now, every speaker has presented workshops for free. They recognize the benefit of presenting at a workshop: it promotes their own small business or simply allows them to give back to the community. We buy Starbucks gift cards for our presenters as a small thank you.

Implementing the Nuts and Bolts

Since its inception in 2015, Biz.ability has provided relevant and timely education to small business owners and entrepreneurs free of cost, along with networking opportunities, resources, mentoring through SCORE, and access to business machines like a fax, photocopier, mobile printer, and Chromebooks and hotspots.

The Biz.ability series of in-person workshops is held twice a year, in the spring and fall, and typically consists of 6–10 workshops per series. Each workshop consists of one session. The program components for each workshop are as follows:

1. A staff member introduces the Round Rock Public Library and explains why our public library holds workshops for small businesses. This introductory spiel covers the library's digital resources available for small businesses, such as Reference Solutions, LinkedIn Learning, Gale Business Plan Builder, and Gale Business-Demographics Now. Resources available through the city of Round Rock are also introduced, especially global information system (GIS) resources. An example of the monetary value of using library resources is shared, such as the Round Rock citizen who renewed his personal subscription to Reference Solutions for $3,000 when he could have used the same resource for free with his library card. And lastly, the requirements to register for a library card at the Round Rock Public Library are shared.
2. Austin SCORE is introduced, and the services that SCORE offers free of charge are explained. We mention their mentoring sessions, located here at the Round Rock Public Library.
3. The workshop speaker and participants do their introductions. The speaker asks each participant to share one line about their business. This promotes networking among participants.
4. The workshop content is shared, and attendees are given time to ask questions.
5. Attendees are also directed to stop by a table with relevant library materials on the topic, which are given to each attendee—print and digital formats are available.

Promoting Your Program

We use Facebook and the library's website to promote Biz.ability. We also collect attendees' e-mail addresses at each Biz.ability workshop and send out flyers to previous attendees. Our local newspaper, the *Round Rock*

Leader, often features a story on Biz.ability a few weeks before a new workshop series begins.

Overcoming Roadblocks and Challenges

The only roadblock we have run into is attendance at the workshops. We use Eventbrite for registration. Since the workshops are free, we have many no-shows. To overcome this challenge, we create 100 tickets per workshop, knowing that only 40 percent of those who registered will attend.

Staff Responsibilities

Staff are a key resource. We have one staff member who organizes the workshops for each series. They meet with SCORE and attend small business events organized by the chamber of commerce, the city, and other organizations. At each workshop, a staff member is present to give an overview of the library resources available to small businesses, as well as answer follow-up e-mails. The staff member must be willing to network and travel. This not only increases the library's visibility in the community, but also facilitates connections with potential speakers.

Tips, Tricks, and Advice

- **Patience is key.** The seed for Biz.ability was planted at a workshop at the 2012 Public Library Association conference. It took three years to find the right partner in SCORE and develop our relationships through networking.
- **Be creative with partnerships and resources.** If you don't have a SCORE chapter or a local chamber, reach out to your local commercial bank. They can present on creating a business plan and financing options. Don't overlook your city government's resources either. For example, the city's GIS manager contacted us because he wanted to teach our small businesses how to use the city's extensive GIS resources. Finally, business database vendors are always willing to present at a chamber event or at the library. Invite them. Before we sign a contract with a business database vendor, we stipulate that they give at least one workshop a year to our community.

- Visit and network with your fellow librarians in the nearest big city or town. You may be able to pool your resources. Your state library is also a good resource.
- Demonstrate the library's role in the business ecosystem to partners, officials, participants, and other stakeholders. Our communities consider us to be knowledgeable about resources and information. We can use this inherent trust to strategically further our library's visibility and relevance in the community by supporting economic development. Embedding ourselves in our business communities shows the mayor, the city council, and other stakeholders that the library is not just a warehouse of books, but a vital player in economic development. For grant-writing, updates to the city council, and for promotional purposes, we use data from our Project Outcome surveys and feedback from our participants.

PROGRAM 22

Business Networking through Community-Building

SBPL Building Business

SANTA BARBARA (CA) PUBLIC LIBRARY

Ahmad Merza and Molly Wetta

Setting the Stage

Santa Barbara Public Library (SBPL) Building Business is a multifaceted approach to bringing business resources to some of our area's most vulnerable populations, including the local Spanish-speaking community. The program leverages community partners and leaders to create tailored programs that will target specific needs. The SBPL Building Business initiative supports the city of Santa Barbara's strategic goals related to economic vitality by helping local businesses and entrepreneurs thrive through hands-on, practical learning opportunities, networking, and specialized resources. These services complement SBPL's workforce development program and other services under the umbrella of our Adult Education division.

Service Area

- Urban
- Medium, less than 99,000 population

Goals and Impact

SBPL empowers business owners and entrepreneurs by connecting them to each other, to resources, and to our partner support agencies through a slate of programs that include classes on business databases, a weekly entrepreneurial networking group, and workshops led by local experts and community partners. While several organizations provide business support in the community, SBPL recognized a need for free, high-quality resources and opportunities for Spanish-speaking business owners and entrepreneurs. SBPL's goal is to identify needs within the community and begin building programs and services that meet those needs. Through outreach and collaboration with local experts, SBPL launched business services in Spanish. To do this, SBPL Building Business provides access to a network of bilingual resources throughout the community.

Getting Started

To get started, you first need to inventory what services and programs already exist in the community, acquaint yourself with all the community agencies and organizations that serve the business community, and reach out to them to understand the gaps in those services. Learn about all the fee-based business programs and services and see if you can replicate a similar program or service for free with the help of grants or community partners. If your library has business databases or other tools, highlight them to your community partners and encourage them to share this information with their audience.

It is important to identify potential community partners. Hosting weekly business discussions and networking meetings helps build community. For the networking meetings, try to recruit community members and business owners to be part of your organizing team.

Key Resources

The key resources our library brought to the initiative included the following:

- Access to two digital database resources that are excellent tools in helping business owners craft the market research portion of their business plans:

    1. ReferenceUSA, which is a great source of business and residential information for reference and research; our patrons use ReferenceUSA to obtain a targeted list of potential clients and see industry trends within a time frame

2. **SizeUp**, which is a business resource tool that provides data-driven insights to help small businesses and entrepreneurs; with SizeUp, local businesses can see how they stack up against similar businesses in their industry, check benchmark performances, assess the competition, learn about target areas for their next advertising campaign, and perform tailored demographic analyses

- Hotspots and laptop checkouts
- Funding for scholarships to courses such as ServSafe Food Handlers and Food Managers
- Print resources in Spanish and English

Key Partners

- Through the **1 Million Cups** program, we have a stellar local organizing team who are passionate and eager to assist small businesses and entrepreneurs in our community. The organizing team is composed of community leaders with specialties in banking, web design, and insurance.
- Our relationship with the **Women's Economic Ventures** (WEV) group enables our library to teach the market research portions of the group's "Live Business Program" courses quarterly in English and Spanish. We also partner with WEV to host business mixers and offer free business-focused financial literacy courses to the community. We are currently working with WEV to develop a curriculum for nannies and childcare providers to get credentialed through the state and work towards opening a business, fulfilling a large need in our community. WEV students may also schedule one-on-one business research consultations with a librarian so they can better understand and use the databases for their business plans. WEV recently gave our library their Partner of the Year Award, reflecting the strength of the partnership we have cultivated, as well as the difference we have made in our shared community.

Budget

Outside of staff time, our program can be achieved with a relatively small budget. The two databases that we utilize have a combined cost of about $15,000 annually. We have a coffee sponsor for our networking meeting group. The ServSafe program is made possible with grant support from the Santa Barbara Adult Education Consortium, and we have worked with ServSafe to get its course prices reduced. Some of our courses on financial literacy were paid through a generous grant through the California State Library; after that grant ended, our partner agencies began hosting business mixers where they covered most food costs and door prizes in exchange for our providing the space and assisting with marketing. Our radio ads on the Radio Bronco station usually run roughly $1,000 a year.

Implementing the Nuts and Bolts

SBPL Building Business began with our hosting a chapter of the Kauffman Foundation's national 1 Million Cups program. We hold weekly networking and business discussion meetings for the community at our Eastside branch library, which serves many BIPOC individuals in our community. The meetings are designed to facilitate networking with entrepreneurs and aspiring business owners. The presenters talk about the obstacles and challenges they have encountered and about recent successes that may be inspirational to others. There is time for Q&A and networking at each meeting.

All of our programming, networking, and reference are offered in both English and Spanish. Library staffers provide one-on-one research consultations using our business databases, financial literacy workshops, and bilingual networking mixers.

As we developed these services, we engaged local business organizations in discussion to learn more about their goals and initiatives. We shared how the library could support them in various ways: helping promote their program, connecting their organization to other community organizations, and using some of our library spaces to host events. By taking this approach, we were able to build a network of like-minded partner organizations which helped us to build our offerings.

Promoting Your Program

Leverage community leaders and partners to help get your message out to businesses. We feature programs in the city's weekly newsletters;

cross-promote programs with other partner agencies; and announce upcoming events in our weekly 1 Million Cups meetings. We typically record all the presenters from our 1 Million Cups meetings and post this to YouTube and the 1 Million Cups website. We promote our upcoming library business events on all our social media accounts and have a dedicated staff member who specializes in graphic design, so our flyers, posters, and social media images are polished and eye-catching.

Be sure to have multilingual promotional outreach if your program serves speakers of other languages. For our community, we have learned that one of the best ways to promote our programs to Spanish-speaking patrons is to do radio ads with Radio Bronco, a local Spanish-language radio station. We have developed a great relationship with the Radio Bronco team, and they go above and beyond to support the library by letting us promote our events on air.

Overcoming Roadblocks and Challenges

We encountered a few challenges in the beginning, particularly with building the initial trust from the business and entrepreneurial communities. When we were launching our 1 Million Cups meetings, we saw some pushback because our community had many networking groups—but none of them were free.

Initially, there were a few 1 Million Cups meetings where we had to redirect attendees who tried to use the group for investor pitches or sales pitches, which goes against the core values of the 1 Million Cups program. We were able to shift and instead let people use our platform to practice pitches and get feedback from the audience on what they could have said or done better. There was also some hesitation initially from partner agencies because they were very protective of the people they support and wanted to attend meetings first with our group before they recommended it to their networks. To overcome this, we made it a point to be very consistent and persistent, and we continued to meet weekly and looked for opportunities where the library could assist and support the organizations. Over time we built community support because people began to see that this was a different type of networking group based on community.

Another challenge was building trust within our Spanish-speaking business community. It was tough to make connections and build community at first. We decided to reach out to local organizations like Casa De La Raza and the Latino Elder Outreach Network that serve these populations, and began

> ### ServSafe Licensure Programs
>
> Providing scholarships and proctoring ServSafe tests met a specific need in our community and supports our core mission of community education.
>
> With the support of one of our partners, the Santa Barbara Adult Education Consortium, the library offers free ServSafe Food Handler and Food Manager courses, a required certification in the state of California for individuals who handle food. Through discussions with small restaurant owners and patrons who utilize our workforce development programs, we were able to identify a need in the community for these certifications. The ServSafe tests were not easily available locally, and the associated costs were a burden to both job seekers and small business owners.
>
> To get the word out, we reach out to business owners who have new staff or staff with expiring certifications, and we cover the cost of the ServSafe course for their staff. We also provide laptops and internet hotspots for those who need to take the course online. To further eliminate barriers, we have staff who are trained proctors to proctor the exams. This saves time for the patrons who would otherwise have to travel outside the county to the nearest proctor, who is over forty-five minutes away.

to build relationships with them. Some of our most successful programs have consisted of two or three partner organizations that all worked towards a common goal. In addition to working with those groups, this has led us to other library partnership opportunities and helped build our reputation in the community.

Staff Responsibilities

Serving the business community is a team effort at our library. We have a lead librarian who coordinates the programs and works with partner agencies; support staff who are trained in the business databases; and a team of Spanish-speaking staff who conduct the training and research consultations for our Spanish-speaking entrepreneurs and community partners. We also get support from our workforce development program staff, who help us work with business owners and build relationships with business owners so that we can promote job openings when they have vacant positions.

Tips, Tricks, and Advice

- Attend business-networking events. If your community doesn't have any, this may be a fruitful opportunity for your library to work with some partner agencies and put one together.
- Your library should not be afraid to work with multiple community partners at once, as this will connect people to different organizations and the library will be seen as a bridge. Once you have built this community and gained its trust, you can begin to identify its needs and help develop partnerships with local organizations.

PROGRAM 23

Be a Neighborhood Champion

Small Business Boot Camp

SPOKANE COUNTY (WA) LIBRARY DISTRICT

Danielle Milton, Stacey Goddard, Crystal Miller, and Sarah O'Hare

Setting the Stage

The Spokane County Library District (SCLD) offers Small Business Boot Camp (SBBC) for business owners and entrepreneurs in the Deer Park area, a rural, low-income community with limited internet access that's over twenty miles north of the Spokane city center, where most support services are located. The district's Deer Park Library is an active member in the Deer Park Chamber of Commerce and has an official role as a Neighborhood Champion, promoting Small Business Saturday (SBS) and the Shop Small movement.

What Is a Neighborhood Champion?

Neighborhood Champions support small businesses by spreading awareness and demonstrating the value in shopping small. They may host events or share resources.

The Deer Park Library's goal in becoming a Neighborhood Champion was to support and drive traffic to local businesses in the community we serve by encouraging people to shop local. The Small Business Boot Camp has grown from 14 participating businesses in 2016 to 43 participating businesses in 2019.

Service Area

- Suburban and Rural
- Large, less than 500,000 population

Goals and Impact

Through working with our local chamber of commerce, we learned that the business community sparingly communicated with each other and rarely shared leads. We also noticed that there was a lack of decoration, special displays, and promotions to catch the eye of shoppers during holidays and throughout the year. It seemed like the local business community could benefit from training on the importance of networking, marketing, and merchandising.

Small Business Boot Camp helps build entrepreneurial skills such as networking, pricing, driving traffic to websites, and effective marketing, and helps support businesses in the community through training and micro-grants. Through grant funding, we were able to offer micro-grant funds, which gave participants the ability to implement something they learned during the program that will further their businesses' success.

The SBBC program allows libraries to provide specific training to entrepreneurs on networking, referrals, using demographic research databases, and more. This gives entrepreneurs the tools they need to thrive year-round. Using a cohort model, where a group of interested and engaged entrepreneurs work together to master skills and concepts, the program can build a stronger business community.

Getting Started

To get started, begin reaching out to local partners, such as your local chamber of commerce and a local volunteer network. From there, begin to develop a program and content that suit your local community, such as marketing and merchandising classes.

Key Resources

Our library brought the following key resources to its initiative:

- **In-person**: Library meeting space, internet access, and staffing for the seminars
- **Virtual**: Hotspots, Zoom subscription, Entrepreneurial Mindset Training workbooks
- **Optional**: Funding for micro-grants, meals during networking events, and childcare

Key Partners

For our program, we partnered with Spokane SCORE, which provides volunteer business counselors and mentors to strengthen the Spokane business community. Our library already had an existing relationship with the local SCORE chapter. Once a month, a volunteer mentor from Spokane SCORE would teach a workshop on a variety of business-related topics for entrepreneurs at the library.

Your local chamber of commerce will have invaluable connections with the business community and would be a great addition to your program by extending the library's reach. Begin by attending the chamber's events regularly to learn about the business community in your area. We worked directly with the Deer Park Chamber of Commerce for our program.

Budget

We budgeted nearly $62,000 for the SBBC program, which we funded through the Libraries Build Business grant. With our funding we provided micro-grants amounting to $500 per participant, which supplied a small incentive for participants to complete the program. This was especially helpful for our year-long program. Upon completion of the program, participants received their micro-grant.

Our budget also included costs for speakers and trainers, a subscription to the EBSCO Entrepreneurial Mindset Training digital resource, direct staff support, promotion and marketing materials, and meals and materials for in-person meetings.

But you can do this program on a smaller scale with a smaller budget. If you're unable to find funding for micro-grants, offer other incentives such as gift cards to local businesses. Partner with community organizations where you can share expertise and use the resources and databases that you already have on hand.

> ### Micro-Grants
>
> As an incentive for completing our program, we offered micro-grants for business owners to use toward their business needs. Some of our participants used their funds to:
>
> - Purchase an enamel kiln to expand mediums in their art business.
> - Expand the marketing and advertising for dentistry with oral health flyers and referral slips created for after-hours dental needs.
> - Print business cards, purchase office supplies, and apply funds toward additional real estate courses for a realtor.

Implementing the Nuts and Bolts

Our library's Small Business Boot Camp was a year-long program, with monthly seminars for a cohort of entrepreneurs and an added online component of the Entrepreneurial Mindset Training. Monthly topics included marketing, goal-setting, tax basics, financial basics, branding, social media, hiring, driving traffic to websites, and a session about how to use the library's databases for businesses. The program included regular networking opportunities and presentations, and assistance with childcare was offered during all sessions meeting in-person. Knowledgeable, trained staff were available for personalized assistance in the form of one-on-one appointments to demonstrate the expanded business resources the library offers, such as how to use our business databases and navigate our physical collection.

In each two-hour session there was time for participants to share updates about what they were currently working on. We also opened a Microsoft Teams channel for participants to communicate and collaborate with each other. Participants had access to the Entrepreneurial Mindset Training course online and were able to complete it at their own pace; in addition, we purchased accompanying physical workbooks for the Entrepreneurial Mindset Training course because we knew there were challenges with internet connectivity. Participants that attended a majority of the sessions received a micro-grant for their business at the end of the year-long program.

We used three surveys and would recommend that libraries looking to offer this program, consider doing the same—surveying participants at the beginning, middle, and end of the program. We also conducted one-on-one interviews with participants at the end of the program to gauge what was beneficial and to serve as a touchpoint to provide resources or answer additional questions. These evaluation tools allow the library to determine how to improve our programs for future cohorts and how to improve our small business resources and services for the wider public.

HOW TO: Small Business Saturday

Small Business Saturday (SBS) is a national event, supported by American Express, which is held on the Saturday after Thanksgiving. American Express sends each library Neighborhood Champion a box full of swag, including promotional SBS cards, posters, stickers, totes, and pens. The shopping totes are a great promotion vehicle for the event, and help to spread the word as people are out shopping.

Leading up to SBS, work with business owners to create interest and excitement among residents at the prospect of patronizing their local shops and restaurants.

1. Create an activity such as a passport or bingo card that participating shoppers need to have stamped by visiting several local shops.
2. Provide marketing materials and promotion for the activity via all outlets and social media channels.
3. Secure small, donated prizes for shoppers who complete the activity, such as gift cards from participating businesses.
4. Ask business owners to provide space for the activity and assist with promotion by posting the marketing materials and using their own social media channels.
5. In the week leading up to SBS, go out to the participating businesses and prepare them with materials for the event (passport or bingo card, a stamper, etc.).
6. On the day of the event, set up a welcome station with additional activities and swag in the library. Shoppers can pick up an activity to begin their shopping and redeem their completed activities at the library station for the prize.

Shop owners have typically reported an increase in revenue on Small Business Saturday, and the library is glad to help give them a boost.

Promoting Your Program

To promote your event, connect with your local chamber of commerce and community business groups. In addition, consider various marketing strategies and word of mouth around your community. We mailed letters out to small business owners in the community, in addition to word of mouth from staff to customers, online promotion, social media, and the local newspaper in the Deer Park area. Because Deer Park is such a small community, staff at the Deer Park Library were the biggest advocates for sharing information about the SBBC program.

Overcoming Roadblocks and Challenges

- **Communication with partners:** Formalize communication with partners and put agreements in place through Memorandums of Understanding (MOUs) when possible. This will help to avoid miscommunications about expectations and roles. Miscommunication led us to end one working relationship on this project.
- **Lack of participation:** A year-long program is a large commitment for a busy entrepreneur. We saw a decline in attendance and participation as the year progressed. We tried to promote continued engagement among participants, but with only limited success. We would recommend a shorter time frame for the program, such as six months.
- **Internet connectivity:** Virtual programming led to challenges for rural participants. The library purchased hotspots for those participants to use for the duration of the program.

Staff Responsibilities

We had two lead librarians for this project. Working together, they designed the program, collaborated with our Communication Department to develop promotional materials, scheduled and hosted the workshops, collaborated with the Spokane SCORE volunteers, and received EBSCO training to facilitate the Entrepreneurial Mindset Training course. Two additional librarians supported the program in a smaller capacity.

Tips, Tricks, and Advice

- The Neighborhood Champion program from American Express is an easy starting point. They have activity templates, information, and marketing materials for the Small Business Saturday program. This is a great way to get to know your business community, build relationships, and learn their needs to plan future programming like our SBBC.
- Collaborate with local organizations that are already providing business support, education, or networking opportunities. If you aren't already active in the business community, reach out to the various organizations, such as chambers of commerce, local SCORE chapters, and other business groups.
- Start listening. Start small by attending regular business partner meetings and listening to discover their needs. By listening, you can start to figure out how the library can help support the organization and develop a strong partnership with it to benefit the community.
- Brainstorm possible roadblocks for your program participants and their experience with your program. Problem-solve beforehand in case any problems arise. For example, we budgeted for childcare to lower the barriers for people with children to attend the program. For virtual programming, we sought hotspots for participants who experienced trouble connecting to the internet.
- Create the topics your program will cover based on feedback from participants, ensuring that the content is relevant to their needs. All communities are unique and may need different resources and approaches.

PROGRAM 24

Meet Them Where They Are
Small Business Outreach

ST. LOUIS COUNTY (MO) LIBRARY

Jennifer Hyun-Lynn Gibson

Setting the Stage

The St. Louis County Library (SLCL) provides free resources and services to increase the success, equity, and inclusion of people of color and underrepresented groups in our business community. Since 2012 we have offered services that include classes at the library, one-on-one teaching sessions, and an annual Small Business Expo. However, entrepreneurs are pulled in many directions and if they are not already coming to the library, it is unlikely they will do so. Only by bringing our services and information to them, where they are, can we connect business owners with our valuable resources and services.

Service Area
- Suburban
- Large, less than 500,000 population

Goals and Impact

The two goals of outreach are to spread awareness of what our library offers and to create new library users. Business owners are unlikely to discover the library's resources themselves. Outreach creates opportunities to find entrepreneurs and demonstrate what the library offers. We can then persuade them to attend programs and learn to use library research to inform their decisions and plans.

We impact entrepreneurs who learn to use the library in new ways: prospective business owners can devise plans and seek funding; existing businesses can save thousands on marketing research; and salespeople can generate leads from consumer and demographic information. These activities have real financial impact on individuals and our community and allow entrepreneurs to redirect their funds elsewhere.

Getting Started

Put yourself in the shoes of a local entrepreneur. Consider what your library offers from their perspective, find places where they gather, and go where they are. Listen and learn as you orient yourself, and be watchful for needs the library can address. Talk one-on-one with every business owner you can and tell them how your library can help. Apply your research skills, and identify local organizations that are helping people to start or grow a small business. The Small Business Administration website is a great place to start, and a simple internet search will help you find local nonprofit organizations. Create a list of contacts, reach out to them, and soon you'll be creating opportunities to promote your library's support for entrepreneurs.

Key Resources
Our library brought the following key resources to its initiative:

- Library card-making supplies
- Technology
  - Laptop/tablet to demonstrate online research and aid in presentations
  - Wi-Fi hotspot
- Promotional materials
  - Giveaways like program flyers, business cards, candy
  - Branded items for exhibiting, like tablecloths, signs, and banners

Key Partners

We work with entrepreneur support organizations (ESOs) that support small businesses at any stage, and we favor partners that help us reach women and people of color. We especially value ESOs that provide expertise and programming at the library in specialty areas like law and finance. We invite our partners to exhibit and give presentations at our annual Small Business & Nonprofit Expo. The following organizations are some of our most productive partners:

- **Legal Services of Eastern Missouri** provides monthly legal office hours for entrepreneurs at the library. They teach library classes on compliance for nonprofits, legal steps to start a business, and trademark for business.
- **Onyx Business Solutions** supports women's economic development through educational programming.
- **SCORE** hosts workshops where we present library resources and make library cards.
- **The local Small Business Administration office** brings classes to the library on topics like finding lenders, retirees starting businesses, federal contracting, and credit-building and banking.
- **The University of Missouri's Small Business Development Center** provides workshops on starting a business, financial management, and online marketing.

Budget

Small business outreach does not require a large budget. When attending mostly free events, transportation costs are the main expense. If funds are available, one-time purchases of a laptop or tablet will make demonstrations and card-making easier. Wi-Fi hotspots are helpful, and you may choose to pay fees to exhibit at large events, but those are optional.

Implementing the Nuts and Bolts

Small business outreach is not one-size-fits-all. Every library develops its own style to suit its specific goals, community, resources, and capacity. Keep your goals in mind and let those objectives guide you. The following four steps provide a general approach to starting outreach.

> **Starting Conversations with Business Owners**
>
> Striking up a conversation with business owners can be daunting. We need to break the ice and lay the groundwork for steering the conversation to the library's resources for business. The following have been useful conversation starters.
>
> - "Tell me about your business—what do you do?
>   How do you find your customers?"
> - "This is a really cool product/service.
>   What are the best ways you've gotten sales leads?"
> - "In your field, how do you find info and demographics
>   to help with decisions and planning?"
> - "Did you know the public library can save small businesses
>   more than $13,000 each year?"

1. Know what you have to offer. This step is crucial. You must have a firm grasp of what you are selling before you can sell it. List everything your library offers entrepreneurs, including spaces, technology, information resources, and services. Consider every item from the entrepreneur's perspective—what is valuable and why? This exercise will give you knowledge and confidence to build your elevator pitch for outreach.
2. Go to free events and places where entrepreneurs gather. Use your research skills to find these places and events. Put yourself in the shoes of someone trying to start a business for the first time. Your goal is to interact with any prospective or current business owner who will listen. Examples include 1 Million Cups events, resource fairs, business conventions, speed networking events, chamber of commerce meetings, craft fairs, and farmer's markets.

    These types of events bring you face-to-face with business owners and plunge you into the experience of pitching the library. Experience doing this outreach will inevitably lead to perfected sales pitches, a tough skin from hearing "no thanks," new library cards, sign-ups for library programs and services, more outreach opportunities, and chances to meet ESOs.

3. Get to know ESOs and make contact with them. Apply your library skills to look for ESOs in your area and think strategically about what you want to accomplish with them. While searching, consider the area and populations served, the services they offer or don't offer, and whether their mission is compatible with the library's mission. Develop a list of ESOs that you would like to start with.

   Examples of ESOs to look for include chambers of commerce, incubators, accelerators, coworking spaces, nonprofits offering educational programs for entrepreneurs, organizations supporting underrepresented groups, SCORE, the Small Business Administration, Small Business Development Centers, and the Urban League.

   When you connect with an ESO, read the room in terms of their interest and needs. Work together to create an outreach approach that suits you both. Examples include sending library flyers and program calendars, attending their upcoming events or meetings, participating in their resource fairs, providing materials and training to their staff so they can promote the library to their clients, and providing workshops directly to their clients. Confirm dates as soon as possible and lock in those events.

4. Outreach grows and can evolve into teaching opportunities. As you fulfill these outreach opportunities, your web of contacts and opportunities will grow exponentially. Every contact could lead to more opportunities to meet entrepreneurs. We reached a point where new outreach opportunities mostly came from previous outreach events, and the types of events shifted to mostly group teaching sessions.

   Teaching a group of entrepreneurs about library services is the most evolved form of outreach—you are now bringing customized library classes to business owners where they are. You have a receptive audience that is primed to learn. We have taught library research sessions in a nonprofit business educational series, a biotech start-up incubator's training program, a YMCA teen summer program, high school special-interest tracks, and even at staff meetings for insurance, real estate, antiques, and radio advertising sales teams.

After a while, outreach opportunities will come to you. You are invited to return to events or to repeat teaching engagements frequently. New people are attending your programs and using the services at your library. You refer library patrons to trusted partners. You've become part of your community's entrepreneurial ecosystem by demonstrating your commitment to supporting small businesses. The expertise you have gained will guide your outreach and collaborations going forward.

Promoting Your Program

Outreach is all about promotion and adopting an entrepreneurial mindset. As we meet new people and ESOs, we are constantly learning and keeping up with the evolving nature of our community. Any interaction is a new chance to promote small business services at the library.

We ask ESOs to distribute flyers about our services and upcoming library programs. We have an opt-in monthly e-mail with updates about small business news and classes. We are always reaching out to ESOs that are new or new to us. We have conversations to build awareness of what the library offers and why it is worthwhile to learn.

When having these conversations, knowing the dollar value of what we can provide gives our library staff confidence about the worth of the services and information we bring to the community. We can determine this dollar value by using the Small Business Value Calculator.

> ### The Small Business Value Calculator
>
> The St. Louis County Library created the Small Business Value Calculator in 2018. Inspired by Library Value Calculators, the purpose of this tool is to put a monetary value on the services we provide. To build the calculator, we listed all of the small business resources and services we offer at SLCL and looked for what they might cost on the open market. The bottom line that we came up with, $13,000 (per patron), is astounding, and that figure allows us to grab the attention of anyone we talk with, including business owners, library staff, and community stakeholders. After hearing this number, entrepreneurs are eager to hear about the library's resources for marketing, demographic, consumer, and industry research.

Overcoming Roadblocks and Challenges

- **Outdated concepts of libraries:** Everyone knows about libraries, but their perceptions may be outdated. When you talk to entrepreneurs, you often need to overcome their ideas of what a library (and librarian) are. Then you can begin exploring library resources for businesses. Your skill in navigating this conversation will grow with practice.
- **Impostor syndrome:** Librarians sometimes feel underqualified for this work. The key to remember is that we are doing research and teaching information literacy, which are quite within our areas of expertise. We are not giving business advice; we are connecting users with research tools and strategies. Business experience is not required.

Staff Responsibilities

The staff doing outreach should be enthusiastic and feel comfortable approaching new people, making cold calls, and hearing no. They must be knowledgeable about what your library offers to effectively sell it. They need to have initiative, display good judgment, and be able to relate to people from diverse backgrounds. Organizational skills are crucial for keeping track of contacts, leads, statistics, and follow-ups.

Tips, Tricks, and Advice

- Start where you are and grow from there. There's no magic formula or perfect timing—just start.
- Listening is just as important as talking. Learn what is important to entrepreneurs in your community. You will build better connections and services by actively listening.
- You will be the only library at many events. Always be prepared to make library cards and promote the library as a whole.
- You are not alone. Contact other libraries that work with entrepreneurs. We are happy to share our insights and experiences.

PROGRAM 25

Untethered and on the Move

TOLEDO LUCAS COUNTY (OH) PUBLIC LIBRARY

Meg Delaney, Miramelinda Arribas-Douglas, Linda L. Fayerweather, and Zachary W. Huber

Setting the Stage

The Business and Workforce Department hubs out of the Toledo Lucas County Public Library's (TLCPL) Main Library and takes programs, resources, and consultative skills out to the community. Our services focus on helping customers who are starting or growing their businesses. Primary clients include entrepreneurs, grant-seekers, and nonprofits—with an emphasis on women, immigrants, refugees, and international newcomers. TLCPL also works with employers and spends time in branches alongside reference librarians throughout the county, demonstrating resources and modeling interview techniques.

When the flagship Main Library closed for major renovations, the Business & Workforce team departed from the role of a traditional public service department and sprang into action out in the community, with a focus on supporting underrepresented communities in pursuit of their entrepreneurial dreams. Now untethered from a traditional service desk, our specialized librarians deliver one-on-one consultations, workshops, and other programming throughout the county and into northwest Ohio.

Service Area

- Suburban and Rural
- Large, less than 500,000 population

Goals and Impact

Nationally and in our region, advancing equity and inclusion for diverse local immigrant populations is a vital strategy for supporting communities and promoting economic success. The efforts of the Business & Workforce team are aligned with TLCPL's Strategic Road Map and its public service priorities. The success of the team's efforts with numerous program components is clear. The initial goal was to provide more one-on-one research and technical assistance. To date, the community's interest in our business programs and services has grown exponentially, and we've provided more consultations, programming, and reference each year.

> **Lucas County: A Certified Welcoming Community**
>
> The national nonprofit Welcoming America designates Certified Welcoming communities by conducting an independent audit of cities and counties that have created policies and programs that reflect their values and commitment to immigrant inclusion. We're proud of the fact that Lucas County is the fourth local government in the country and the second local government in Ohio to achieve status as a Certified Welcoming community. Locally, the Welcome Toledo-Lucas County (TLC) initiative was launched in 2014, with resolutions of support from Lucas County and the Toledo City Council to support that vital strategy. Now housed at the Main Library and coordinated in partnership with Lucas County and LISC Toledo, the initiative is governed by a steering committee of community partners and leaders, including immigrants and refugees. The Welcome TLC librarian is a vital member of the Business & Workforce team.

Several reports highlight the need for services to local entrepreneurs in our community. Chief among them is the "New Americans in Toledo and Lucas County" report, which illustrates the demographic and economic contributions of immigrants and refugees in Toledo-Lucas County. The report, produced in partnership with the New American Economy and the Toledo Regional Chamber of Commerce, among others, found that immigrants in the Toledo region:

- Contributed more than $200 million to local communities
- Helped offset local population loss

- Paid more than $30 million in federal taxes and more than $19 million in state and local taxes in 2017

The report also details the contributions that immigrants make to Toledo's workforce, including major roles in key industries that are vital to Toledo's economic stability. This analysis has been transformative in helping the library better understand and communicate the importance of being a welcoming, diverse community and the connection to creating a strong, sustainable economy.[1]

Getting Started

- Adopt a "test and try" stance so that team members, administrators, and others are comfortable critiquing your service model, process, and goals. Remember, excellence is a moving target.
- Determine the scope of your pilot project. What will you do? For whom? For how long? Who are your internal stakeholders? Assess whether you have enough customers/clients and potential partners for a successful pilot.
- Establish what success will look like and the measures you'll use. Measure and document everything as you go.
- Build both internal and external communication plans. Report out to stakeholders regularly.
- Celebrate every success.

Key Resources
The library's key resources for our initiative included:

- Staff equipped with laptops, individual phone numbers, and cell phones
- A consultation space equipped with a smart board and webcam
- Zoom for webinars and interactive meetings
- Our purpose-built Work Space, which is available by application to individuals, groups, and organizations to further their efforts in nonprofit and business development (Components of the space include a projection system, teleconferencing equipment,

Toledo Lucas County Public Library's Work Space
Photo by Roger Mastroiani, Design by HBM Architects

flipping/nesting tables, study and laptop tables, and a keycode system that allows users to access the room before and after the library's business hours.)

Key Partners

- **The Toledo Business Growth Collaborative** supports the library in serving specific audiences: African American, Hispanic/Latinx, and members of other minority racial or ethnicity groups; immigrants and refugees; and low- to moderate-income individuals.
- **The Urban Libraries Council** asked TLCPL to be an inaugural member of its Strengthening Libraries as Entrepreneurial Hubs cohort. The purpose of the program is to advance equity and community economic health by increasing support for all entrepreneurs and particularly women, people of color, immigrants, and veterans.
- **Upwardly Global**'s "Jobversity Practitioner Learning Pathway" online training program, Welcome TLC, and the Lucas County

Department of Planning and Development coordinated training for thirty-four local workforce and service provider practitioners to better understand how to assist immigrants, refugees, and internationals with finding jobs and building careers in the region's job market.

Budget

The biggest part of our budget is staffing. Creating the Business & Workforce team was revenue-neutral for the library. Some of the team's positions existed before, and the Welcome TLC librarian came from a vacant position elsewhere in the library system. Other budget items to consider are speakers, events, printing and copying, and perhaps clerical support.

Implementing the Nuts and Bolts

Being untethered from an information desk is a key aspect of what makes our team different. We take many consultations, programs, and workshops outside of the Main Library to the branches and other community locations. This gives us inroads to different neighborhoods. It also helps to build trust with individuals and partners.

If a service already exists in your ecosystem of partners, you can make connections with it. If it doesn't yet exist, begin the dialogue to build shared services or a referral process. For example, one of our branches serves a community with a high concentration of Spanish speakers. To address the unique needs of that community, one of our business partners—the Minority Business Assistance Center—now offers monthly business services and assistance in Spanish at this branch.

HOW TO: Be a Strong Partner

1. Find external entities in your community (SBDC, SCORE, colleges, etc.) that are already engaged in this space and show them how the library can assist, lessen their burden, and be a partner. Our aim is to complement, not compete with, other organizations. Create formal partnerships. Librarians are more likely to be viewed as colleagues in the field when they can attend community events such as chamber of commerce meetings and maintain memberships in

area professional organizations. Those experiences and contacts then open new opportunities to collaborate and partner.
2. When considering adding a potential partner, identify how the partnership could bring real value to both the customers and the library. Determine if the partner provides services that fill a gap in the library's services and vice versa. Establish shared protocols as to how the partners will help hold each other accountable and share information between them.
3. Understand that setting up a network of partners is not easy work, and not all potential partners are created equal. Partners need to be vetted thoroughly by library staff to ensure that those organizations have shared values with the library. The library's trust with its customers is on the line with every referral.
4. Develop an ecosystem of partners to create a wider set of connections, casting a net that includes and leverages the expertise of an entire community; the end result will be beneficial for library users. While many partner resources are freely accessible to your customers, individuals may be hesitant to approach some of these organizations on their own. Their trust in a library's recommendation can help overcome that hesitancy.
5. While some of the partner organizations in the local ecosystem may provide overlapping services, each individual organization provides its own specific nuance and depth in the services it makes available to customers. Several organizations in our locality specialize in providing services to traditionally under-resourced groups such as women and communities of color, bolstering our library's initiative to reach these groups. These examples include:

- Northwest Ohio Hispanic Chamber of Commerce
- Ohio Minority Supplier Development Council
- Toledo African American Chamber of Commerce
- Minority Business Assistance Center
- Women of Toledo

Promoting Your Program

Produce materials that make it easy for both staff and customers to understand the breadth of your services and the network of partners available to them. We are able to do this through our dedicated business services support page.

We also assembled a business resources booklet for starting a business and creating a customized business plan. This booklet includes our numerous business-service partners, their mission statements, and their contact information. We also have specific newsletters for our various audiences, and we attend our partners' events.

Overcoming Roadblocks and Challenges

There have been several challenges in building our program. Most notable are the inequities that customers face related to technology. The Business & Workforce team members have laptops, cell phones, a dedicated Zoom account and a smart board. With these tools, they can meet customers out in the community or in the library. Meeting customers where they are, helping them to better use their own technology, and demonstrating the tech and resources that are available in all of our locations helps to overcome this challenge.

Staff Responsibilities

Three lead librarians consult with a manager/administrator in building and implementing their plans. The librarians' primary activities include consulting one-on-one with customers, creating and presenting seminars and workshops, arranging for and collaborating with external speakers, and writing newsletters to their core audiences. The three librarians are as follows:

- Small business specialist, 1 FTE
- Grants and nonprofit specialist, 1 FTE
- Welcome TLC librarian, 1 FTE

Tips, Tricks, and Advice

- **Examine your service area's demographic data closely.** Identify any opportunities for achieving early success with your target population group. Having successes and sharing those positive examples will provide interesting stories for local media and partners and will help build momentum and "buzz" around your services.
- **Sometimes just having space is a real plus.** SCORE and other organizations use our library's conference rooms and community meeting rooms to meet with their clients and conduct their events and programming.

NOTE

1. "New Americans in Toledo and Lucas County: The Demographic and Economic Contributions of Immigrants," 2019, New American Economy, Welcome Toledo-Lucas County, and Toledo Regional Chamber of Commerce, www.newamericaneconomy.org/wp-content/uploads/2019/08/G4G_Toledo.pdf. A summary of the report is available at https://research.newamericaneconomy.org/report/new-americans-in-toledo-and-lucas-county/.

PROGRAM 26

Support Rural Business

Employment and Business Entrepreneur Center

TOPSHAM (ME) PUBLIC LIBRARY

Susan M. Preece

Setting the Stage

The Topsham Public Library in mid-coast Maine has been actively involved in supporting small businesses, entrepreneurs, and job seekers since before the Brunswick Naval Air Station closed in 2005. Our library's mission is to be a community center for all. With a reputation as a trusted source, we are in a unique position to be a conduit of information connecting people, organizations, programs, and resources. As such, we can connect to all members of the community. In addition, with our connection to the town of Topsham staff, especially the economic development director and the General Assistance Office, we can reach out to those who might not know what we offer. Finally, our own Business Support Program offers us a channel to the local business community to find out what kinds of work are available to those looking for employment, changing their career, or starting their own business.

Our Employment and Business Entrepreneur Center provides a comprehensive and coordinated series of programs, drop-ins, informational opportunities, and collection enhancements in collaboration with our partners.

Service Area

- Rural
- Very small, less than 10,000 population

Goals and Impact

In 2005, the Brunswick Naval Air Station closed. Hundreds of people who had worked for the Navy and the supporting community businesses found themselves facing a new workforce model. In addition, many longtime factory and industrial workers have been displaced due to the use of technology in the workplace. Many businesses have been severely stressed due to the lack of broadband access, a drop in tourism, and the shrinking industrial segment of the local economy.

The Employment and Business Entrepreneur Center can provide individual, tailored support to members of our local community who are pivoting in their careers. With support from our existing partners, we can connect fledgling small businesses and entrepreneurs to resources, including mentoring and resource development. In turn, supporting our local entrepreneurs bolsters some of the state's ten-year strategic goals, particularly those to grow talent in Maine, promote innovation, improve connectivity, and promote hubs of excellence. The goals for our program are to reach patrons where they are and connect them to what they need, whether that is career counseling, mentoring, support in the use of technology, and more. We hope to be a "one-stop shop" to move people forward to reach their personal goals and to enhance the economic vitality of Topsham and the mid-coast area.

According to a 2016 Pew Research study on libraries, 8 out of 10 people (78 percent) believe that libraries can help them find reliable and trustworthy information. As cornerstone institutions, all libraries—large and small, urban and rural—can provide business support for their communities. Partnering with experts and connecting people is what libraries do, and our goal is to provide tailored services to each individual patron based on their needs. This program is a natural extension of our core mission. We are a community center for all.

Getting Started

The Topsham Public Library has been actively involved in supporting small businesses, entrepreneurs, and job seekers since before the Brunswick Naval Air Station closed in 2005. By partnering with the Maine CareerCenters, the Southern Midcoast Chamber of Commerce, and Topsham Development Inc., we found ways to assist the newly unemployed in rebuilding and expanding their skills.

Key Resources

Our library brought the following key resources to our initiative:

- **Zoom connections through Maine InfoNet:** Zoom was available for any patron to use for business meetings or one-to-one consultations with the local CareerCenter.
- **Laptops and equipment:** We provided laptops, keyboards, and a small desk space for entrepreneurs to use in the library. We are in the process of exploring the circulation of laptops and potentially hotspots.
- **Meeting/convening space:** We have a small meeting space and a larger 150-seat community room that can be used for business meetings and events.

Key Partners

- **CareerCenters–Maine State program:** Maine CareerCenters provide a variety of employment and training services at no charge for the state's workers and businesses. The CareerCenters are located all across the state. The Southern Midcoast CareerCenter worked with us by providing a staff member to assist patrons via a Zoom link at the library. Patrons could reserve a 45-minute session to work one-on-one with a CareerCenter expert.
- **Southern Midcoast Maine Chamber of Commerce:** This chamber of commerce helped us connect with many local businesses and offered to provide a course on entrepreneurship for our program. The chamber works with businesses and nonprofits in mid-coast Maine. The chamber has used our library's meeting room spaces to hold Lunch and Learn events over the course of the past few years. We provide the venue and occasionally a speaker to connect local businesses informally with one another.
- **Topsham Development Inc.:** The town of Topsham's economic development director has worked with the library for several years, along with the Topsham Development board, to support our vision of the public library as a convening space. Our library's ability to reach a broad audience in the community helps Topsham Development to explain the many reasons why Topsham is a good place to start a business.

Budget

We received $42,200 from the Libraries Build Business grant. We used this funding to hire part-time administrative staff, purchase laptops and equipment, develop promotional materials, provide training and workshops, and cover transportation and facilities costs.

Implementing the Nuts and Bolts

Our established job information and entrepreneur collection provides books, articles, example business planning, information on local funding opportunities, and connections to local resources, including the Maine CareerCenters and Topsham Development Inc. The Digital Maine database collection offers our customers 24/7 access to the latest information, news, and research available through curated full-text databases; these databases offer scholarly journals, local newspapers, and e-books for on-the-spot answers to any business-related question.

Our program relied on one-on-one connection and provided customized sessions to patrons with our partner at the Southern Midcoast CareerCenter. After a session, we administer a survey to our Entrepreneur Center participants. We have consistently received good reviews from those using the CareerCenter virtual meetings. Several survey responses expressed surprise at the ease of use and support from the library staff. Others were pleased that the library was involved in this type of activity. Many mentioned their comfort level with the library as a definitive reason why they chose to participate. Finally, we heard that because the process was easy for participants, they were more likely to return for follow-up sessions on their own timeline. Evaluating our program helped us check on what was useful to participants and plan for the future as we slowly build our program.

HOW TO: Provide One-to-One Business Support

1. Find a partner or consultant that has business expertise. In our case, we partnered with the Maine CareerCenters.
2. Set up an online registration that the library, patrons, and partner can access.
3. At the library, book appointments and provide the CareerCenters (or other partner) with a short statement about what the patron is looking for so that the counselor can prepare in advance of the meeting.

4. On the day of the appointment, set up a virtual meeting with the CareerCenters's counselor by using a computer in a private room or kiosk at the library. Our library provides all the equipment needed for a virtual session, including a laptop, videoconferencing software, camera, and microphone for quality audio and visual.
5. Have library staff available for technical support. Should there be a computer problem, attendees can easily ask us to troubleshoot.
6. Build in flexibility so that patrons get the support they need. Some members come in for one session only (45 minutes). Others book several appointments to work on skills and other issues. (For example, topics could include interviewing practice, a sales pitch review, or resume or business plan support.)
7. Support patrons with appropriate business resources and information. Check in with patrons after their one-to-one business support sessions to see if they need help searching for suggested resources or information. Ask for feedback about the experience.

Promoting Your Program

In a small community, there may be unique outlets for you to take advantage of. Word of mouth can be a great way to spread the word, too. For us, we connected with print and electronic media, blog posts, Twitter and Facebook, and e-mail blasts with Mailchimp. As a small rural community, we have unique access to print news outlets. *The Cryer* is a local monthly with which we have a regular page. We also rely on word of mouth along with our blog, social media posts, and our in-house e-mail list of 1,500 addresses.

Overcoming Roadblocks and Challenges

While the library has good bandwidth and fiber-optic connections, many of the people we needed to reach did not. Wi-Fi hotspots were not effective for us due to the lack of cell service in the community.

Ultimately, we pushed through and were able to provide a Zoom option set up in the library, so we could begin focusing on CareerCenter one-on-one virtual help. Our partnership with the CareerCenters encouraged other Maine libraries to do the same. During our first three months, five other libraries have adopted this plan.

Staff Responsibilities

As a small rural library, our staff members wear many different hats. Our main role is to facilitate and provide a supportive environment for our community. To run this program, our library director, adult services, and tech support manager provided support to the program, connecting with partners and patrons, and doing promotion of our services. We also had administrative support for a time, and this was helpful in planning our services and doing outreach.

Tips, Tricks, and Advice

- Expect to feel overwhelmed and unsure when starting a business program, especially if you are in a small community. Small successes will pay off over time, though, so it is okay to start small and slowly add on as you go. Peer learning and sharing are critical. As a result of the launch of our Entrepreneur Center, five other Maine libraries are offering this program at their libraries, just from hearing about our successful partnership with the CareerCenter.
- Don't undervalue the services offered by your library. Many libraries do not tout their expertise. We may not have had advanced training in business management, but we are good researchers and know how to connect people with the resources they need. As a profession, we need to be proactive about how to support our communities even if it means dipping our feet into an area formerly dominated by other community sectors— like adult literacy, the chamber of commerce, and other workforce development programs.
- Our brand strength is trust and accuracy. We can bring these to the table and provide more outreach to areas of the community that other programs can't reach.

RESOURCES

Libraries Build Business

Libraries Build Business is an initiative of the American Library Association, supported by Google.org, to partner with a cohort of thirteen public libraries around the country. Those libraries are building local capacity and expanding services for small businesses and entrepreneurs, with a focus on businesses owned by people from low-income and underrepresented groups. The initiative has created a variety of resources and a community of practice for the field. For more information about Libraries Build Business and to join the community, contact Megan Janicki (mjanicki@alawash.org) or visit the website at www.ala.org/advocacy/workforce/grant.

Libraries Build Business Products and Media

Zulkey, Claire. "Big Ideas for Small Business: How Libraries Strengthened Their Small Business Programs to Reach Those Who Needed Them Most." *American Libraries*, November 1, 2021. https://americanlibrariesmagazine.org/2021/11/01/big-ideas-for-small-business/.

Whitman, J., M. Janicki, and M. Visser. "Open to Change: Libraries Catalyze Small Business Adaption to COVID-19." ALA Policy Perspectives, November 2020. www.ala.org/advocacy/sites/ala.org.advocacy/files/content/Workforce/Open-to-Change_WEB_111320.pdf.

Project Outcome

www.ala.org/pla/data/performancemeasurement

Project Outcome is a free toolkit designed to help public libraries understand and share the impact of essential library services and programs by providing them with simple surveys and an easy-to-use process for measuring and analyzing outcomes. Project Outcome also provides libraries with the resources and training support needed to apply their results and confidently advocate for their library's future.

Flourish Agenda
https://flourishagenda.com
A healing-centered approach is a holistic one involving culture, spirituality, civic action, and collective healing. A healing-centered approach does not view trauma simply as an individual isolated experience, but rather highlights the ways in which trauma and healing are experienced collectively. For more information about healing centered engagement, visit Flourish Agenda for resources and information.

Association for Rural & Small Libraries
www.arsl.org
The Association for Rural & Small Libraries (ARSL) is a network of people throughout the country who are dedicated to the positive growth and development of libraries. The ARSL believes in the value of rural and small libraries and strives to create resources and services that address national, state, and local priorities for libraries situated in rural communities.

ODLOS Glossary
www.ala.org/aboutala/odlos-glossary-terms
The American Library Association's Office for Diversity, Literacy and Outreach Services (ODLOS) maintains a glossary of terms. The intent is to provide guidance and open discussion in the spirit of creating a more equitable, diverse, and inclusive society.

SWOT and PESTLE Analyses
PESTLE and SWOT are analytical tools to help you during the process of developing a strategic plan or starting a needs assessment.

> **Gray, Byron.** "How to Effectively Conduct a PESTLE & SWOT Analysis." www.linkedin.com/pulse/how-conduct-pestle-swot-analysis-byron-gray/.

Community Business Resources
The following are a few common business resources for small business owners and entrepreneurs. You might also consider business associations

and alliances in your community that support an underrepresented group, such as a local Hispanic Business Alliance or Women in Business networking group.

SCORE
www.score.org
SCORE, the Service Core of Retired Executives, has the largest network of free volunteer small-business mentors in the nation.

U.S. Chamber of Commerce
www.uschamber.com
The U.S. Chamber of Commerce is the world's largest business organization. Its members range from small businesses and chambers of commerce across the country that support their communities, to leading industry associations and global corporations that innovate and try to meet the world's challenges, to emerging and fast-growing industries that are shaping the future. Check for a local chamber of commerce, business networking group, or board of trade in your community.

U.S. Black Chambers, Inc.
https://usblackchambers.org
The U.S. Black Chambers, Inc. (USBC) provides leadership and advocacy in the realization of economic empowerment. The USBC offers resources, initiatives, and a network of African American Chambers of Commerce and business organizations to support their work of developing and growing Black enterprises.

National Federation of Independent Business
www.nfib.com
The National Federation of Independent Business (NFIB) is the voice of small business and advocates on behalf of America's small and independent business owners, both in Washington, DC, and in all fifty state capitals. The NFIB is nonprofit, nonpartisan, and member-driven.

Small Business Development Centers
https://americassbdc.org
America's Small Business Development Centers (SBDCs) form the most

comprehensive small-business assistance network in the United States and its territories. SBDCs are hosted by leading universities, colleges, state economic development agencies, and private partners, and are funded in part by the U.S. government through a partnership with the U.S. Small Business Administration. There are nearly 1,000 local centers available to provide no-cost business consulting and low-cost training to new and existing businesses.

INDEX

A

academic libraries
    business resources of, 42
    partnership with public libraries, 46–48
Academy, SB-BI, 64, 67
access
    accessibility of library programs, 36–37
    digital inclusion/access at small/rural libraries, 5–6
ACE Women's Business Center, 128
Addison (IL) Public Library, business and job seeker services, 55–60
Adobe Creative Suite software, 134, 135
Adobe Pro, 176
AdvancedTech Cell Phone Repair, 59
advocacy, 26
agency, 34
AiR (artist-in-residence), 187
ALA
    See American Library Association
Alan Levan Institute, 91
Allen County Public Library (ACPL), 50–52
Alliance of Entrepreneurial Resources (AERO), 88, 90–91
American Express
    Neighborhood Champion program, 214
    Small Business Saturday, 57, 212
American Library Association (ALA)
    EDI, commitment to, xvi, 30–35
    Libraries Build Business initiative, xi, xiii, xiv–xvi
    ODLOS Glossary, 238
Andrew, Maud, 78–85
Apple iPads, 157
Appleton (WI) Public Library
    belonging, cultivation of sense of, 38–39
    in Libraries Build Business initiative, xiv–xv
    partnership with ColorBold Business Association, 37
    "Small Business—Big Impact" (SB-BI) initiative, 61–68
Arribas-Douglas, Miramelinda, 222–229
artist-in-residence (AiR), 187
Arts and Media manager, 193
Asana, 153
aspirations, 34
assessment, 26
    See also community assessment; evaluation; needs assessment
Association for Rural & Small Libraries, 238
attendance
    See participants; program attendance
audience
    building, 60
    for ESOL class, 186
    for Invest in Yourself, 141, 143
    target audience, engaging, 89–90
    for Women's EXPO, 171
    See also program attendance
Austin SCORE
    in Biz.ability workshops, 198
    as partner for Biz.ability workshops, 197, 199
A-Z Database
    for MAGIC, 176, 177
    PWPL information compiled from, 178
    for Small Business Hub, 182

B

badges, 136, 137
"B-A-I-L" team, 163

INDEX

Baltimore County (MD) Public Library
    Entrepreneur Academy, 70–77
    Libraries Build Business initiative, xiv–xv
    nonprofit academy of, 25
    training for small business support, xiii
    Zoom for, 26
banks
    as partners, 23, 196, 199
    as potential partners, 18
Barbakoff, Audrey, 140–146
BCCC (Brookhaven Chambers of
    Commerce Coalition), 169
"Be a Neighborhood Champion: Small
    Business Boot Camp" (Milton,
    Goddard, Miller, & O'Hare), 208–214
BeanStack, 134, 136–138
Beckett, Samuel, 104
"Becoming a Resource Hub: The Dallas
    B.R.A.I.N." (Lowe), 106–112
belonging, 38–39
Benedict College Women's Business
    Center, 190–191
BFA (BKLYN Fashion Academy), 78, 84
biases, institutional, 39
BIC
    See Business Insight Center (BIC),
    Central Library of Rochester
    and Monroe County
BIDs (business improvement districts), 18
"Big Ideas for Small Business: How Libraries
    Strengthened Their Small Business
    Programs to Reach Those Who
    Needed Them Most" (Zulkey), 237
bilingual resources, 202, 204
bilingual staff, 160, 206
BIPOC
    See Black, Indigenous, and people of color
"BIPOC Business Community and
    Connections: Small Business—Big
    Impact" (McCleer & Vue), 61–68
Biz.ability workshops
    getting started, 196–197
    goals/impact of, 195–196
    implementation of, 197–198
    promotion of, 198–199
    roadblocks/challenges, 199
    setting the stage, 195
    staff responsibilities, 199
    tips, tricks, advice for, 199–200
"Biz.ability Workshops: Tools to Empower
    You" (Halley), 195–200
BizKids Club, 48–50
Bizminer, 182
BKLYN Fashion Academy (BFA), 78, 84
Black, Indigenous, and people
    of color (BIPOC)
    Built in Broward program for
        tech businesses, 86–92
    entrepreneur storytelling series, 64–66
    Sea Un Vendedor Ambulante
        Exitoso/Successful Street
        Vending program, 155–160
    "Small Business—Big Impact"
        initiative for, 61–68
    See also minorities
Black Valley Digital
    Built in Broward program, 86, 87
    as partner for Built in Broward, 88
blog post, 89
"books to go" kits, 177
Bourret, Christopher
    "Identifying Stakeholders, Building
        Partnerships, Finding Funding,
        and Sustaining It All," 13–27
    on Small Business Hub of Providence
        (RI) Public Library, 180–186
BPL
    See Brooklyn (NY) Public Library (BPL)
B.R.A.I.N.
    See Dallas Business Resource and
        Information Network (B.R.A.I.N.)
branding
    branded auto reply for e-mail, 178
    Invest in Yourself branding, King
        County Library System, 140–146
    of professional business product, 175
    of program, 118
Brian Hamilton's Starter U course, 127
brochure, 130
Brookhaven Chambers of Commerce
    Coalition (BCCC), 169
Brooklyn (NY) Public Library (BPL)
    BKLYN Fashion Academy, 84
    Business & Career Center, 84

INDEX   243

Power UP! background, 78-79
Power UP! getting started, 79-81
Power UP! goals/impact of, 79
Power UP! implementation of, 81-84
Power UP! tips, tricks, advice for, 85
Brophy, Julie
    on Entrepreneur Academy of Baltimore County Public Library, 69-77
    "Identifying Stakeholders, Building Partnerships, Finding Funding, and Sustaining It All," 13-27
    on small business support, training for, xiii
    "Specialized Library Supports for Entrepreneurs," 41-52
Broward Black Chamber of Commerce, 90-91
Broward County Library
    Built in Broward program, 86-92
    Libraries Build Business initiative, xiv-xv
    marketing library program to potential partners, 19
Brown, Sara, 41-52
Brunswick Naval Air Station, 230, 231
budget
    for Biz.ability workshops, 197
    for Building Business initiative, 204
    for Built in Broward program, 88
    for business and job seeker services, 57
    for "Business Help at Your Library" program, 121-122, 123
    for Business Insight Center, 96
    for Cultivate Indy, 135
    for Encore Entrepreneurs/Key Advanced Entrepreneurs, 103
    for Entrepreneur Academy, 72
    for Entrepreneur Workshop Series, 162
    for Entrepreneurial Launch Pad, 189, 191
    for Invest in Yourself branding, 143
    for MAGIC, 176-177
    for Miller Business Center, 169-170
    for New Start Entrepreneurship Incubator, 128
    for PowerUP! 81
    for Sea Un Vendedor Ambulante Exitoso/Successful Street Vending program, 157-158
    for SLCL's small business outreach, 217
    for Small Business Boot Camp, 210-211
    for Small Business Hub, 183
    for "Small Business—Big Impact" initiative, 63
    for Stamford Small Business Resource Center, 115
    for TLCPL's Business and Workforce team initiative, 226
    for Wyoming Library to Business, 150
    See also funding
"Build Your Business Brand through Community Engagement: Invest in Yourself" (Barbakoff), 140-146
Building Business initiative, Santa Barbara (CA) Public Library
    budget for, 204
    goals/impact of, 201-202
    implementation of, 204
    partners for, 203
    promotion of, 204-205
    resources for, 202-203
    roadblocks/challenges, 205-206
    ServSafe licensure programs, 206
    setting the stage, 201
    staff responsibilities, 206
    tips, tricks, advice for, 207
"Building Support for Rural Entrepreneurs: A Statewide Initiative" (Svoboda), 147-154
building trades contractors, 141
Built in Broward, Broward County Library program
    budget for, 88
    components of, 88-89
    goals/impact of, 87
    partners for, 87-88
    promotion of/community connection, 89-91
    resources for, 87
    roadblocks/challenges, 91
    setting the stage, 86
    staff responsibilities, 91
    tips, tricks, advice for, 91-92
"Built to Last" (Burke), 86-92
Burke, Sheldon
    on Built in Broward program, 86-92

244 INDEX

Burke, Sheldon (*cont.*)
    "Identifying Stakeholders, Building Partnerships, Finding Funding, and Sustaining It All," 13–27
Burnard, Nathaniel, 41–52
Burton D. Morgan Foundation, 102
business alliances, 18
Business and Careers manager, 193
business and job seeker services, Addison (IL) Public Library
    flagstone initiatives, 57–58
    getting started, 56–57
    goals/impacts of, 56
    promotion of program, 58–59
    roadblocks/challenges, 59
    setting the stage, 55
    staff responsibilities, 60
    tips, tricks, advice, 60
Business and Workforce Team, Toledo Lucas County Public Library
    budget for, 226
    goals/impact of business programs/services, 223–224
    outreach by, 222
    partners for initiative, 225–226
    promotion of program, 227–228
    resources for initiative, 224–225
    roadblocks/challenges, 228
    staff responsibilities, 228
    strong partner, how to be, 226–227
    tips, tricks, advice for, 229
business card, 144–145
business classes
    in business plan competition, 83
    of Cultivate Indy, 132, 135
    in PowerUP! 81
business community
    involvement in, 163
    library's role in, 200
    listening to, 214
    MAGIC's involvement in, 175–176
    Miller Business Center and, 172, 173
    packaging existing services for, 73, 75
    Small Business Boot Camp's goals for, 209
"Business Help at Your Library" program, Ferguson Municipal Public Library
    budget for, 121–122
    goals/impact of, 120
    implementation of, 122–123
    partners for, 121
    promotion of, 123
    resources for, 121
    roadblocks/challenges, 123
    setting the stage, 119–120
    staff responsibilities, 123
    tips, tricks, advice for, 123–124
business improvement districts (BIDs), 18
business incubators
    Black Valley Digital for, 87
    Built in Broward component, 87, 88–89
    New Start Entrepreneurship Incubator, 125–131
    RIT Venture Creations, 95
Business Insight Center (BIC), Central Library of Rochester and Monroe County
    budget for, 96
    goals/impact of, 94
    implementation of, 96–97
    partners for, 95–96
    promotion of, 97
    resources for, 95
    roadblocks/challenges, 97–98
    setting the stage, 93
    staff responsibilities, 98
    tips, tricks, advice for, 98–99
business librarians
    commitment to helping business community, 172
    for Entrepreneur Workshop Series, 163
    learning from, 165–166
    of Miller Business Center, 169
Business Maker Space (Yakama Nation Library), 10–12, 36
business mixers
    attending, 207
    of Building Business initiative, 203, 204
"Business Networking through Community-Building" (Merza & Wetta), 201–207
business owners
    BIPOC business community/connections, SB-BI initiative for, 61–68
    BIPOC entrepreneur storytelling series, 65–66
    Biz.ability workshops for, 195–200

Building Business initiative for, 201–207
"Business Help at Your Library" program for micro-entrepreneurs, 119–124
conversations with, 218
Dallas B.R.A.I.N. for, 106
Invest in Yourself branding for, 141
MAGIC for, 174–179
small business outreach for, 215–221
Stamford Small Business Resource Center for, 113–118
See also entrepreneurs
business plan
BeanStack for Small Business Challenge, 136–138
Entrepreneur Academy's curriculum, 73
business plan competition
creation of, 79–81
goals/impact of, 79
how to run, 82–83
implementation of, 81
promotion of, 83
roadblocks/challenges, 83–84
setting the stage, 78–79
staff responsibilities for, 84
Business Resource and Information Network
See Dallas Business Resource and Information Network (B.R.A.I.N.)
business resources
booklet of TLCPL, 228
business resource packets, 121, 123
Dallas B.R.A.I.N. for access to, 106–112
See also resources
Business Start-Up Kit, 177
business stations, 149
Business Support Program, Topsham Public Library, 230
business workshops, 195–200
buy-in, 26
Byrnes, Jennifer, 93–99

C

Calendly, 190
California State Library, 204
Canal Connection Chamber of Commerce, 162
Candid, 176
CAP Services, 63
capacity, 5

capitalism, 9–10
CareerCenters, 7–8, 9
Carlson Center for Intellectual Property
art searches for patents/trademarks, 94
at Business Insight Center, 93
manager for, 98
Casa De La Raza, 205
case studies
Biz.ability workshops, 195–200
BizKids Club, 48–50
Built in Broward, 86–92
Business and Job Seeker Services, 55–60
"Business Help at Your Library" program, 119–124
Business Insight Center, 93–99
Cultivate Indy, 132–139
Dallas B.R.A.I.N., 106–112
Employment and Business Entrepreneur Center, 230–235
Encore Entrepreneurs/Key Advanced Entrepreneurs, 100–105
Entrepreneur Academy, 69–77
Entrepreneur Workshop Series, 161–166
Entrepreneurial Launch Pad, 187–194
Invest in Yourself branding, 140–146
LA Law Library, legal support for business services, 44–46
MAGIC, 174–179
Miller Business Center, 167–173
New Jersey State Library's work towards statewide professional development, 42–44
New Start Entrepreneurship Incubator, 125–131
Sea Un Vendedor Ambulante Exitoso/Successful Street Vending program, 155–160
Small Business Boot Camp, 208–214
Small Business Hub, 180–186
small business outreach of SLCL, 215–221
"Small Business—Big Impact" (SB-BI) initiative, 61–68
Stamford Small Business Resource Center, 113–118
Team Read, Allen County Public Library, 50–52

case studies (*cont.*)
    Wyoming Library to Business
        (WL2B) initiative, 147–154
CASH Campaign of Maryland, 72
Cell-Ed
    budget for licenses/content, 158
    learning units for street
        vendor program, 158
    micro-entrepreneurship skills
        program, 155–156
    partnership with Los Angeles
        Public Library, 156, 157
    promotion of program, 159–160
    provision of safety/healing strategies, 39
    for resources that resonate with ESL, 37
Central Library of Rochester and Monroe
    County, Business Insight Center, 93–99
challenges
    See roadblocks/challenges
chambers of commerce
    attending events of, 196
    for business community connections, 210
    as potential partners, 16–17
Chicago Metropolitan Agency for Planning, 56
Chinn Park Library (VA), 174–179
churches, 138
Citizens' Review Panel (CRP) Fund
    Distribution Process, 48–49
City of Appleton Comprehensive
    Plan, 2010-2030, 62
City of Columbia, Office of Business
    Opportunities, 22, 191
classroom spaces, 182
clerk, 98
Cleveland Foundation, 102
coffee, 142
collaboration
    for entrepreneurship support, 41–42
    importance of, 179
    investment in, 37
    with local organizations, 214
    for WL2B initiative, 5
    See also partnerships
collection, 80
ColorBold Business Association, 37, 63
Commissary, 96
communication
    conversations with business owners, 218
    with partners, 91, 213
    for partnerships/programs, 9
    with partners/stakeholders, 90
    shared terms/understanding, 31
    for Stamford Small Business
        Resource Center, 116
    of steps/timelines to customer, 178
    for Wyoming Library to Business, 152–153
community
    Baltimore County Public
        Library's mission, 70
    being led by, 146
    connecting with, 89–90, 142
    EDI, LBB initiative's
        commitment to, 29–30
    Entrepreneur Workshop Series
        for economic needs of, 162
    Entrepreneurship's benefits for, 35
    library collaboration with, 38
    needs of, meeting, 25–26
    networking for library business and
        job seeker services, 56–57
    New Jersey State Library's work,
        principles of, 42–43
    partnerships for business
        plan competition, 85
    partnerships with library and, 19
    PowerUP! partners, 80–81
    rural libraries, importance
        to community, 3–4
    SB-BI initiative and, 62
    stakeholders, identifying, 13–16
    street vendors, working with, 158–159
    support of small business
        owners in, xii–xiii
    TLCPL's Business and Workforce
        team's outreach to, 222–223
    trust in library program, 160
    trust of SBPL's Building Business
        initiative, 205–206
    See also business community
community assessment
    for branding, 140, 141
    for building relationships, 144
    for Invest in Yourself, 143
community business resources, 238–239
community centers, 4
community college libraries, 46–48

Community College of Baltimore County, 46
community database, 110
Community Economic Development Fund, 115
community experts, 102
community members, 14
community organizations
    outreach in immigrant communities, 186
    partnerships with, 20
    for promotion of business program, 164
    reaching out to, 202
community partners
    identification of potential, 202
    of Stamford Small Business Resource Center, 115
    for working with street vendors, 158–159
Community Power Collective (CPC), 157
community-based social justice organizations, 17–18
competition
    See business plan competition
computers
    computer help from small/rural libraries, 6
    for Cultivate Indy, 134, 135
    for Employment and Business Entrepreneur Center, 232
    for Entrepreneur Workshop Series, 162
    for Sea Un Vendedor Ambulante Exitoso/ Successful Street Vending program, 157
    for Small Business Hub, 182
    See also technology
"Connect with Immigrant Entrepreneurs: Sea Un Vendedor Ambulante Exitoso/ Successful Street Vending" (Ildefonso), 155–160
"Considerations for Small and Rural Libraries" (West, Preece, Svoboda, Sekaquaptewa, & Hall), 3–12
Constant Contact, 66
consultants, 102
coworking space, 19
CPC (Community Power Collective), 157
Creation Station Business (Broward County Library)
    Built in Broward program, 86
    business librarian as lead for Built in Broward, 91
    partnerships with coworking spaces, 19
    for promotion of Built in Broward, 90

creative freelancers, 141
credit unions, 18, 21
criminal record, 126
The Cryer (newspaper), 234
Cultivate Indy, Independence (KS) Public Library
    BeanStack, Small Business Challenge on, 136–138
    budget for, 135
    goals/impact of, 133
    implementation of, 135
    partners for, 134–135
    promotion of, 138
    resources for, 133–134
    roadblocks/challenges, 138
    setting the stage, 132
    staff responsibilities, 138
    tips, tricks, advice for, 139
Cultivate Indy Small Business Lab, 132, 135
"Cultivate Small Business with BeanStack: Cultivate Indy" (West), 132–139
cultural humility
    EDI principles, integration of, 31
    power imbalances, identifying, 38
    as tool for healthy engagement, 32–33
culture
    as healing-centered engagement principle, 34
    of innovation/inclusivity, 142
curriculum
    of Encore Entrepreneurs/Key Advanced Entrepreneurs, 103–104
    of ESOL course, 184, 186
Cuyahoga County (OH) Public Library, Encore Entrepreneurs/Key Advanced Entrepreneurs, 100–105
Cuyahoga Works, 100
Cyrier, Lesley, 55–60

D

Dallas (TX) Public Library, 106–112
Dallas Business Resource and Information Network (B.R.A.I.N.)
    budget for, 109
    getting started, 107
    goals/impact of, 107
    implementation of, 109–110
    partners for, 108–109

Dallas Business Resource and Information
   Network (B.R.A.I.N.) *(cont.)*
   promotion of, 110
   resources for, 108
   roadblocks/challenges, 111
   setting the stage, 106
   staff responsibilities for, 111
   tips, tricks, advice for, 111–112
Dallas Entrepreneur Center (DEC), 108
Dallas Office of Economic Development, 106
data, 23–24
databases
   for Building Business initiative,
      202–203, 204
   business database vendors, 199
   for "Business Help at Your
      Library" program, 121, 122
   of Business Insight Center, 96, 97
   for Cultivate Indy, 134
   for Dallas B.R.A.I.N., 108, 109, 110
   for Encore Entrepreneurs/Key
      Advanced Entrepreneurs, 102
   for Entrepreneur Workshop Series, 163
   for MAGIC, 175, 176
   for Miller Business Center, 169
   packaging existing services, 75
   for PowerUP! 80
   for Small Business Hub, 182
DEC (Dallas Entrepreneur Center), 108
Deer Park Chamber of Commerce, 210
Deer Park Library, Spokane County
   (WA), 208–209, 213
Delaney, Meg, 222–229
demographic data, 229
"Develop an ESOL for Business
   Owners Class: Small Business
   Hub" (Bourret), 180–186
Devereux, Andrea, 125–131
diversity, 132–139
   See also equity, diversity, and inclusion
division head, 98
documentation, 124
dollar value, 220
donations, 173

E

EBSCO
   for Cultivate Indy, 134

Entrepreneurial Mindset Training
   digital resource, 210, 211
Economic Community Development
   Institute (ECDI), 100, 102
Economic Roundtable, 155
Economically Needed Diversity Options
   for Wyoming (ENDOW)
   Executive Council, 148
economy
   entrepreneurship's benefits for, 35
   immigrants' impact on, 223–224
   library's role in business community, 200
EDI
   See equity, diversity, and inclusion
educational opportunities, 109
EiR
   See entrepreneur-in-residence
elected officials, 14
e-mail list, 164, 172
e-mail newsletter
   of Addison Public Library, 59
   for promotion of Small Business Hub, 185
   for SB-BI initiative promotion, 66
e-mails
   branded auto reply for, 178
   for promoting program, 75
   for promotion of Women's EXPO, 171
employment, 126
Employment and Business Entrepreneur
   Center, Topsham (ME) Public Library
   getting started, 231–233
   goals/impact of, 231
   implementation of, 233
   one-to-one business support, 233–234
   promotion of, 234
   roadblocks/challenges, 234
   setting the stage, 230
   staff responsibilities, 235
   tips, tricks, advice for, 235
employment centers, 164
"Empowering New Businesses with a
   Business Plan Competition"
   (Andrew & Robinson), 78–85
Encore Cleveland, 100
Encore Entrepreneurs/Key Advanced
   Entrepreneurs, Cuyahoga
   County (OH) Public Library
   budget for, 103

getting started, 101–102
goals/impact of, 101
implementation of, 103–104
promotion of, 104
resources for, 102
roadblocks/challenges, 104
setting the stage, 100–101
staff responsibilities, 104
tips, tricks, advice for, 105
English skills, 184–185
Enoch Pratt Free Library (Baltimore), 69, 72
Entrepreneur Academy, Baltimore County Public Library
    curriculum, creation of, 72–73
    getting started, 71–72
    goals/impacts of, 70–71
    promotion of, 75
    roadblocks/challenges, 75–76
    setting the stage, 69–70
    staff responsibilities, 76
    survey results from cohorts of, 74
    tips, tricks, advice for, 76–77
Entrepreneur Engagement Group, 75–76
entrepreneur storytelling series, 64
entrepreneur support organizations (ESOs)
    partnership with St. Louis County Library, 217
    promotion of small business outreach, 220
    small business outreach, development of, 219
Entrepreneur Workshop Series, Macedon (NY) Public Library
    getting started, 162
    goals/impact of, 161
    implementation of, 162–164
    Melinda Kelsey, 165
    promotion of, 164
    roadblocks/challenges, 164
    setting the stage, 161
    staff responsibilities, 164–165
    tips, tricks, advice for, 165–166
entrepreneurial ecosystem, xi–xiv
Entrepreneurial Launch Pad, Richland Library (Columbia, SC)
    budget for, 191
    EiR, definition of, 189
    EiR program, how to create, 192–193
    getting started, 188–190
    goals/impact of, 188
    partners for, 190–191
    promotion of, 193
    resources for, 190
    roadblocks/challenges, 193
    setting the stage, 187–188
    staff responsibilities, 193
    tips, tricks, advice for, 194
Entrepreneurial Library of Things (LoT)
    description of, 190
    Entrepreneurial Launch Pad for access to, 187
    funding for, 189
    staff responsibilities for, 193
entrepreneurial mindset
    modeling, 105
    for new entrepreneur initiative, 101
Entrepreneurial Mindset Academy, 127
"The Entrepreneurial Mindset: Encore Entrepreneurs and Key Advanced Entrepreneurs" (Kelly), 100–105
Entrepreneurial Mindset Training digital resource, EBSCO, 210, 211
entrepreneur-in-residence (EiR)
    definition of, 189
    meeting space for, 190
    program, creation of, 192–193
    program of Richland Library, 187–188
    of Stamford Small Business Resource Center, 113, 116
    in Team Read program, 51
entrepreneurs
    formerly incarcerated individuals, NSEI for, 125–131
    one-to-one support for micro-entrepreneurs, 119–124
    packaging existing services for business community, 73
    PowerUP! business plan competition for, 78–85
    Sea Un Vendedor Ambulante Exitoso/Successful Street Vending program, 155–160
    small business outreach for, 215–221
    support of, with research, 177–178
    See also business owners
entrepreneurs, specialized library supports for
    academic libraries, 46–48

250 INDEX

entrepreneurs, specialized library supports for academic libraries *(cont.)*
    LA Law Library, legal support for business services, 44–46
    libraries working together for, 41–42
    New Jersey State Library, statewide professional development, 42–44
    partnerships/networking for services, 52
    youth entrepreneurship programs, 48–52
"Entrepreneurs Launch and Grow: The Entrepreneurial Launch Pad" (Luccy & Quillivan), 187–194
entrepreneurship
    academic libraries, partnership with, 46–48
    Libraries Build Business initiative, xiv–xvi
    purpose of, 35–36
    small and rural libraries, 3–10
    understanding of, 36
    Yakama Nation Library and, 9–12
    youth entrepreneurship programs, 48–52
    See also library entrepreneurship programs; small business and entrepreneurship programs
environmental scan, 15–16
equipment, 197
    See also computers; technology
equity, diversity, and inclusion (EDI)
    ALA/Libraries Build Better and, xvi
    continuing work of, 40
    engaging accessibly, equitably, authentically, 36–39
    entrepreneurship and, 35–36
    LBB commitment to, xv, 30–35
    in library entrepreneurship programs, 29–30, 42
    TLCPL's Business and Workforce team initiative, 223
"Equity, Diversity, and Inclusion in Library Entrepreneurship Programs" (McCleer, Ildefonso, Kimbrough, & Sekaquaptewa), 29–40
Equity in Energy, Innovation, and Entrepreneurship Summit, 86
"ESOL for Business Owners" course
    budget for, 183
    development of, 184–185
    goals/impact of, 181
    implementation of, 183–184
    partners for, 182–183
    resources for, 182
    Small Business Hub, services of, 180–181
    staff responsibilities for, 185
    tips, tricks, advice for, 186
ESOs
    See entrepreneur support organizations
Etsy Craft Entrepreneurship Program, 109, 110
evaluation
    of business program, 105
    of Cultivate Indy, 135–136
    of NSEI, 129, 130
events
    business mixers, 203, 204, 207
    going to, 218
    kickoff event, 90
    Women's EXPO event, hosting, 170–171
Ewing Marion Foundation, 188

F

FabLab ICC, 47, 135
Factiva, 95
Fades Barbershop, Round Rock (TX), 196
fashion, 84
FastTrac for Female Entrepreneurs, 21–22
Fayerweather, Linda L., 222–229
feedback
    about funding proposal, 24
    for assessment of library program, 26
    on Entrepreneur Academy, 70–71
    on Small Business Hub programs, 184
    from Stamford Small Business Resource Center participants, 116
Feinberg, Karly, 13–27
Ferguson (MO) Municipal Public Library
    "Business Help at Your Library" program, 119–124
    in Libraries Build Business initiative, xiv–xv
    micropreneurs, support of, 8
    packets for entrepreneurs/small businesses, 6–7
Ferguson Library (Stamford, CT), Stamford Small Business Resource Center
    budget for, 115
    goals/impact of, 114
    implementation of, 115–116
    partners for, 115

promotion of, 116
resources for, 114–115
roadblocks/challenges, 116–-117
setting the stage, 113–114
staff responsibilities, 117
tips, tricks, advice for, 117–118
"FIT Oshkosh," 61
flexibility
community needs and, 159, 160
importance of, 105
for partnerships/programs, 9
Florida International University, 86
Flourish Agenda, 238
flyers
for MAGIC, 178
for promoting program, 75, 123
for promotion of Small Business Hub, 185
for promotion of small business outreach, 220
YNL Business Maker Space and, 11
follow up, 90
FOREFRONT, 48
formerly incarcerated individuals
New Start Entrepreneurship Incubator for, 125–128
promotion of NSEI to, 130
working with, 129–130
Fort Lauderdale, Florida, 86
Foundation Directory Online grant database, 174–175, 177
Fox Valley Technical College, 61
Friends of the Round Rock Public Library, 197
Frost & Sullivan, 95
funders, 14
funding
for business plan competition, 82
creativity with, 160
for Entrepreneur Workshop Series, 162
local credit unions/banks as partners, 18
opportunities, leveraging, 22–24
for PowerUP! 81
seed capital from PowerUP! 78
for small/rural libraries, 5
See also budget

G

Gale Business Package, 122
Gauthier, Ronald M., 125–131
GCIC (Google Columbia Impact Challenge Grant), 189
General Assembly, 19
General Assembly Miami, 86, 87, 88
General Provision, 91, 92
Georgia Department of Community Supervision, 127
Georgia Department of Labor, 127
Getting Addison Back to Work program, 58
Gibson, Jennifer Hyun-Lynn, 215–221
Ginwright, Shawn, 33
Glimco, Emily, 55–60
global information system (GIS) resources, 198, 199
goals
of Biz.ability workshops, 195–196
of Building Business initiative, 201–202
of Built in Broward program, 87
of "Business Help at Your Library" program, 120
of Business Insight Center, 94
of Cultivate Indy, 133
of Dallas B.R.A.I.N., 107
of Employment and Business Entrepreneur Center, 231
of Encore Entrepreneurs/Key Advanced Entrepreneurs, 101
of Entrepreneur Academy, 70–71
of Entrepreneur Workshop Series, 161
of Entrepreneurial Launch Pad, 188
of Invest in Yourself branding, 141–142
of MAGIC, 175
of Miller Business Center, 168
of New Start Entrepreneurship Incubator, 126
of PowerUP! 79
of SLCL's small business outreach, 215–216
of Small Business Boot Camp, 209
of Small Business Hub, 181
of "Small Business—Big Impact" initiative, 62
of Stamford Small Business Resource Center, 114
of TLCPL's Business and Workforce team, 223–224
of Wyoming Library to Business, 148

Goddard, Stacey
    "Identifying Stakeholders, Building Partnerships, Finding Funding, and Sustaining It All," 13–27
    on Small Business Boot Camp, 208–214
Goldman Sachs, 108
Google Columbia Impact Challenge Grant (GCIC), 189
Google.org, xiv
Grant Resources Kit, 177
grants
    applying for, 22–23
    Foundation Directory Online grant database, 174
    micro-grants, 209, 210, 211
    opportunities, 166
    for Stamford Small Business Resource Center, 115
    in W2LB initiative, 151
    See also Libraries Build Business (LBB) initiative
graphic design, 11, 12
Gray, Byron, 238
Greater Gwinnett Reentry Alliance (GGRA)
    partnership with GCPL, 22
    partnership with New Start Entrepreneurship Incubator, 125, 126–127
    promotion of NSEI, 130
Greater Middle Country Chamber of Commerce, 169
Grow with Google
    for Cultivate Indy, 133
    for MAGIC, 175, 176
Gunia, Eva, 174–179
Gwinnett County (GA) Public Library
    in Libraries Build Business initiative, xiv–xv
    New Start Entrepreneurship Incubator, 39, 125–131
    partnerships of, 22
    shared terms/understanding, 31
Gwinnett Parole Board, 130
Gwinnett Reentry Intervention Program, 130
Gwinnett Sheriff's Office, 130

H

Hall, Taneesa R.
    "Considerations for Small and Rural Libraries," 3–12
    "One-to-One Support for Micro-Entrepreneurs: Business Help at Your Library," 119–124
Halley, Geeta, 195–200
Hamilton, Brian, 127
handout, 7, 177–178
Hauppauge Industrial Association—Long Island (HIA-LI), 169
Healing Justice Transformative Leadership Institute, 157
healing-centered engagement (HCE)
    EDI principles, integration of, 31
    principles of, 33–35
    trauma, response to, 39
Hench, Lori, 13–27
historical context, 31–32
Honeywell, Marra, 41–52
hotspots
    lack of cell service and, 234
    for Small Business Hub, 182
    for small business outreach, 217
    for street vending program, 157
"How Libraries Build Business" (Janicki & Visser), xi–xvii
how to
    launch BIPOC entrepreneur storytelling series, 65–66
    package existing services for business community, 73, 75
    promote business program/connect with community, 89–90
    provide business services on a shoestring, 122–123
    run a business plan competition, 82–83
    Small Business Saturday, 212–213
    use BeanStack for small business programming, 136–138
    work with formerly incarcerated individuals, 129–130
"How to Effectively Conduct a PESTLE & SWOT Analysis" (Gray), 238
Huber, Zachary W., 222–229

humility
    See cultural humility

I

IBISWorld, 95, 176–177, 178
Ice House Entrepreneurship
    Program, EBSCO, 134
"Identifying Stakeholders, Building
    Partnerships, Finding Funding,
    and Sustaining It All" (Brophy,
    Hench, Feinberg, Luccy, Burke,
    Milton, Goddard, Logan,
    Pitts, & Bourret), 13–27
Ildefonso, Madeleine
    "Equity, Diversity, and Inclusion in Library
        Entrepreneurship Programs," 29–40
    on Sea Un Vendedor Ambulante
        Exitoso/Successful Street
        Vending program, 155–160
immigrants
    immigration services of Los
        Angeles Public Library, 156
    Invest in Yourself branding for, 141
    Lucas County as Certified
        Welcoming community, 223
    SB-BI initiative for, 61–68
    Sea Un Vendedor Ambulante
        Exitoso/Successful Street
        Vending program, 155–160
    Small Business Hub services for, 180–186
    TLCPL's Business and Workforce
        team initiative for, 222–229
impact
    of Biz.ability workshops, 195–196
    of Building Business initiative, 201–202
    of Built in Broward program, 87
    of "Business Help at Your
        Library" program, 120
    of Business Insight Center, 94
    of Cultivate Indy, 133
    of Dallas B.R.A.I.N., 107
    of Employment and Business
        Entrepreneur Center, 231
    of Encore Entrepreneurs/Key
        Advanced Entrepreneurs, 101
    of Entrepreneur Academy, 70–71
    of Entrepreneur Workshop Series, 161
    of Entrepreneurial Launch Pad, 188
    of Invest in Yourself branding, 141–142
    of MAGIC, 175
    measuring success by, 145
    of Miller Business Center, 168
    of New Start Entrepreneurship
        Incubator, 126
    of PowerUP! 79
    of SLCL's small business outreach, 215–216
    of Small Business Boot Camp, 209
    of Small Business Hub, 181
    of "Small Business—Big
        Impact" initiative, 62
    of Stamford Small Business
        Resource Center, 114
    of TLCPL's Business and
        Workforce team, 223–224
    of Wyoming Library to Business, 148
imposter syndrome, 221
incarcerated individuals
    See formerly incarcerated individuals
incentives, 131, 135
inclusion
    belonging, library cultivation of, 38–39
    digital inclusion/access at small/
        rural libraries, 5–6
    formerly incarcerated individuals,
        working with, 129–130
    See also equity, diversity, and inclusion
Independence (KS) Public Library
    Cultivate Indy, 132–139
    in Libraries Build Business
        initiative, xiv–xv
    makerspace partnership, 46–47
    small business resources for patrons of, 4
Independence Chamber of Commerce, 134
Independence Community College, 47
Independence Main Street, 134
industry jargon, 117
InnovationQ, 95
in-person services, 121
instructor development program, 89
intellectual property, 94
internet access
    digital inclusion/access at small/
        rural libraries, 5–6
    at Ferguson Municipal Public Library, 120

internet access (*cont.*)
    for MAGIC, 176
    for Small Business Boot Camp, 213
    at Yakama Nation Library, 10–12
interviews, 212
Invest in Yourself branding, King County Library System
    budget for, 143
    goals/impact of, 141–142
    implementation of, 143–144
    partners for, 142
    promotion of program, 144–145
    resources for, 142
    roadblocks/challenges, 145
    setting the stage, 140
    staff responsibilities for, 145
    tips, tricks, advice for, 145–146

J

Janicki, Megan
    "How Libraries Build Business," xi–xvii
    "Open to Change: Libraries Catalyze Small Business Adaption to COVID-19," 237
Jenkins, Karen R., 189
job seekers programs, 120
Joseph, Elizabeth, 113–118
judges, 83

K

Kajabi, 87
Kauffman Foundation, 113, 204
Kelly, William, 100–105
Kelsey, Melinda, 165
Key Advanced Entrepreneurs
    See Encore Entrepreneurs/Key Advanced Entrepreneurs, Cuyahoga County (OH) Public Library
Key Foundation
    funding for Key Advanced Entrepreneurs, 100
    grants for entrepreneurs from, 101
    as partner of Cuyahoga County Public Library, 102
key resources
    See resources
keyboards, 157
kickoff event, 90

Kimbrough, LaKesha, 29–40
King County (WA) Library System, Invest in Yourself branding
    budget for, 143
    goals/impact of, 141–142
    implementation of, 143–144
    partners for, 142
    promotion of program, 144–145
    resources for, 142
    roadblocks/challenges, 145
    setting the stage, 140
    staff responsibilities for, 145
    tips, tricks, advice for, 145–146
kiva.org, 51
knowledge, 37

L

LA Law Library, 44–46
landing page, 87, 92
language
    of Cell-Ed learning modules, 155
    shared terms/understanding, 31
    structural change, conditions for, 33
laptops, 232
Laramie County (WY) Library System, Wyoming Library to Business (WL2B) initiative
    areas of focus, 150–151
    budget for, 150
    getting started, 148–149
    goals/impact of, 148
    Libraries Build Business initiative, xiv–xv
    partners for, 5, 149–150
    promotion of, 152
    resources for, 149
    roadblocks/challenges, 152–153
    setting the stage, 147
    staff responsibilities, 153
    technical support component, 47
    tips, tricks, advice for, 153–154
    video production studio, 151–152
Latin American Association, 22, 125
Latino Elder Outreach Network, 205
Latinx Small Business Roundtable, 141
Launchpad event, 128–129
LaVallee, Katherine, 174–179
law libraries, 44–46

INDEX

LBB
 See Libraries Build Business
  (LBB) initiative
Legal Services of Eastern Missouri, 217
legal support for business services, 44–46
Levandowski, Andrea, 41–52
LibGuides, 80
librarians
 for Built in Broward program, 91
 for Business Insight Center, 98
 imposter syndrome, 221
 for Miller Business Center, 172
 New Jersey State Library's work
  towards statewide professional
  development, 42–44
 one-to-one consultations with, 123
 of Small Business Hub, 185
 valuing services of, 235
 visiting/networking with, 200
 See also business librarians; staff;
  staff responsibilities
libraries
 belonging, cultivation of sense of, 38–39
 collaboration for entrepreneurship, 41–42
 funding opportunities, leveraging, 22–24
 Libraries Build Business initiative, xi–xvii
 outdated concepts of, 221
 partnerships, building, 16–20
 small/rural libraries,
  considerations for, 3–12
 trust in, 231
Libraries Build Business (LBB) initiative
 accessible, equitable, authentic
  engagement, 36–39
 EDI, commitment to, xvi
 EDI principles in library
  entrepreneurship programs, 29
 EDI principles, integration of, 40
 entrepreneurial ecosystem,
  integrating into, xi–xiv
 equity, diversity, and inclusion,
  commitment to, 30–35
 grant for Built in Broward program,
  88
 grant for "Business Help at Your
  Library" program, 121
 grant for Cultivate Indy, 135
 grant for Entrepreneurial
  Launch Pad, 189, 191
 grant for Los Angeles Public
  Library, 157–158
 grant for New Start Entrepreneurship
  Incubator, 128
 grant for Small Business Boot Camp, 210
 grant for Small Business Hub, 183
 grant for "Small Business—Big
  Impact" initiative, 63
 grant for Topsham Public Library, 233
 grant for Wyoming Library to Business, 150
 information about, 237
 map of libraries in, xv
 overview of, xiv–xvi
 partners of libraries in, 18
 partnerships, successful, 21–22
 profiles of libraries in LBB cohort, xvii
 program possibilities, xi
 relationships/power balances and, 36
 small/rural libraries,
  considerations for, 5–9
 small/rural libraries, help for community, 4
 Wyoming Library to Business
  (WL2B) initiative, 47
Libraries Lead with Digital Skills grant, 57, 58
library administration, 168
library card-making supplies, 216
library entrepreneurship programs
 with academic libraries, 46–48
 EDI, LBB initiative's commitment to, 30–35
 engaging accessibly, equitably,
  authentically, 36–39
 equity, diversity, and inclusion in, 29–30
 LA Law Library, legal support for
  business services, 44–46
 libraries working together for, 41–42
 New Jersey State Library, statewide
  professional development, 42–44
 partnerships/networking for services, 52
 small/rural libraries,
  considerations for, 3–12
 youth entrepreneurship programs, 48–52
 See also small business and
  entrepreneurship programs
library leadership, 14
library services, 73, 75

library small business programs
  funding opportunities, leveraging, 22–24
  marketing library program to potential partners, 19
  partnership, formalizing, 20–21
  partnerships, building, 16–18, 20
  partnerships, examples of successful, 21–22
  stakeholders, finding, 13–16
  sustaining, 24–27
  See also library entrepreneurship programs; small business and entrepreneurship programs
library staff
  See librarians; staff
Library Value Calculators, 220
lighting, 152
lightning talk, 89, 90
LinkedIn Learning, 127
listening
  to business community, 214
  to community members, 159
  to entrepreneurs, 221
LivePlan, 95
Logan, Atlas
  "Identifying Stakeholders, Building Partnerships, Finding Funding, and Sustaining It All," 13–27
  on New Start Entrepreneurship Incubator, 125–131
Los Angeles (CA) Public Library
  Cell-Ed units, 39
  in Libraries Build Business initiative, xiv–xv
  partnership with LA Law Library, 45–46
  resources that resonate with ESL, 37
  Sea Un Vendedor Ambulante Exitoso/Successful Street Vending program, 155–160
  workforce development/immigration services, 156
Los Angeles, California, 155–156
Lowe, Heather, 106–112
Lucas County (OH), 223
Luccy, Diane
  on Entrepreneurial Launch Pad, 187–194

"Identifying Stakeholders, Building Partnerships, Finding Funding, and Sustaining It All," 13–27
Luminate, 96

M

Macedon (NY) Public Library, Entrepreneur Workshop Series
  getting started, 162
  goals/impact of, 161
  implementation of, 162–164
  Melinda Kelsey, 165
  promotion of, 164
  roadblocks/challenges, 164
  setting the stage, 161
  staff responsibilities, 164–165
  tips, tricks, advice for, 165–166
MAGIC
  See Management and Government Information Center
"The MAGIC Touch: Management and Government Information Center" (LaVallee & Gunia), 174–179
Maine CareerCenters
  connection to, 233
  one-to-one business support, 233–234
  partnership with Topsham Public Library, 231, 232, 235
makerspace
  academic library partnership for, 46–47
  of Cultivate Indy Small Business Lab, 135
  of Small Business Hub, 181, 182
  Yakama Nation Library Business Maker Space, 10–12, 36
Malafi, Elizabeth, 167–173
Management and Government Information Center (MAGIC)
  background on, 174–175
  budget for, 176–177
  getting started, 175–176
  goals/impact of, 175
  partners for, 176
  promotion of, 178
  resources for, 176
  roadblocks/challenges, 179
  staff responsibilities, 179

support of local entrepreneurs, 177–178
tips, tricks, advice for, 179
market research
    Business Insight Center for, 94, 95–96
    for Dallas B.R.A.I.N., 107, 108
    from MAGIC, 174
    Women's Economic Ventures and, 203
marketing
    of business and job seeker services, 58–59
    of business plan competition, 82
    of library program to potential partners, 19
    for library small business initiative, 26
    plan of Stamford Small Business Resource Center, 114
    See also promotion
Maryland Department of Labor, 72
Maryland Small Business Development Center, 72
McCleer, Adriana
    "BIPOC Business Community and Connections," 61–68
    "Equity, Diversity, and Inclusion in Library Entrepreneurship Programs," 29–40
meaning, 34
"Meet Them Where They Are: Small Business Outreach" (Gibson), 215–221
meeting space
    for "Business Help at Your Library" program, 121
    for Employment and Business Entrepreneur Center, 232
    for MAGIC, 176
    of SBPL Building Business initiative, 204, 205
Memorandum of Agreement (MOA), 20–21
Memorandum of Understanding (MOU)
    for clear terms for partners' expectations, 23
    for communication with partners, 213
    formalizing partnership with, 20–21
    for partnerships, 139
mentors
    entrepreneur-in-residence (EiR), 189
    in Entrepreneur Workshop Series, 163
    for New Start Entrepreneurship Incubator, 128

    as partners for NSEI, 128
    of SCORE, 162
mentorship
    by Austin SCORE, 198
    in BizKids Club, 49
    in business plan competition, 83
    in Team Read program, 51
Mergent Intellect, 95
Merza, Ahmad, 201–207
Metheny, Ryan, 41–52
micro-entrepreneurs
    "Business Help at Your Library" program for, 119–124
    Invest in Yourself branding for, 141
    library support of, 8
    Sea Un Vendedor Ambulante Exitoso/Successful Street Vending program, 155–160
micro-grants
    budget for SBBC program, 210
    from Small Business Boot Camp, 209
    use of by participants, 211
Microsoft Teams, 153, 211
Middle Country (NY) Public Library, Miller Business Center, 167–173
Midlands Regional Competitiveness Report, 188
Midlands Technical College, 21–22, 191
Miller, Crystal, 208–214
Miller Business Center, Middle Country (NY) Public Library
    budget for, 169–170
    description of, 167–168
    goals/impact of, 168
    partners for, 169
    planning for, 170
    promotion of, 171–172
    resources for, 168–169
    roadblocks/challenges, 172
    staff responsibilities, 172
    tips, tricks, and advice for, 172–173
    Women's EXPO event, hosting, 170–171
Milton, Danielle
    "Identifying Stakeholders, Building Partnerships, Finding Funding, and Sustaining It All," 13–27
    on Small Business Boot Camp, 208–214

minorities
- Encore Entrepreneurs/Key Advanced Entrepreneurs serving, 101
- Entrepreneurial Launch Pad for, 187–194
- Invest in Yourself, mission of, 141
- Sea Un Vendedor Ambulante Exitoso/Successful Street Vending program, 155–160
- Small Business Hub for, 180–186
- Stamford Small Business Resource Center for, 114
- *See also* Black, Indigenous, and people of color

Minority Business Assistance Center, 226, 227
MOA (Memorandum of Agreement), 20–21
mobile learning modules, 155
mobile resources, 6–7
money
- *See* budget; funding

Montgomery County Action Council, 135
Moore, Delores, 36
MOU
- *See* Memorandum of Understanding

mutually beneficial relationships, 32–33
My Librarian, 75
MyTurn software, 190

N

National Community Reinvestment Coalition, 30
National Federation of Independent Business (NFIB), 239
needs
- of business owners, 216
- of community, identification of, 186
- of community, meeting, 25–26

needs assessment
- business needs assessment, 58
- library small business programs and, xiii
- of local small business landscape, 133
- SWOT/PESTLE analyses for, 238

Neighborhood Champion program, 214
networking
- attending business-networking events, 207
- for Entrepreneur Workshop Series, 163–164
- by Entrepreneurial Launch Pad, 192
- as essential, 52
- for funding for small/rural libraries, 5
- for library business and job seeker services, 56–57
- offering in business program, 76
- for promotion of business program, 89
- in SBPL Building Business initiative, 204
- "Small Business—Big Impact" initiative for, 64
- Women's EXPO event, 170–171

"New Americans in Toledo and Lucas County" report, 223–224
New Jersey Business Action Center, 43
New Jersey Economic Development Authority, 43
New Job Toolkits, 58
"A New Start: Entrepreneurship for the Formerly Incarcerated" (Pitts, Logan, Gauthier, Serrie, & Devereux), 125–131
New Start Entrepreneurship Incubator (NSEI)
- budget for, 128
- formerly incarcerated individuals, working with, 129–130
- getting started, 126–127
- goals/impact of, 126
- implementation of, 128–129
- Libraries Build Business grant to fund, 22
- partners for, 127–128
- promotion of, 130
- purpose of, 39
- resources for, 127
- roadblocks/challenges, 130
- setting the stage, 125–126
- staff responsibilities, 130–131
- tips, tricks, advice for, 131

New York State Small Business Development Center, 95
newspapers, 138
Nextcorp, 96
NFIB (National Federation of Independent Business), 239
NIIC (Northeast Indiana Innovation Center), 50–52
NJLibsGrowBiz Committee, 43–44
Non-Profit Academy, Baltimore County Public Library, 71
nonprofits
- Grant Resources Kit for, 177
- partnerships with, 57

INDEX **259**

Northeast Indiana Innovation
  Center (NIIC), 50–52
Northwest Ohio Hispanic Chamber
  of Commerce, 227
NSEI
  See New Start Entrepreneurship Incubator

O

OCLS (Orange County Library System), 48–50
ODLOS Glossary, 238
Office of Economic Development
  one-on-one assistance, 109–110
  as partner for Dallas B.R.A.I.N.,
    106, 108, 111
O'Hare, Sarah, 208–214
Ohio Minority Supplier Diversity/
  Development Council, 227
1 Million Cups
  Entrepreneurial Launch Pad
    and, 187–188, 192
  SBPL Building Business and, 203, 204,
    205
one-to-one assistance
  of Dallas B.R.A.I.N., 109–110
  with Employment and Business
    Entrepreneur Center, 233
  for micro-entrepreneurs, 119–124
  provision of, 233–234
  TLCPL's Business and Workforce
    team initiative, 222, 223
"One-to-One Support for Micro-
  Entrepreneurs: Business Help at
  Your Library" (Hall), 119–124
Onyx Business Solutions, 217
"Open to Change: Libraries Catalyze Small
  Business Adaption to COVID-19"
  (Whitman, Janicki, & Visser), 237
"Opening the Doors to Economic Success:
  The Miller Business Center" (Serlis-
  McPhillips & Malafi), 167–173
Orange County Library System (OCLS), 48–50
Orengo, Tony, 41–52
outcomes, 145
Outlook Quick Parts, 176
Outlook Task, 178
outreach
  coordinator, 128, 131
  SLCL's small business outreach, 215–221

TLCPL's Business and Workforce
  team initiative, 222–229
Wyoming Library to Business for, 147
See also promotion

P

participants
  in Baltimore County Public Library's
    business programs, 70–71
  in business plan competition, 82–84
  in entrepreneur Academy, 73
  following up with, 76–77
  in PowerUP! 81–82
  in Stamford Small Business Resource
    Center program, 116
  in Women's EXPO, 171
  See also audience; program attendance
partners
  of Baltimore County Public Library, 72
  for Biz.ability workshops, 197
  for Brooklyn Public Library's
    PowerUP! 80–81
  for Building Business initiative, 203, 204
  for Built in Broward program, 87–88
  for "Business Help at Your
    Library" program, 121
  for Business Insight Center, 95–96
  communication with, 90, 213
  for Cultivate Indy, 134–135
  of Cuyahoga County Public Library, 102
  for Dallas B.R.A.I.N., 108–109
  for Employment and Business
    Entrepreneur Center, 231, 232
  for Entrepreneur Workshop Series, 162
  for Entrepreneurial Launch
    Pad, 190–191, 193
  of Ferguson Library, 113, 114
  of Gwinnett County Public Library, 125
  for Invest in Yourself branding, 142
  for MAGIC, 176
  for Miller Business Center, 169
  for New Start Entrepreneurship
    Incubator, 127–128
  for promotion of business program, 104
  for SBPL's Building Business initiative, 203
  for Sea Un Vendedor Ambulante Exitoso/
    Successful Street Vending program, 157
  for SLCL's small business outreach, 217

partners *(cont.)*
    for Small Business Boot Camp, 209, 210
    for Small Business Hub, 182–183
    as stakeholders in library small business program, 14
    for Stamford Small Business Resource Center, 115
    strong partner, how to be, 226–227
    for TLCPL's Business and Workforce team initiative, 225–226
    for Women's EXPO, 170
    working with multiple community partners, 207
    for Wyoming Library to Business, 149–150
partnerships
    for Addison Public Library's business and job seeker services, 57
    for budget stretching, 123
    building, 16–18, 20
    for Built in Broward program, 86, 90–91
    for business plan competition, 85
    for business program, 76
    for business program of small/rural libraries, 7–8
    community assessment for, 144
    creativity with, 199
    for Dallas B.R.A.I.N., 106, 107, 111
    for Entrepreneur Academy, 75
    for Entrepreneur Workshop Series, 161, 162
    equity/inclusion vision and, 37
    as essential, 52
    examples of successful, 21–22
    formalizing, 20–21
    for funding for small/rural libraries, 5
    funding opportunities and, 23
    keeping/deepening, 25
    Libraries Build Business initiative, xiv–xvi
    of libraries for entrepreneurship support, 41–42
    libraries/small businesses, xii
    Los Angeles (CA) Public Library/LA Law Library, 45–46
    marketing library program to potential partners, 19
    Memorandum of Understanding for, 139
    of New Jersey State Library, 42–44
    for New Start Entrepreneurship Incubator, 126–128
    for small business outreach, 219
    for "Small Business—Big Impact" initiative, 63, 66, 67
    strong partner, how to be, 226–227
    trust for, 205–206
    for W2LB initiative, 147
patent, 94
"Pathway to Entrepreneurial Success: The Stamford Small Business Resource Center" (Joseph), 113–118
patience, 146, 199
Penn State University, 151
people-first language, 129
persistence, 24
PESTLE, 15, 238
Pew Research, 231
pilot project, 224
pitch competition, 85
pitch deck contests, 110
PitchBook, 95
Pitts, Adam
    "Identifying Stakeholders, Building Partnerships, Finding Funding, and Sustaining It All," 13–27
    on New Start Entrepreneurship Incubator, 125–131
positive attitude, 154
postcards, 171
Potomac Health Foundation
    Capacity Building grant for PWPL, 174–175
    grant for MAGIC, 177
    as partner of MAGIC, 176
power imbalances
    in cultural humility framework, 32, 33
    identification of, 38
PowerUP! Brooklyn Public Library (BPL)
    BKLYN Fashion Academy, 84
    creation of, 79–81
    goals/impact of, 79
    how to run business plan competition, 82–83
    implementation of, 81
    promotion of, 83
    roadblocks/challenges, 83–84
    setting the stage, 78–79

INDEX **261**

staff responsibilities, 84
tips, tricks, advice for, 85
Preece, Susan M.
   "Considerations for Small and Rural Libraries," 3–12
   "Support Rural Business: Employment and Business Entrepreneur Center," 230–235
press release
   for promotion of business program, 75, 89, 164
   of Stamford Small Business Resource Center, 116
Prince William County's Department of Economic Development, 177
Prince William Public Library (Woodbridge, VA), 174–179
printed materials, 115
privacy concerns, 129
privilege, 143–144
prizes, 79, 81, 83
professional development, 42–44
program attendance
   Biz.ability workshops, 199
   as roadblock, 179
   for Small Business Boot Camp, 213
   transportation/connectivity issues, 185
program outline, 16
program plan, 114
project management software, 153
Project Outcome
   Appleton Public Library's use of, 64
   for Biz.ability workshops, 197
   information about, 237–238
promotion
   of BIPOC entrepreneur storytelling series, 65
   of Biz.ability workshops, 198–199
   of Building Business initiative, 204–205
   of Built in Broward program, 89–91
   of business and job seeker services, 58–59
   of "Business Help at Your Library" program, 123
   of Business Insight Center, 97
   of business plan competition, 83
   of Cultivate Indy, 138
   of Dallas B.R.A.I.N., 110
   of Employment and Business Entrepreneur Center, 234
   of Encore Entrepreneurs/Key Advanced Entrepreneurs, 104
   of Entrepreneur Academy, 75
   of Entrepreneur Workshop Series, 163–164
   of Entrepreneurial Launch Pad, 193
   of Invest in Yourself branding, 144–145
   of MAGIC, 178
   of Miller Business Center, 171–172
   of New Start Entrepreneurship Incubator, 130, 131
   of PowerUP! 83
   promotional materials for small business outreach, 216
   of Sea Un Vendedor Ambulante Exitoso/Successful Street Vending program, 159–160
   of Small Business Boot Camp, 213
   of Small Business Hub, 185
   of small business outreach, 219, 220
   of "Small Business—Big Impact" initiative, 66
   of Stamford Small Business Resource Center, 116
   of TLCPL's Business and Workforce team initiative, 227–228
   of WL2B, 152
   of Women's EXPO, 171
Providence (RI) Public Library, Small Business Hub
   budget for, 183
   "ESOL for Business Owners" course, development of, 184–185
   getting started, 182
   goals/impact of, 181
   implementation of, 183–184
   in Libraries Build Business initiative, xiv–xv
   partners for, 182–183
   program feedback, 24
   promotion of, 185
   resources for, 182
   roadblocks/challenges, 185
   setting the stage, 180–181
   staff responsibilities, 185
   tips, tricks, advice for, 186

public libraries
    academic libraries, partnership with, 46–48
    collaboration with other libraries, 41–42
Public Library Association, 64, 197

Q
questionnaire, 26
Quillivan, Mary Kate, 187–194

R
racial equity analysis, 143–144
Radio Bronco, 204, 205
reading, 50–52
recidivism, 126
reentry organizations, 129
Reference Solutions, 198
ReferenceUSA, 202
reflection, 32, 33
relationships
    for business and job seeker services, 60
    with community, building, 91
    for developing business program, 59
    for Entrepreneur Workshop Series, 166
    entrepreneurship and, 35–36
    as healing-centered engagement principle, 34
    Invest in Yourself branding and, 144, 145
    investment in, 37
    mutually beneficial relationships, 32–33
    partner relationships, strategies for, 20
    with potential partners, building, 89
    staying connected, 194
    See also partners; partnerships
relevancy, 26
requests for information, 178
research, 177–178
    See also market research
resource fair, 127
resources
    for Addison Public Library's business and job seeker services, 57
    Association for Rural & Small Libraries, 238
    for Biz.ability workshops, 197, 198
    for Building Business initiative, 202–203
    for Built in Broward program, 87
    for "Business Help at Your Library" program, 121
    for Business Insight Center, 95
    for business plan competition, 79, 80
    business program resources handout, 7
    community business resources, 238–240
    community resources for entrepreneurs, 181
    for Cultivate Indy, 133–134
    for Dallas B.R.A.I.N., 108
    for Employment and Business Entrepreneur Center, 232
    for Encore Entrepreneurs/Key Advanced Entrepreneurs, 102
    for Entrepreneur Academy, 72
    for Entrepreneur Workshop Series, 162, 163
    for Entrepreneurial Launch Pad, 190
    for entrepreneurs, knowledge of, 120
    evaluation of, 37
    Flourish Agenda, 238
    high barrier to entry, 111
    for Invest in Yourself branding, 142
    Libraries Build Business, 237
    for MAGIC, 174, 176
    for Miller Business Center, 168–169
    for New Start Entrepreneurship Incubator, 127
    ODLOS Glossary, 238
    packaging existing services for business community, 73, 75
    Project Outcome, 237–238
    for Sea Un Vendedor Ambulante Exitoso/Successful Street Vending program, 157
    for Small Business Boot Camp, 210
    for Small Business Hub, 182
    for small business outreach, 216, 218
    for "Small Business—Big Impact" initiative, 63
    for Stamford Small Business Resource Center, 114–115
    SWOT/PESTLE analyses, 238
    for TLCPL's Business and Workforce team initiative, 224–225
    transformational practices, 38
    for Wyoming Library to Business, 149
responsibilities, 21
    See also staff responsibilities

RI Department of State Business Services, 183
RI Hispanic Chamber of Commerce, 183
RI Small Business Development Center, 183
Richland County, Office of Small
    Business Opportunities, 191
Richland Library (Columbia, SC),
    Entrepreneurial Launch Pad
  budget for, 191
  EiR, definition of, 189
  EiR program, how to create, 192–193
  getting started, 188–190
  goals/impact of, 188
  in Libraries Build Business
      initiative, xiv–xv
  partners for, 190–191
  partnerships of, 21–22
  promotion of, 193
  resources for, 190
  roadblocks/challenges, 193
  setting the stage, 187–188
  staff responsibilities, 193
  tips, tricks, advice for, 194
RIT Venture Creations, 95
roadblocks/challenges
  for Biz.ability workshops, 199
  brainstorming about possible, 214
  for Building Business initiative, 205–206
  for Built in Broward program, 91
  for "Business Help at Your
      Library" program, 123
  for Business Insight Center, 97–98
  to business program, overcoming, 59
  for Cultivate Indy, 138
  for Dallas B.R.A.I.N., 111
  for Employment and Business
      Entrepreneur Center, 234
  of Encore Entrepreneurs/Key
      Advanced Entrepreneurs, 104
  for Entrepreneur Academy, 75–76
  for Entrepreneur Workshop Series, 164
  for Entrepreneurial Launch Pad, 193
  for Invest in Yourself branding, 145
  to MAGIC, 179
  for Miller Business Center, 172
  for New Start Entrepreneurship
      Incubator, 130
  for PowerUP! 83–84
  for Sea Un Vendedor Ambulante Exitoso/
      Successful Street Vending program, 160
  for SLCL's small business outreach, 221
  for Small Business Boot Camp, 213
  for Small Business Hub, 185
  "Small Business—Big Impact"
      initiative, 66–67
  for Stamford Small Business
      Resource Center, 116–-117
  for TLCPL's Business and Workforce
      team initiative, 228
  for Wyoming Library to Business, 152–153
Robert Wood Johnson Foundation
    Culture of Health Prize, 56
Robinson, Arcola, 78–85
Rochester, New York, 93
"Rochester—Innovation Was Born
    Here" (Byrnes), 93–99
Rochester Institute of Technology, 95–96
Rochester Public Library, 165–166
roles, in MOU, 21
Round Rock Chamber of Commerce, 197
Round Rock Leader (newspaper), 198–199
Round Rock (TX), 197
Round Rock (TX) Public Library, 195–200
rural business, 230–235
rural entrepreneurs, 147–154
rural libraries
  challenges facing, xvi
  Cultivate Indy, Independence (KS)
      Public Library, 132–139
  Employment and Business
      Entrepreneur Center of Topsham
      Public Library, 230–235
  See also small and rural libraries

S

safe space, 9
Santa Barbara Adult Education
    Consortium, 204, 206
Santa Barbara (CA) Public Library,
    Building Business initiative
  budget for, 204
  goals/impact of, 201–202
  implementation of, 204
  partners for, 203
  promotion of, 204–205

Santa Barbara (CA) Public Library, Building Business initiative *(cont.)*
    resources for, 202–203
    roadblocks/challenges, 205–206
    ServSafe licensure programs, 206
    setting the stage, 201
    staff responsibilities, 206
    tips, tricks, advice for, 207
SBA
    See Small Business Administration
SBDC
    See Small Business Development Center
SBDC (SC Small Business Development Centers), 191
SBRC (Small Business Resource Center), 165–166
SBS
    See Small Business Saturday
SC Small Business Development Centers (SBDC), 191
scaling, 194
SCORE
    See Service Core of Retired Executives
Sea Un Vendedor Ambulante Exitoso/ Successful Street Vending program
    budget for, 157–158
    goals/impact of, 156
    partners for, 157
    promotion of, 159–160
    resources for, 157
    roadblocks/challenges, 160
    setting the stage, 155–156
    staff responsibilities, 160
    street vendors, how to work with, 158–159
    tips, tricks, advice for, 160
seed capital
    insufficient, as roadblock, 129
    for winning plans in PowerUP! 78, 81
Sekaquaptewa, Michael
    "Considerations for Small and Rural Libraries," 3–12
    "Equity, Diversity, and Inclusion in Library Entrepreneurship Programs," 29–40
self-reflection, 32
Serlis-McPhillips, Sophia, 167–173
Serrie, Ann, 125–131
ServSafe program, 204, 206

Service Core of Retired Executives (SCORE)
    Austin SCORE, 197, 198, 199
    Entrepreneur Workshop Series, partnership for, 161–166
    information about, 239
    North Metro Atlanta, 127
    as partner for Dallas B.R.A.I.N., 108
    as partner of Stamford Small Business Resource Center, 115
    partnership with Business Insight Center, 97
    partnership with GCPL, 22, 125
    partnership with St. Louis County Library, 217
    as potential partner for library small-business initiatives, 17
    SCORE RI/Providence Public Library partnership, 180–183
shared terms and understanding, 31
signage, 123
Simone Center for Innovation and Entrepreneurship, 95–96
SizeUp, 203
Slack
    for Built in Broward program, 87, 89
    for communication with stakeholders, 153
small and rural libraries
    entrepreneurial mindset for, 12
    opportunities/limitations facing, 3–4
    reach of, 3
    special considerations for, 5–9
    Yakama Nation Library, 9–12
Small Biz Ally, 125
Small Business & Nonprofit Expo, 217
Small Business Administration (SBA)
    as partner for Biz.ability workshops, 197
    as partner for Entrepreneurial Launch Pad, 191
    as partner for W2LB initiative, 150
    as partner of Baltimore County Public Library, 72
    as partner of Stamford Small Business Resource Center, 115
    partnership with St. Louis County Library, 217
small business and entrepreneurship programs
    Biz.ability workshops, 195–200

BizKids Club, 48–50
Built in Broward, 86–92
Business and Job Seeker Services, 55–60
"Business Help at Your Library" program, 119–124
Business Insight Center, 93–99
Cultivate Indy, 132–139
Dallas B.R.A.I.N., 106–112
Employment and Business Entrepreneur Center, 230–235
Encore Entrepreneurs/Key Advanced Entrepreneurs, 100–105
Entrepreneur Academy, 69–77
Entrepreneur Workshop Series, 161–166
Entrepreneurial Launch Pad, 187–194
Invest in Yourself branding, King County Library System, 140–146
MAGIC, 174–179
Miller Business Center, 167–173
New Start Entrepreneurship Incubator, 125–131
PowerUP! Brooklyn Public Library, 78–85
Sea Un Vendedor Ambulante Exitoso/Successful Street Vending program, 155–160
of small and rural libraries, 3–12
Small Business Boot Camp, 208–214
Small Business Hub of Providence (RI) Public Library, 180–186
small business outreach of SLCL, 215–221
"Small Business—Big Impact" (SB-BI) initiative, 61–68
Stamford Small Business Resource Center, 113–118
Team Read, Allen County Public Library, 50–52
Wyoming Library to Business (WL2B) initiative, 147–154
Small Business Boot Camp, Spokane County (WA) Library District
budget for, 210–211
goals/impact of, 209
implementation of, 211–212
partners for, 210
promotion of, 213
resources for, 210
roadblocks/challenges, 213

setting the stage, 208–209
Small Business Saturday, 212–213
staff responsibilities, 213
tips, tricks, advice for, 214
Small Business Challenge, 136–138
Small Business Development Center (SBDC)
Independence Public Library's partnership with, 4
information about, 239–240
IPL programs through, 133
as partner for Biz.ability workshops, 197
as partner of Stamford Small Business Resource Center, 115
Small Business Expo, 215
Small Business Hub, Providence (RI) Public Library
budget for, 183
"ESOL for Business Owners" course, 184–185
getting started, 182
goals/impact of, 181
implementation of, 183–184
partners for, 182–183
promotion of, 185
resources for, 182
roadblocks/challenges, 185
setting the stage, 180–181
staff responsibilities, 185
tips, tricks, advice for, 186
small business outreach, St. Louis County (MO) Library
budget for, 217
goals/impact of, 215–216
implementation of, 217–220
partners for, 217
promotion of, 220
resources for, 216
roadblocks/challenges, 221
setting the stage, 215
Small Business Value Calculator, 220
staff responsibilities, 221
tips, tricks, advice for, 221
small business owners
See business owners
Small Business Resource Center (SBRC), 165–166

Small Business Saturday (SBS)
    at Addison Public Library, 57–58
    celebrating, 212–213
    Neighborhood Champion program, 214
Small Business Team, 193
Small Business Value Calculator, 220
"Small Business—Big Impact" (SB-BI) initiative at Appleton Public Library
    BIPOC entrepreneur storytelling series, 65–66
    getting started, 62–63
    goals/impacts of, 62
    implementation of, 64
    promotion of program, 66
    roadblocks/challenges, 66–67
    setting the stage, 61–62
    staff responsibilities, 67
    tips, tricks, advice for, 67–68
small businesses
    Libraries Build Business initiative, xi–xvii
    library programs/services for, xi–xiv
small food businesses, 141
SmallBiz Ally, 22, 127
social entrepreneurship, 51
social media
    for promotion of Building Business initiative, 205
    for promotion of business program, 89–90, 164
    for promotion of Cultivate Indy, 138
    for SB-BI initiative promotion, 66
    for Stamford Small Business Resource Center, 115
    Yakama Nation Library and, 11
Southern Midcoast CareerCenter, 233
Southern Midcoast Maine Chamber of Commerce, 231, 232
space
    for "Business Help at Your Library" program, 121, 122
    for Dallas B.R.A.I.N., 108
    for Employment and Business Entrepreneur Center, 232
    for Entrepreneurial Launch Pad, 190
    library conference rooms for meetings, 229
    meeting space for MAGIC, 176
    for Miller Business Center, 169
    size of, 172
    for small and rural libraries, 6–7
    for Small Business Hub, 182
    for Stamford Small Business Resource Center, 115
    for TLCPL's Business and Workforce team initiative, 224
    for video production studio, 150, 151–152
Spanish-speaking business owners, 201–207
speakers
    for BIPOC entrepreneur storytelling series, 65–66
    for Entrepreneur Academy, 72
    for Entrepreneur Workshop Series, 163
    for ESOL course, 186
    for New Start Entrepreneurship Incubator, 128
    in Team Read program, 50–51
special considerations, 5–9
"Specialized Library Supports for Entrepreneurs" (Metheny, Levandowski, Brown, Orengo, Burnard, Honeywell, Brophy, Svoboda, & West), 41–52
Spilyay (Coyote), 10
Spokane County (WA) Library District, Small Business Boot Camp
    budget for, 210–211
    goals/impact of, 209
    implementation of, 211–212
    in Libraries Build Business initiative, xiv–xv
    partners for, 21, 210
    promotion of, 213
    resources for, 210
    roadblocks/challenges, 213
    setting the stage, 208–209
    Small Business Saturday, 212–213
    staff responsibilities, 213
    tips, tricks, advice for, 214
Spokane SCORE, 210
St. Louis County Library (SLCL), small business outreach
    budget for, 217
    goals/impact of, 215–216
    implementation of, 217–220
    partners for, 217

promotion of, 220
resources for, 216
roadblocks/challenges, 221
setting the stage, 215
Small Business Value Calculator, 220
staff responsibilities, 221
tips, tricks, advice for, 221
staff
    as biggest resource, 173
    for business program of small/
        rural libraries, 7
    for Entrepreneur Academy, 72
    for hosting Women's EXPO, 170
    for MAGIC, 174, 176
    PowerUP! budget for staff, 81
    sustaining small business
        program and, 24–25
    time as key resource, 142
    for TLCPL's Business and Workforce
        team initiative, 224, 226
    working relationships with colleagues, 60
staff responsibilities
    for Addison Public Library's business
        and job seeker services, 60
    for Biz.ability workshops, 199
    for Building Business initiative, 206
    for Built in Broward program, 91
    for "Business Help at Your
        Library" program, 123–124
    for Business Insight Center, 98
    for Cultivate Indy, 138
    for Dallas B.R.A.I.N., 111
    for Employment and Business
        Entrepreneur Center, 235
    for Encore Entrepreneurs/Key
        Advanced Entrepreneurs, 104
    for Entrepreneur Academy, 76
    for Entrepreneur Workshop Series, 164–165
    for Entrepreneurial Launch Pad, 193
    for Invest in Yourself branding, 145
    for MAGIC, 179
    for Miller Business Center, 172
    for New Start Entrepreneurship
        Incubator, 130–131
    for PowerUP! 84
    for Sea Un Vendedor Ambulante Exitoso/
        Successful Street Vending program, 160

    for SLCL's small business outreach, 221
    for Small Business Boot Camp, 213
    for Small Business Hub, 185
    for "Small Business—Big
        Impact" initiative, 67
    for Stamford Small Business
        Resource Center, 117
    for TLCPL's Business and Workforce
        team initiative, 228
    for Wyoming Library to Business, 153
stakeholders
    in business plan competition, 82
    communication with, 90, 153
    of Entrepreneur Academy, 71, 72–73
    finding, 13–16
    library working with, xiii
    listening to, 143
Stamford 1 Million Cups, 113
Stamford Next, 115
Stamford Partnership, 115
Stamford Small Business Resource
      Center, Ferguson Library
    budget for, 115
    goals/impact of, 114
    implementation of, 115–116
    partners for, 115
    promotion of, 116
    resources for, 114–115
    roadblocks/challenges, 116–-117
    setting the stage, 113–114
    staff responsibilities, 117
    tips, tricks, advice for, 117–118
"Starting & Growing a Business: Legal and
      Financial Knowledge You Need to
      Succeed" (LA Law Library), 45–46
"starting a business" workshop series, 183
start-up capital
    See seed capital
Startup Week, Techstars, 107
start-ups
    "Business Help at Your Library" program
        for micro-entrepreneurs, 119–124
    Business Insight Center for, 93–99
    PowerUP! for, 78–85
    program as business start-up, 117
statewide professional development, 42–44
Statista, 95

"Stories and Strategies" storytelling series, 64
storytelling
    BIPOC entrepreneur storytelling series, 64, 65–66
    equity/inclusion through, 39
street vendors
    goals/impact of program for, 156
    how to work with, 158–159
    Sea Un Vendedor Ambulante Exitoso/Successful Street Vending program, 155–160
Strictly Business networking events, 167, 169
study rooms, 73
subject matter experts, 72
success, 76
Success Council, 79
Successful Street Vending program
    See Sea Un Vendedor Ambulante Exitoso/Successful Street Vending program
support group, 79–80
"Support Rural Business: Employment and Business Entrepreneur Center" (Preece), 230–235
"Supporting the Local Economy" (Cyrier & Glimco), 55–60
surveys
    for "Business Help at Your Library" program, 122
    for Dallas B.R.A.I.N., 112
    for Entrepreneur Academy, 70–71, 73, 74
    for Entrepreneurial Launch Pad, 192
    for "ESOL for Business Owners" course, 184
    for NSEI, 129
    Project Outcome for, 64
    for Small Business Boot Camp, 212
    for Stamford Small Business Resource Center, 116
    of street vendors, 158
sustainability
    advocacy/buy-in, 26
    assessment for relevancy, 26
    community's needs, targeting, 25–26
    partnerships, keeping/deepening, 25
    of project in original program plan, 117
    of small business programs, 24–27
    staff engagement/planning for change, 24–25
success, setting up for, 27
Svoboda, Rachael
    "Building Support for Rural Entrepreneurs: A Statewide Initiative," 147–154
    "Considerations for Small and Rural Libraries," 3–12
    "Specialized Library Supports for Entrepreneurs," 41–52
SWOT, 15, 238
Syracuse University Innovation Law Center, 96

T

"Taking a Shot with SCORE: Entrepreneur Workshop Series" (Wicksall), 161–166
"Taking Budding Entrepreneurs from Business Idea to Business Plan" (Brophy), 69–77
Task, 176
teaching opportunities, 219
technology
    for Biz.ability workshops, 197
    Built in Broward program for tech businesses, 86–92
    for "Business Help at Your Library" program, 122
    for Cultivate Indy, 134, 135
    for Employment and Business Entrepreneur Center, 232
    iniquities for customers, 228
    packaging existing services for business community, 75
    resources for W2LB initiative, 149
    for small business outreach, 216
    for Stamford Small Business Resource Center, 115
    for street vending program, 157
    tech workshops, 86, 87, 88–89
    technical support, 47
    for video production studio, 150
    YNL Business Maker Space for learning, 11, 12
Techstars, 107
terms, 31
"test and try" stance, 224
3D printer
    for "Business Help at Your Library" program, 121, 122

packaging existing services for business community, 75
Thriving Communities, 158
time
    scheduling "ESOL for Business Owners" course, 185
    staff time for Cultivate Indy, 138
    as valuable resource for staff/patrons, 123–124
timeline, 156
tips, tricks, and advice
    for Biz.ability workshops, 199–200
    for Building Business initiative, 207
    for Built in Broward program, 91–92
    for business and job seeker services, 60
    for "Business Help at Your Library" program, 123–124
    for Business Insight Center, 98–99
    for Cultivate Indy, 139
    for Dallas B.R.A.I.N., 111–112
    for Employment and Business Entrepreneur Center, 235
    for Entrepreneur Academy, 76–77
    for Entrepreneur Workshop Series, 165–166
    for Entrepreneurial Launch Pad, 194
    for ESOL course, 186
    for Invest in Yourself branding, 145–146
    for MAGIC, 179
    for Miller Business Center, 172–173
    for New Start Entrepreneurship Incubator, 131
    for PowerUP! 85
    for Sea Un Vendedor Ambulante Exitoso/Successful Street Vending program, 160
    for SLCL's small business outreach, 221
    for Small Business Boot Camp, 214
    for "Small Business—Big Impact" initiative, 67–68
    for Stamford Small Business Resource Center, 117–118
    for TLCPL's Business and Workforce team initiative, 229
    for Wyoming Library to Business, 153–154
Toledo African American Chamber of Commerce, 227
Toledo Business Growth Collaborative, 225
Toledo Lucas County (OH) Public Library (TLCPL)
    budget for, 226
    Business and Workforce team, outreach by, 222
    goals/impact of business programs/services, 223–224
    partners for initiative, 225–226
    promotion of program, 227–228
    resources for initiative, 224–225
    roadblocks/challenges, 228
    staff responsibilities, 228
    strong partner, how to be, 226–227
    tips, tricks, advice for, 229
Topsham (ME) Public Library
    Employment and Business Entrepreneur Center, 230–235
    federal government resources, help with accessing, 4
    Internet access offered by, 6
    in Libraries Build Business initiative, xiv–xv
    partnership with CareerCenter, 9
Topsham Development Inc.
    connection to, 233
    partnership with Topsham Public Library, 231, 232
Towson University, 46
trademark, 94
training
    Academy for business owners, 64
    Entrepreneur Academy of Baltimore County Public Library, 69–77
    instructor development program, 89
    for library staff, 24
    in PowerUP! 81
    in W2LB initiative, 150
transformational practices, 38
trauma
    Cell-Ed units addressing, 158
    of formerly incarcerated individuals, 130
    trauma-informed programming, 39
Trello, 153
tribal libraries, 9–12
trust
    branding for, 175
    building, 159
    community trust in library program, 160

trust (cont.)
    formerly incarcerated individuals and, 130
    with individuals/partners, 226, 227
    in libraries, 231
    as library strength, 235
    of SBPL's Building Business initiative, 205–206

U

UCEDC, 43
ULC (Urban Libraries Council), 94, 225
underrepresented populations
    BizKids Club for, 48–50
    Built in Broward program for tech businesses, 86–92
    community-based social justice organizations for, 17–18
    Cultivate Indy for, 132–139
    EDI, LBB initiative's commitment to, 30–35
    EDI principles in library entrepreneurship programs, 29
    entrepreneurship, purpose of, 35–36
university libraries, 46–48
University of Georgia's Small Business Development Center, 22, 125
University of Kansas Community Tool Box, 141, 142
University of Missouri's Small Business Development Center, 217
University of Wisconsin Extension, 61
University of Wyoming, 149
"Untethered and on the Move" (Delaney, Arribas-Douglas, Fayerweather, & Huber), 222–229
Upwardly Global, 225–226
Urban Libraries Council (ULC), 94, 225
U.S. Black Chambers, Inc., 239
U.S. Chamber of Commerce, 239
U.S. Department of Energy (DOE), 86

V

value proposition, 98
vendor fellow, 157
vendors
    See street vendors
Ventura Cafe, 90
Venture Wisconsin, 63
Veteran Women's Enterprise Center, 109

video, 130
video production studio
    budget for, 150
    description of, 151
    evaluation of space for, 151–152
    promotion of, 152
    as resource for W2LB initiative, 149
    tips for, 153
    training for use of, 150
virtual meeting kits, 121–122
virtual platforms, 190
virtual program, 179
virtual resources, 210
virtual services, 121
vision, 166
visitors bureaus, 18
Visser, Marijke, xi–xvii, 237
volunteer coordinator, 131
Volunteer Prince William, 176
Vue, Yee Lee, 61–68

W

Ward, Tina, 196
Wayne County Business Council, 162
wealth, 10
web page, 149
WebEx, 179
website
    of ALA's Libraries Build Business initiative, xvi
    of Invest in Yourself, 144
    for marketing business resources/services, 177
    for promotion of business program, 164
    Small Business Hub page, 182
    of Stamford Small Business Resource Center, 115
Welcome Toledo-Lucas County (TLC) initiative, 223, 226
Welcoming America, 223
welcoming space, 68
West, Brandon
    "Considerations for Small and Rural Libraries," 3–12
    on Cultivate Indy, 132–139
    "Specialized Library Supports for Entrepreneurs," 41–52
Wetta, Molly, 201–207

WEV (Women's Economic Ventures), 203
Whitman, J., 237
Wicksall, Stacey, 161–166
Wisconsin United Coalition of Mutual
    Assistance Association (WUCMAA), 63
Wisconsin Women's Business initiative
    Corporation (WWBIC), 63
WL2B
    See Wyoming Library to Business
        (WL2B) initiative
women
    Encore Entrepreneurs/Key Advanced
        Entrepreneurs serving, 101
    Entrepreneurial Launch Pad for, 187–194
    Stamford Small Business
        Resource Center for, 114
    WL2B initiative and, 5
    Women's EXPO event, hosting, 170–171
    Women's EXPO, purpose of, 167–168
    Wyoming Library to Business for, 147, 148
Women of Toledo, 227
Women's Business Center, Benedict
    College, 22, 190–191
Women's Business Development Center, 115
Women's Economic Ventures (WEV), 203
Women's EXPO
    budget for, 169–170
    hosting, 170–171
    purpose of, 167–168
Wong, Patricia "Patty," xi
word of mouth
    for promotion of Miller
        Business Center, 172
    for promotion of program, 159, 164, 234
    for promotion of Small Business
        Boot Camp, 213
    for promotion of Small Business Hub, 185
Work Space, 224–225
workshop area devices, 182
wraparound services, 130
WUCMAA (Wisconsin United Coalition of
    Mutual Assistance Association), 63
WWBIC (Wisconsin Women's Business
    initiative Corporation), 63
Wyoming, economy of, 148
Wyoming Library to Business
    (WL2B) initiative
    areas of focus, 150–151

budget for, 150
creation of, 151
getting started, 148–149
goals/impact of, 148
mobile stations, 6
partners for, 5, 149–150
promotion of, 152
resources for, 149
roadblocks/challenges, 152–153
setting the stage, 147
staff responsibilities, 153
technical support component of, 47
tips, tricks, advice for, 153–154
video production studio, 151–152
Wyoming Small Business Development
    Center Network, 5, 150
Wyoming State Library, 5, 149–150
Wyoming Women's Business Center, 5, 149, 152

Y

Yakama Nation Library (Toppenish, WA)
    Business Maker Space, goal of, 36
    in Libraries Build Business
        initiative, xiv–xv
    program for local makers/
        entrepreneurs at, 4
    Yakama Nation Library Business
        Maker Space, 10–12
Yakama Small Business Network, 12
young people, 48–52
youth entrepreneurship programs
    agency fostered by, 42
    BizKids Club, 48–50
    Team Read, 50–52

Z

Zoom
    background for profile, 179
    for Built in Broward program, 87
    for Employment and Business
        Entrepreneur Center, 232, 234
    for Sea Un Vendedor Ambulante Exitoso/
        Successful Street Vending program, 157
    for TLCPL's Business and Workforce
        team initiative, 224
Zulkey, Claire, 237

You may also be interested in ...

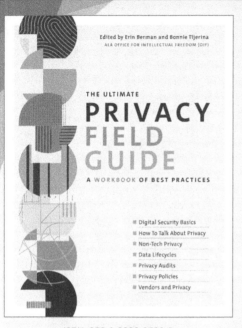

ISBN: 978-0-8389-3730-3

ISBN: 978-0-8389-1901-9

ISBN: 978-0-8389-4631-2

ISBN: 978-0-8389-4945-0

For more titles, visit **alastore.ala.org**

Printed in the USA
CPSIA information can be obtained
at www.ICGtesting.com
LVHW011211041124
795636LV00003B/9